Learning about the

Holocaust

A Student's Guide

Learning about the

Holocaust

A Student's Guide

RONALD M. SMELSER

Editor in Chief

volume 2 F-K

Macmillan Reference USA

an imprint of the Gale Group

New York • Detroit • San Francisco • London • Boston • Woodbridge, CT

Learning About the Holocaust

Macmillan Reference USA
1633 Broadway
New York, NY 10019

Gale Group
27500 Drake Road
Farmington Hills, MI 48331

Library of Congress Catalog Card Number: 00–062517

Printed in the United States of America

Printing Number
1 2 3 4 5 6 7 8 9 10

Library of Congress Cataloging-in-Publication Data
Learning About the Holocaust: a student's guide / Ronald M. Smelser, editor in chief.
    p. cm.
    Includeds bibliographical references (p.) and index.
    ISBN: 0-02-865536-2 (set) – ISBN 0-02-865537-0 (v. 1) –
ISBN 0-02-865538-9 (v. 2) – ISBN 0-02-865539-7 (v. 3) –
ISBN 0-02-865540-0 (v. 4)
    1. Holocaust, Jewish (1939–1945)–Study and teaching (Secondary)
I. Smelser, Ronald M., 1942-

D804.33 .L4 2000
940.53'18—dc21   00-062517

Contents

VOLUME 1

A

B

Contents

VOLUME 2

F

G

H

I

Contents

VOLUME 3

R

Contents

VOLUME 4

S

Timeline:
The Holocaust in the Context of World Events

1918 November 9: The Weimar Republic is established in Germany.

November 11: The war that would come to be called World War I ends after four years. Germany is defeated.

1919 June 28: The Treaty of Versailles is signed. It establishes the League of Nations and punishes Germany for its aggression in World War I.

September 16: Adolf Hitler joins the German Workers' Party, precursor of the National Socialist German Workers (Nazi) Party.

1920 January 16: The League of Nations convenes for the first time.

August 8: National Socialist German Workers' Party (known as the Nazi party) is founded.

1921 Adolf Hitler takes control of the National Socialist party.

1922 October 27: Benito Mussolini is appointed the premier of Italy.

1923 November 11: Adolf Hitler is arrested for his attempt to overthrow the German government in Bavaria in the Beer Hall Putsch.

1924 April 1: Adolf Hitler is sentenced to five years in prison for the Beer Hall Putsch. While there, he writes *Mein Kampf*.

December 20: Hitler is released from prison after only eight months.

1925 April 26: Paul von Hindenburg is elected president of Weimar Republic (Germany).

November 11: Adolf Hitler's personal guard, the SS (*Schutzstaffel*), is founded.

1926 September 8: Germany joins the League of Nations.

1929 January 6: Heinrich Himmler appointed Reichsführer-SS.

October 24: "Black Tuesday"—the U.S. stock market crash on Wall Street. The Great Depression begins and spreads around the world.

1930 September 14: In Reichstag (Parliament) elections, the Nazi party emerges as a serious new force in German politics, earning 107 seats in the 577-member Reichstag. In the face of massive unemployment, antisemitism in Germany intensifies and spreads throughout Eastern Europe.

1932 April 10: Paul von Hindenburg is re-elected president of Germany, defeating challenger Adolf Hitler.

July 31: In Reichstag elections, National Socialists (Nazis) become the largest party in Germany, taking 230 of 608 seats.

November 8: Franklin D. Roosevelt is elected president of the United States.

November 9: In Reichstag elections Nazis lose 2,000,000 votes and drop to 196 seats

1933 January 30: Adolf Hitler becomes the chancellor of Germany.

February 28: After a fire in the Reichstag on February 27, the Nazis declare a state of emergency, suspending freedom of speech, restricting freedom of assembly, and ending freedom of the press.

March 4: Franklin D. Roosevelt takes office for his first term as U.S. president. In his inaugural address, he says, "We have nothing to fear but fear itself."

March 23: Political prisoners arrive at Dachau.

March 24: The Reichstag approves the Enabling Act, giving Adolf Hitler dictatorial powers.

April 1: Nazis unleash a nationwide one-day boycott of Jewish businesses.

April 7: Jews are expelled from the German civil service.

April 11: Nazi definitions of "Aryan" and "non-Aryan" are adopted.

April 26: The Gestapo is established.

May 10: Nazis begin staging public book burnings, targeting works by political opponents and Jews. Eventually millions of books will be destroyed.

July 14: The Nazi Party is named the only legal political party in Germany.

July 20: An agreement (concordat) is signed between the Vatican and Nazi Germany.

October 14: Germany leaves the League of Nations.

1934 January 26: Germany and Poland sign a ten-year pact of non-aggression.

June 30–July 2: The Night of the Long Knives—also known as the Röhm Purge. Under Adolf Hitler's orders, the SS purges the SA (Storm Troopers); many SA leaders are killed.

July 20: The SS becomes an independent organization, with Heinrich Himmler as its chief.

August 2: German president Paul von Hindenburg dies.

August 3: Adolf Hitler becomes both president and chancellor. Soon all German officials and soldiers are required to swear allegiance to Hitler personally, not to the people or the country. At the September Nazi Party Congress in Nuremberg, Hitler proclaims his "Third Reich," which he says will last for one thousand years.

1935 January 13: A plebiscite in the Saarland overwhelmingly favors returning to Germany.

March 16: Hitler announces reintroduction of military conscription in violation of the Versailles treaty.

September 15: The Reichstag passes the first two "Nuremberg Laws," the Reich Citizenship Law and the Law for the Protection of German Blood and German Honor, which prohibit marriage and sexual intercourse between Germans and Jews and strip Jews of their remaining civil rights in Germany. These later serve as a model for the Nazis' treatment of Gypsies.

December 31: Jews are dismissed from the civil service in Germany.

1936 March 7: Germany sends troops into Rhineland, breaking the terms of the Treaty of Versailles.

May 9: Italy defeats Ethiopia, which it invaded in October, 1935.

July 18: A civil war erupts in Spain which will last for three years and foreshadows World War II.

August 1: The Summer Olympic Games begin in Berlin. African American runner Jesse Owens wins four gold medals during the games, but Adolf Hitler refuses to recognize the spectacular achievement.

October 25: The Rome-Berlin Axis Pact is signed, cementing an alliance between Adolf Hitler and Italian fascist leader Mussolini.

1937 March 14: In the face of increasing violence toward Jews in Europe, Pope Pius XI condemns racism and extreme nationalism in his encyclical "With Burning Concern."

July 16: Buchenwald concentration camp is opened.

September 7: Hitler declares the end of the Treaty of Versailles.

November 25: Germany and Japan sign a military and political pact.

1938 March 12–13: The *Anschluss*—Germany invades and annexes Austria.

April 26: Jews are required to register their property and financial holdings. It is now illegal for Aryans to pretend to own businesses still run by Jews; the push for "Aryanization" of businesses and property increases.

June 14: Jewish-owned businesses are forced to register with Nazi authorities.

June 15: Fifteen hundred German Jews are put into concentration camps.

July 6–13: Representatives of 32 countries meet at the Evian Conference in France to discuss the Jewish refugee and immigration problem. No solution emerges because virtually every country refuses to increase immigration quotas for Jews.

July 25: Jewish physicians are limited to treatment of Jewish patients.

August 17: Male Jews are required to add "Israel" to their names; female Jews must add "Sarah."

September 27: Jews may no longer work as lawyers.

September 29: At the Munich Conference, the Allies appease Adolf Hitler, granting Sudetenland—part of Czechoslovakia—to Germany.

October 15: Germany occupies Czechoslovakia's Sudetenland.

October 20–21: Jews are first deported to Poland from Vienna, Hamburg, and Prague.

November 9–10: The massive pogroms known as Kristallnacht explode across Germany and Austria. Synagogues are defaced and destroyed; Jewish homes and businesses are looted and vandalized.

November 15: Jewish children may no longer attend German schools.

December 3: Aryanization of Jewish businesses is mandated by law and carried out by force and intimidation.

1939 March 15–16: Germany invades Czechoslovakia.

April 22: Italy and Germany cement their alliance by signing the Pact of Steel.

May 15: The Ravensbrück concentration camp for women is established.

May 19: The MacDonald White Paper issued by the British government strengthens limits on Jewish emigration to Palestine.

August 23: The Germans and Soviets sign a non-aggression pact.

September 1: Germany invades Poland. Within the month, Poland falls.

September 2: Stutthof camp is established.

September 3: Great Britain and France declare war on Germany.

September 17: The Soviets invade eastern Poland, challenging the Germans.

September 21: SS official Reinhard Heydrich orders the creation of Jewish ghettos and Judenrate (Jewish Councils) in occupied Poland.

October 8: The first ghetto for Jews is established in Poland, in Piotrkow.

October 12: The Germans establish the Generalgouvernement in Poland.

November 23: Jews in occupied Poland are required to wear badges in the shape of the Star of David.

December 5–6: Jewish property in Poland is seized by German authorities.

1940 January 25: Nazis select the town of Auschwitz as the location for a new concentration camp.

February 12: The Nazis begin deporting Jews from Germany to occupied Poland.

April 9: Denmark and Norway are invaded by the Germans.

April 30: Łódź ghetto, established in February, is sealed; more than 200,000 Jews are not able to leave.

May 10: Germany invades the Netherlands, Belgium, Luxembourg, and northern France.

May 10: Winston Churchill becomes the prime minister of Great Britain.

May 20: Auschwitz concentration camp is established.

July 10: The Battle of Britain begins, with a major dogfight over the English Channel, and Germany's blitzkrieg bombing of London.

September 15: Battle of Britain Day—London is heavily blitzed by German bombers and fighter planes. The Luftwaffe meets with stiff resistance in the English Channel, resulting in an important Allied victory and turning point in the war.

September 27: The Tripartite Pact—Japan joins Germany and Italy in the Axis alliance.

October 16: Warsaw ghetto is established; the following month, it is sealed, holding in 400,000 Jews.

1941 March 1: Heinrich Himmler visits Auschwitz and orders an expansion that will increase capacity by at least 100,000 prisoners.

March 3: Krakow ghetto is established.

April 6: Germany invades Yugoslavia and Greece.

May 27: The German warship *Bismarck* is sunk by the British. U.S. president Franklin D. Roosevelt declares a national emergency in May because of events in Europe and Asia.

June 22: Operation Barbarossa—the Germans invade the Soviet Union.

July 8: Jews in the German-occupied Baltic countries are ordered to wear the Star of David badge.

July 21: Hermann Göring appoints Reinhard Heydrich to develop a plan for carrying out the "Final Solution of the Jewish Question"—the extermination of European Jews.

August 14: The Atlantic Charter is signed by Great Britain and the United States; the document outlines basic principles of postwar global rights and responsibilities and forms the beginnings of what will one day be the charter of the United Nations.

September 3: Zyklon B is first used in experiments at Auschwitz.

September 6: The Vilna ghettos are established with 40,000 Jews.

September 29–30: More than 33,000 Jews are massacred at Babi Yar.

October 23: Jewish emigration from Germany is prohibited.

November 24: Theresienstadt ghetto is established in Bohemia-Moravia as the Nazis' "model" Jewish ghetto. Also this month, construction begins on Bełżec extermination camp.

December 7: Japan attacks the United States at Pearl Harbor. Four days later, Germany and Italy declare war on the United States. The United States reciprocates by declaring war on the Axis powers.

December 8: The Chełmno extermination camp opens. Among its first victims are 5,000 Gypsies.

1942 January 20: At the Wannsee Conference, the Nazis coordinate plans for the "Final Solution."

January 21: The United Partisan Organization forms in Vilna.

February 23: The *Struma*, an unsafe cattle boat carrying more than 700 Jewish refugees from a port in Romania, sinks after being refused entry into Palestine.

June 1: Jews in the Netherlands, Belgium, Croatia, Slovakia, and Romania are ordered to wear the yellow Star of David badge.

March: Sobibór and Bełżec camps are established. The first transfer of French Jews to Auschwitz occurs. Marshal Petain approves French collaboration with

the Nazis. The United States starts supplying the Allies with war materials through the Lend-Lease Bill.

May 27: SS official Richard Heydrich is wounded; he dies early in June. A week later, the Nazis avenge his death by destroying the town of Lidice, in the Protectorate of Bohemia and Moravia (formerly Czechoslovakia).

June 4–6: The Allies win the Battle of Midway. Japan's eastward thrust is decisively thwarted.

June 23: Systematic gassing begins at Auschwitz.

July 19: Heinrich Himmler orders the start of Operation Reinhard.

July 23: Treblinka camp opens. The first victims and prisoners are from the Warsaw Ghetto. The Jewish Fighting Organization (ŻOB) is established in Warsaw.

August 23: The battle for Stalingrad begins. Three months later, the Soviets launch a successful counteroffensive against the Germans.

October 5: All Jews in concentration camps in Germany are to be sent to Auschwitz and Majdanek, on orders of Heinrich Himmler.

November 11: In a crucial turning point victory for Allied forces, the Germans are defeated at El Alamein, Egypt.

1943 January 18–21: A major, armed act of resistance occurs in the Warsaw ghetto.

January 29: All Gypsies in German-occupied territories are ordered arrested and sent to concentration camps.

February 26: The first transport of Gypsies is placed in the "Gypsy Camp" at Auschwitz.

March 5: Allied forces begin bombing Ruhr, a region central to Germany's coal, iron and steel industries.

April 19–30: At the Bermuda Conference, the Allies discuss the rescue of Jews in occupied Europe, but the talks are fruitless. Also this month, the Bergen-Belsen camp is opened.

April 19: The Warsaw ghetto uprising erupts and continues through May 16.

May 19: The Nazis declare Berlin *Judenfrei* (free of Jews).

June 11: Heinrich Himmler orders the liquidation of the Jewish ghettos of Poland and the Soviet Union.

June 22: German U-boats are withdrawn from the North Atlantic; the Allies win the Battle of the Atlantic.

July 5: The Sobibór extermination camp is made a concentration camp.

August 2: Prisoners at the Treblinka camp revolt; 200 escape, but the Nazis hunt them down.

October 2: The Danes rescue more than 7,200 Jews from the Nazis.

October 14: Prisoners at the Sobibór camp revolt; 300 escape. Of these, 50 survive.

November 3: Erntefest ("Harvest Festival") begins, in which 42,000 Jews are killed.

1944 January 24: War Refugee Board is created in the United States.

March 19: Germany invades Hungary; Hungarian Jews are required to wear the Star of David badge. During the next several months, more than 400,000 Hungarian Jews are deported to Auschwitz.

June 6: D-Day: The Allies land in Normandy, France. Throughout the year, Allied forces penetrate into more and more parts of Europe.

July 20: German officers fail in an assassination attempt against Adolf Hitler.

July 24: Soviet troops liberate the Majdanek camp.

July 28: The first major death march begins: Warsaw to Kutno.

August 4: Anne Frank and her family are arrested in Amsterdam and sent to Auschwitz. Anne and her sister are later sent to Bergen-Belsen.

September 1: Warsaw Polish Uprising begins and lasts until October 2 when the Polish Home Army is defeated by the Nazis.

October 6–7: Prisoners in Special Commandos (*Sonderkommandos*) at Auschwitz stage an uprising.

October 23: The Allies recognize Charles de Gaulle as the head of the provisional French government.

October 30: The last gassings at Auschwitz-Birkenau take place.

December 16–27: The Battle of the Bulge in Luxembourg and Belgium—the Germans are defeated.

1945 January 1: Germans begin full retreat on the Eastern Front.

January 17: Soviet troops enter Warsaw.

January 18: Death March from Auschwitz begins.

January 27: Soviet troops liberate Auschwitz-Birkenau.

February 4–11: Franklin D. Roosevelt, Winston Churchill, and Soviet leader Joseph Stalin meet at Yalta as the Allied forces meet with increasing success worldwide.

April 12: U.S. president Franklin D. Roosevelt dies and is succeeded by Harry S Truman.

April 12: Buchenwald and Bergen-Belsen camps are liberated. As more camps are released from Nazi control, the number of displaced persons (DPs) rises dramatically throughout Europe.

April 28: Benito Mussolini is shot by Italian partisans.

April 29: Dachau camp is liberated by American troops.

April 30: In his Berlin bunker, Adolf Hitler writes his Last Will and Testament, then commits suicide.

April–May: Allied troops liberate Dachau, Ravensbrück, Bergen-Belsen, Buchenwald, Mauthausen, and Theresienstadt camps. With liberation and the end of war in Europe, Displaced Persons (DP) camps are inundated.

May 7: Germany surrenders unconditionally to the Allies.

May 8: V-E Day—Victory in Europe.

June 5: The victorious Allies divide Germany into four occupation zones.

July 16: The first atomic bomb is tested, at Alamogordo, New Mexico.

July 17–August 2: Allied leaders Winston Churchill, Harry Truman, and Joseph Stalin meet in Potsdam.

August 6: The United States drops an atomic bomb on Hiroshima, and, three days later, on Nagasaki.

August 14: Japan surrenders. World War II is over.

November 20: The Nuremberg War Trials begin in Germany.

1946 January 7: The United Nations holds its first meeting, in London.

January 20: President Charles de Gaulle of France resigns.

October 1: The Nuremberg War Trials conclude.

October 16: The first convicted Nazi War criminals are executed by hanging at Nuremberg.

December 9: Twenty-three former Nazi doctors and scientists are tried at Nuremberg. Sixteen are found guilty; seven are executed by hanging.

1947 June 5: The Marshall Plan is instituted, to help Europe rebuild.

September 15: Twenty-one former SS Operational Squad leaders are tried at Nuremberg. Although fourteen of them are sentenced to death, only four who were group commanders are executed.

1948 May 14: The State of Israel is proclaimed.

June 25: The U.S. Congress creates a Displaced Persons Commission.

October 30: The first boatload of war refugees arrives in the United States.

1949 April 4: The North Atlantic Treaty Organization—NATO—is formed.

May 23: West Germany becomes a separate state, under occupation forces. East Germany becomes a Soviet-bloc state later in the year.

December 9: The United Nations approves the Genocide Convention.

1957 The last Displaced Persons (DP) camp closes.

1960 May 11: Adolf Eichmann is captured in Argentina. He is tried in Jerusalem starting on April 11, 1961. Found guilty, he is executed by hanging on May 31, 1962.

Fascism

Fascism is a political and cultural movement that arose in twentieth-century Europe. Fascism, in political form and ideology, ruled ITALY from 1922 to 1945. The term was later applied to similar political regimes and beliefs in other countries.

Fascism encourages elitism and rejects materialism, calling for absolute political rule, with no pretenses toward principles of democracy. For fascists, the state, or government, is the expression of national unity. The state is responsible for control of society and the economy. Thus, it is anti-individualist. Fascism claims to purify, strengthen, and revitalize the state, in which the individual is no more than a cell in the collective entity.

Fascism rejects the theory of "natural rights" and the individualist view of society. For the fascist ideologists, both those from the beginning of the twentieth century and those of the 1930s, liberalism and Marxism are ideologies of social warfare. Fascists believe that both of those systems destroy the natural unity of the nation. Fascism's proclaimed purpose is to restore society's solidarity and unity. It developed as an expression of the rapid modernization processes that Europeans experienced in the late 1800s. Many profound social and economic changes occurred in the Western world at that time, and fascism was a reaction to those changes.

Roots of Fascism in Europe

Italian Benito Mussolini was attracted to these new political thoughts in the early 1900s. He belonged to a movement known as "revolutionary syndicalism," which gradually transformed into fascism. In Mussolini's eyes, World War I (1914–1918) demonstrated the sweeping power of nationalism and provided the opportunity to put socialism into practice. Thus the emerging ideology of fascism had found a leader; the war provided the social and psychological conditions for its practical application.

World War I opened up new vistas for the functions of the state. It proved that the state was able to control the economy, the means of production, and labor relations. The war showed that governments could dictate the basic elements of economic planning and mobilize all sections of society for a concentrated national effort. The war also revealed the great extent to which people were prepared to accept state authority, to forego their freedoms, to accept what was in effect a dictatorship, and even to sacrifice their lives. In other words, total war demonstrated that the national state was able to control the individual in every part of life. It showed

that totalitarianism—whose initial ideological features had been outlined by earlier theorists—could really exist. Italy's revolutionary syndicalists, including Mussolini, were the first to have the opportunity to translate that lesson into terms of political victory and the seizure of power.

Fascist beliefs were found throughout Europe. They differed from place to place, depending upon the particular cultural, social, and political circumstances. However, even the vast differences between the industrial centers of Northern Europe and the agricultural areas of Southern Europe could not hide the common denominator of fascism in all these countries.

Elements of Fascism

Fascism came up with two tools to maintain "the unity of the nation"— corporatism and the totalitarian state. "Corporatism" symbolizes fascists' belief in the power of politics to dominate market forces and class interests. The corporatist system is designed to allow the authoritarian state to plan the economy and settle labor relations and the differences between social classes. Once political and personal rights and freedoms are outlawed, the workers' right to organize is also canceled. Corporatism puts an end to the power of special interests and allows the social and economic system be controlled by the state. It represents the real basis on which the totalitarian state rests.

The authoritarian state seeks to control every sphere of life—politics, the economy, society, and culture. It does away with all institutions or organizations that express multiple ideas and beliefs—parliaments, political parties, a free press, and a choice of educational opportunities. It demands not only discipline but also identification and unconditional readiness for sacrifice.

Indeed, totalitarianism is the cornerstone of the fascist revolution's ideology. For Mussolini and others, the totalitarian state signified the beginning of a new era, an era in which the state has absolute priority over the individual. The individual exists only to perform his or her duty and is only a means to an end—the state's achievement of the goals it sets itself. This means the end of liberal culture. It follows that the fascist revolution is a total revolution, a moral and spiritual revolution, which creates a new order for all sectors of society.

Influence of Fascist Ideology

Mussolini, in his work *The Fascist Doctrine* (on which he collaborated with philosopher Giovanni Gentile), left no doubt that the state should embrace all spheres of human activity, organize them, and determine what their content should be. There was no aspect of society's life that was not political, and there was therefore nothing that could be excluded from the state's grip.

In this sense, fascist ideology was truly revolutionary. It provided a complete alternative to the established order. Fascism's idealism and appeal to the emotions provided the instruments for a total revolution. This revolution of the spirit had a tremendous appeal in those days all over Europe, especially among young people who had only contempt for the political and economic world of their parents. In fact, the influence of fascist ideology went far beyond the hard core of its founders and devoted followers. Much wider circles, to one degree or another, were drawn to its promise of a violent rebellion of spiritual forces and basic instincts, of primitive and unrestrained reaction against routine and convention. To many, the clarity of

Benito Mussolini (l.) and Adolf Hitler (r.), 1939.

dictatorship seemed a more natural form of government than the messy give-and-take of a democracy.

The impact of the fascist revolution was felt all over Europe, though politically, Italy was the only true fascist state. But, like any other ideology, fascism ran into a constant struggle with reality. It was extremely difficult to overcome social and economic interests and the influence of the traditional centers of power—the monarchy, the church, and high finance. As is true in every other movement, fascism was also forced into various compromises, which saved Italy from becoming an entirely totalitarian state.

Still, in the case of Italian Fascism, the correlation between ideology and practice was very high. The abolition of parliamentary and democratic institutions, along with deliberate and planned violence, political murder, and the physical or political crushing of the opposition, were all expressions of the fascist system's essential character. Mobilizing the masses—through marches, mass rallies, militias, and uniformed youth movements—was an effective translation into practice of the theories taught by some of Europe's greatest scientists. Thus a new political culture

To many disillusioned by post-World War I politics and economics, the clarity of dictatorship seemed a more natural and preferable form of government than the messy give-and-take of a democracy

3

was born, in which the state came before the individual and could demand of the individual whatever sacrifice it wanted.

In the economically depressed conditions that prevailed in Europe in the 1920s and the 1930s, this political culture gathered destructive force. No society was immune to it. Interest in fascism was not limited by social class, educational level, age, religion, or origin. Everywhere, in all sectors of society and in all religious groupings, there were people ready to accept fascism as a legitimate and original third way, with a stature equal to that of Marxism and liberalism.

Fascism and Antisemitism

It is important to note that **ANTISEMITISM** was not a basic element of fascist ideology. This was the great difference between fascism and Nazism. Nazi ideology was based on the doctrine of biological determinism, in which hatred of Jews was a central element. In fascism, antisemitism differed from place to place. Italian Fascism, in its early period, was generally free of antisemitism; it developed in its later stages, gradually and often as a result of external events. The 1938 Italian racist legislation resulted from the growth of extremist nationalist trends in Italian Fascism as well as from Italy's relationship with Nazi **GERMANY**.

There were fascist groups in **FRANCE** (such as *Action Française*) whose ideology differed only slightly from that of Nazism, and others that were practically untouched by antisemitism. As World War II approached, however, the antisemitic dimension in French fascism increased in strength. By October 1940, the Vichy government, which was not formally a fascist government, introduced racist laws closely resembling the **NUREMBERG LAWS**. British fascism was extremely antisemitic, as was fascism in **BELGIUM**, Romania, and **HUNGARY**. Spanish fascism, in contrast, was free of antisemitism. Italy had an official anti-Jewish policy that followed the introduction of racist legislation. But the persecution and hatred of Jews never came close to that in Central and Eastern Europe.

SEE ALSO **GREAT BRITAIN; RACISM**.

Vichy
The region of France not occupied by Germany and governed from the spa town of Vichy.

SUGGESTED RESOURCES

Blum, George P. *The Rise of Fascism in Europe.* Westport, CT: Greenwood Press, 1998.

Delzell, Charles F. *Mediterranean Fascism, 1919–1945.* New York: Walker, 1971.

Eatwell, Roger. *Fascism: A History.* New York: Allen Lane, 1996.

Laqueur, Walter. *Fascism: Past, Present, Future.* New York: Oxford University Press, 1995.

Mussolini, B. *Fascism: Doctrine and Institutions.* New York: H. Fertig, 1968.

Payne, Stanley G. *A History of Fascism, 1914–1945.* Madison: University of Wisconsin Press, 1995.

Feiner, Leon

(1888–1945)

A Bund activist and member of the Jewish underground in **POLAND**, Feiner was born in **KRAKÓW** and studied law at the Jagiellonian University there. As a longtime member of socialist movements and a **Bund** activist in independent Poland, he frequently defended leftist political activists in court. Feiner came from a background of assimilated Jews, so his cultural identity was more Polish than Jewish, but his loyalty to the Bund, as well as the increasingly anti-Jewish policy that

Bund
The Jewish Socialist Party, which was founded in 1897; members of the Bund worked for equal rights for Jews and many took part in underground resistance activities during World War II.

Poland was pursuing, brought him closer to the Jewish masses and made him want to share their fate. In the second half of the 1930s he was imprisoned in Bereza-Kartuska, a Polish concentration camp in which a large number of opposition figures, of various shades of political opinion, were held.

When the war broke out, Feiner fled to the Soviet-occupied part of Poland, only to be put in prison. Following the German conquest of the area in 1941, he escaped and made his way back to **WARSAW**. There he lived under an assumed identity on the Polish ("Aryan") side of the city and was an underground representative of the Bund and of the Jews in the ghetto. When the Bund joined the **JEWISH FIGHTING ORGANIZATION** (Żydowska Organizacja Bojowa; ŻOB), Feiner was appointed Bund representative on the "Aryan" side. With Abraham Berman (who represented the Jewish National Committee), Feiner formed the coordinating committee for contacts with the Polish underground. Feiner drafted and sent most of the Bund's reports and messages to London and the United States. In the fall of 1942 Jan Karski, a member of the Polish underground who was sent to London in its behalf, took a message from Feiner addressed to Samuel Zygelbojm, for transmission to all the Jews in the free world. Feiner asked Zygelbojm to tell the Jews "to lay siege to all important offices and agencies of the British and the Americans, and not to move from there until these Allied powers give guarantees that they will embark upon the rescue of the Jews. They [the demonstrators] should abstain from food and water, waste away before the eyes of the apathetic world, and starve to death. By doing so they may perhaps shock the conscience of the world."

Leon Feiner.

In the last few months of 1942, Feiner helped establish a Polish organization for giving aid to Jews and trying to rescue them. This project had been initiated by various Polish circles—Catholics, liberal intellectuals, and representatives of moderate and liberal political parties. From January 1943 to July 1944 Feiner was deputy chairman of Zegota, the Polish Council for Aid to Jews, and was its chairman from November to December 1944, until the liberation of Warsaw in January 1945.

After the liberation, Feiner, who was terminally ill, was transferred to **LUBLIN**, the temporary seat of Poland's new regime. One month later he died.

SUGGESTED RESOURCES

Korbonski, Stefan. *The Polish Underground State: A Guide to the Underground, 1939–1945.* New York: Columbia University Press, 1978.

Rescue and Resistance: Portraits of the Holocaust. New York: Macmillan Library Reference USA, 1999.

A Teacher's Guide to the Holocaust: Rescuers. [Online] http://fcit.coedu.usf.edu/holocaust/people/rescuer.htm (accessed on August 22, 2000).

A Teacher's Guide to the Holocaust: Resisters. http://fcit.coedu.usf.edu/holocaust/people/resister.htm (accessed on August 22, 2000).

Fighting Organization of Pioneer Jewish Youth

The Fighting Organization of Pioneer Jewish Youth (He-Haluts ha-Lohem) was created in **KRAKÓW** in mid-August 1942, as a Jewish underground organization; not in order to save lives but out of a desire "to die as Jews without the shame of dying as slaves." The initiative for its creation came from the pioneer youth movement Akiva, which was also the guiding force in its activity. Other members came from such Jewish youth organizations as Dror, Ha-Shomer ha-Dati, Ha-

> The aim of the group was to undermine the self-confidence of the authorities, destroy weapons and support systems, and injure as many Germans as possible.

Shomer ha-Tsa'ir, and the Pioneer Youth Organization (*see* **YOUTH MOVEMENTS**). He-Haluts ha-Lohem had about one hundred members.

The organization was formed after the deportation of about 6,000 of the Jews of Kraków in June 1942 (*see* **DEPORTATIONS**), when news had arrived of mass slaughter in parts of German-occupied eastern **POLAND** and the **SOVIET UNION**. It was led by a four-member command: Aharon **LIEBESKIND**, who was responsible for obtaining arms; Avraham Leibovich ("Laban"), a member of Dror, who was appointed treasurer; Shimshon Draenger, who was in charge of the "technical office" for forging official documents; and Manik Eisenstein, a member of the Pioneer Youth Organization.

Planning for Resistance

He-Haluts ha-Lohem kept in close contact with the **JEWISH FIGHTING ORGANIZATION**(Żydowska Organizacja Bojowa; ŻOB) in **WARSAW**, but was independent in determining the timing and the place of its actions. The group intended to undertake anti-Nazi action primarily outside the ghetto, in order to hide their Jewish identity so that responsibility for their actions would not be placed on the ghetto, and thereby lead to the ghetto's liquidation.

There were several reasons for this method of struggle:

1. The organization felt a sense of responsibility for the ghetto's fate; it was better for all the Jews if no link could be established between the sabotage activities outside the ghetto and residents inside.

2. The ghetto in Kraków was small. Between the June 1942 deportation and December of the same year the ghetto area had been reduced twice; there were few hiding places inside.

3. The Kraków ghetto population was small and unstable. After June 1942 many of the residents were not from Kraków. As strangers to the members of the local underground, they were sometimes considered unreliable.

4. The creation of a labor camp in Płaszów, near the city, gave many of the Jews a sense of hope for survival. Without a feeling of desperation, it was difficult to obtain resistance support from most ghetto inhabitants.

5. Since Kraków was the capital of the **GENERALGOUVERNEMENT**, the area outside the ghetto offered many sabotage possibilities. Furthermore, it was not impossible to operate in the "Aryan" part of the city with a handful of men and a meager supply of weapons. The aim of the group was to undermine the self-confidence of the authorities, to harm their position, and to injure as many Germans as possible.

Many preparations were made for the armed struggle. Forged documents were prepared to ensure freedom of movement for members of the organization. Money for guns came from the sale of forged documents and by "expropriations" (forcible collection of money from rich Jews). Weapons were also acquired by attacking German soldiers in the middle of the night on the city boulevards. Membership in He-Haluts ha-Lohem was increased by adding members from youth movements, principally Akiva and Dror, in cities close to Kraków. He-Haluts ha-Lohem was organized by groups of five, each with a commander in contact with the principal command.

Carrying out the Plans

On September 20, 1942, the first group of five went out to the forests in the Rzeszów district. Operations were not successful; expected support from a Polish underground group never materialized.

In October a group was sent to the forests in the Dębica area. This attempt also ended in failure and in severe battle losses. From then on, the organization chose to limit opposition activities to Kraków itself. There were also plans to organize support in Warsaw and **Lvov**, where members could take refuge after carrying out their activities.

Until November 1942, operations within the ghetto consisted of attacks on German soldiers and **Gestapo** men, seizure of their weapons, and surveillance of informers in order to liquidate them. A second fighting organization, which operated in the ghetto, carried out similar activities and also sabotaged German installations in the city and its surroundings.

During that period, the ghetto served as a base for operations outside the ghetto. After members of the command had been traced, the location was transferred to the "Aryan" part of the city, and members of the organization were dispersed outside the ghetto. A large-scale operation was planned for December 22, 1942, just before Christmas, when the city would be flooded with German soldiers on holiday leave. This was to be executed with the help of several groups, including the Polish Workers' Party.

The targets of the action were cafés in the center of town where the German soldiers passed their time. Best known was the Cyganeria, which was attacked with homemade hand grenades. The Germans announced twenty dead and wounded. None of the attackers was injured in the attack, but about twenty He-Haluts ha-Lohem fighters, returning to their base in the deserted Jewish hospital, walked into a Gestapo ambush and were taken to the Montelupich Prison. Among those captured was command member "Laban"; Aharon Liebeskind was killed in the struggle.

That action concluded the organization's operations in the city. Activity was renewed in the Wisnicz Forest after the escape on April 29, 1943, of Shimshon Draenger and Gusta Draenger, two of the primary leaders, from the Montelupich prison, where they had been held since January 1943. The Draengers and Hillel Wodzisławski, a member of the command from Wisnicz, worked to assemble any remaining fighters. In November 1943, after its leaders were captured by the Germans, the He-Haluts ha-Lohem organization ceased to exist. Only fifteen members of He-Haluts ha-Lohem survived. Almost all of them emigrated to Israel.

SUGGESTED RESOURCES

Cohen, Asher. *The Halutz Resistance in Hungary 1942–1944.* New York: Institute for Holocaust studies at the City University of New York, 1986.

The Ghetto Fighters' House Museum of the Holocaust and Resistance. [Online] http://www.amfriendsgfh.org/Docs/gfh.html (accessed on August 28, 2000)

Rescue and Resistance: Portraits of the Holocaust. New York: Macmillan Library Reference USA, 1999.

A Teacher's Guide to the Holocaust: Resisters. [Online] http://fcit.coedu.usf.edu/holocaust/ people/resister.htm (accessed on August 22, 2000).

"Final Solution"

The "Final Solution" (in German, Endlösung) was the Nazis' program to solve their "Jewish question"—what to do with the Jews?—by murdering every Jew in Europe. The program was started by Adolf **Hitler** in the summer of 1941. At that

time, Germans were flush with their military successes in Europe and their expected victory over the **SOVIET UNION**.

Evolution of the Concept

The "Final Solution" was the result of a long evolution of policy stemming from Nazi **ANTISEMITISM**. Hitler first expressed a "solution" to the "Jewish question" in 1919. Once he and his **NAZI PARTY** won power in Germany in 1933, they tried to force Jewish emigration. When World War II started in September 1939 with Germany's invasion of **POLAND**, the Nazis planned mass expulsions of Jews. They made the leap to mass murder with the assault by the **OPERATIONAL SQUADS** (*Einsatzgruppen*) on Soviet Jews in 1941. Each new direction in Jewish policy evolved as the Germans encountered new obstacles in their drive for totalitarian control over Europe.

In the very earliest document of Hitler's political career—a letter written on September 16, 1919, to Adolf Gemlich—he expressed the view that the "Jewish question" would be solved not through emotional antisemitism and pogroms (attacks) but only through an "antisemitism of reason." This would lead to a systematic legal struggle to deprive the Jews of their privileges and classify them as foreigners. He wrote: "The final goal, however, must steadfastly remain the removal of the Jews altogether."

The "Jewish question" remained central for Hitler in the 1920s. For Nazis, he declared, it was the "pivotal question." The Nazi party was determined to solve it "with well-known German thoroughness to the final consequence." For the most part, the "final consequence" was expressed in terms such as "removal," "expulsion," and "exclusion." But on occasion Hitler's language was more ominous. He made the analogy between the tuberculosis bacillus, which had to be destroyed, and the Jew— the "racial tuberculosis" which had to be removed if the German people (*Volk*) were to recover their health. On one occasion in 1922, he fantasized about publicly hanging every Jew in Germany and leaving the bodies dangling until they stank.

Such statements indicate the depth of Hitler's obsession with the Jews. He viewed them as the source of all of Germany's historical misfortunes and current problems. In fact, he saw the Jews as the "greatest evil." He was determined to get rid of the Jews in one way or another. Hitler's statements also reveal his violent and murderous tendencies. In the 1920s, though, they did not form a grand design, blueprint, or decision for the "Final Solution" of 1941 to 1945— the comprehensive and systematic mass murder of all European Jewry.

In the early 1930s, the Nazi Party did little preparation for its Jewish policy. After it took power in 1933, various Nazi factions pursued different and often conflicting policies. Hitler generally favored making laws to bring about systematic discrimination—the "antisemitism of reason" of the Gemlich letter— over the public violence of pogroms and "wild actions." But there was not any expression of what had been so common in Hitler's statements during the early 1920s—namely, the determination of the final goal of Nazi Jewish policy. Few Nazis seemed to be looking ahead to where the persecution of the Jews might lead. In the **SS**, however, as early as 1934, a report for Heinrich **HIMMLER** on the "Jewish question" emphasized the need to work toward a total emigration of Jews from Germany.

Emigration then became the centerpiece of SS Jewish policy. But it remained a "voluntary solution" until Germany annexed **AUSTRIA** (the Anschluss) in March 1938. Then Adolf **EICHMANN**, the "Jewish expert" of Reinhard **HEYDRICH**'s **SD** (*Sicherheitsdienst*; Security Service), was sent to the Austrian capital, **VIENNA**. He

The emergence of the "Final Solution" as both a concept and a program was a complex phenomenon shaped by Hitler's antisemitic beliefs, by the nature of the Nazi regime, and by the changing circumstances in which the Nazis found themselves.

organized assembly-line procedures for speeding up and forcing Jewish emigration.

Forced Emigration and Economic Isolation for the Jews

In 1938, expulsion began to define Nazi Jewish policy throughout Germany. Soviet Jews were ordered out of the country in the spring, followed by Polish Jews in the fall. Hermann Göring began the systematic **ARYANIZATION** (transfer of ownership from Jewish to non-Jewish) of Jewish property. This radical step threatened to pauperize the Jews—to strip them of their financial resources within months, making emigration even more difficult. Joseph **GOEBBELS** made his bid for power over Nazi Jewish policy by setting off the massive **KRISTALLNACHT** pogrom of November 9 and 10, 1938.

In the wake of Kristallnacht, the Nazis moved to organize their various Jewish policies into a cohesive whole. Göring announced Hitler's instructions to the Nazi leaders gathered before him on November 12, 1938: "The Jewish question is to be summed up and coordinated once and for all and solved one way or another....; If the German Reich should in the near future become involved in conflict abroad then it is obvious that we in Germany will first of all make sure of settling accounts with the Jews...."

In the following months, Hitler approved plans for the resettlement of German Jewry. Göring established the Reich **CENTRAL OFFICE FOR JEWISH EMIGRATION**, using Eichmann's Vienna experiment as a model. The office was placed under Heydrich's control, with the charge that the "emigration of the Jews from Germany [was] to be furthered by all possible means."

In a speech to the Reichstag (parliament) on January 30, 1939, Hitler scolded countries that criticized Germany's treatment of its Jews, for their own reluctance to accept Jews as immigrants: "The world has sufficient space for settlements." If, however, war broke out first, "then the result will not be the Bolshevization [communization] of the earth, and thus the victory of Jewry, but the annihilation of the Jewish race in Europe."

Hitler's Priorities

Were these threats a literal statement of Hitler's intention to kill the Jews upon the outbreak of war? He may have had other motives. Hitler may have been pressuring governments that he thought to be under Jewish influence to accept Germany's Jewish refugees, and not to interfere with its destruction of Czechoslovakia. Or he may have wanted to give his followers the idea that to solve the "Jewish question," a policy more radical than emigration would be needed after the outbreak of war. Several facts support this second interpretation. First, less than two weeks before the Reichstag speech, Hitler made the same threat to the Czech ambassador, František Chvalkovsky—an unlikely person in whom to confide premeditated mass murder, but an entirely appropriate target for diplomatic pressure. Second, when war did break out in September 1939, Hitler did not immediately begin the systematic mass murder of the Jews under German control. Instead, with his clear approval, Nazi Jewish policy became more radical in a different way; solving the "Jewish question" still meant removing the Jews one way or another.

The conquest and breakup of Poland brought an additional 2 million Jews into the German sphere, including more than half a million in the "incorporated territories" annexed directly to Nazi Germany. In addition, 7 million Poles lived in the incorporated territories. If the "Jewish question" was one major obsession in

Hitler let it be known that there was no longer enough territory in Poland to spare any for deported Jews. Another solution to the "Jewish issue" would need to be developed.

Hitler's world view, the conquest of "living space" (*Lebensraum*) in Eastern Europe was the other. Poland thus presented a major challenge to the Nazis. According to a plan approved by Hitler in late September 1939, the Poles and Jews of the incorporated territories were to be expelled into a region called the **GENERALGOUVERNEMENT**. The very concept of Polish nationhood was to be erased through the "liquidation" (including physical destruction) of the Polish intelligentsia, considered the bearers of Polish nationalism. The incorporated territories were to be repopulated with ethnic Germans (**VOLKSDEUTSCHE**) sent from the Baltic countries and eastern Poland. Those areas had been surrendered to the Soviets as the price of the Nazi-Soviet Non-Aggression Pact of August 1939. As for the Jews, they were to be expelled not just from the incorporated territories but from all of Nazi Germany, into a reservation on the outer edge of the German empire. At that time, this was the **LUBLIN** region, on the demarcation line with Soviet-occupied eastern Poland.

The "Jewish Question" Becomes More Complicated

The Nazis set in motion a massive upheaval among the populations, but Hitler's overall plan could not be realized. Very quickly, **DEPORTATIONS** of Jews from within Germany's pre-war boundaries were forbidden. Deportations of Jews from the incorporated territories were scaled down. Priority was given to deporting Poles, whose farms, businesses, and homes could be turned over to incoming ethnic Germans. By the spring of 1940, Hitler had decided that the Lublin Reservation was no longer the target of a solution to the "Jewish question" (*see* **NISKO AND LUBLIN PLAN**). There was not enough territory in Poland to spare for the Jews.

Himmler was receptive to this hint. In late May 1940, he gave Hitler a memorandum discussing the treatment of the populations of Eastern Europe. He included the notion of expelling all the Jews to some colonial territory in Africa. Other Eastern Europeans not suitable for "Germanization" were to be turned into slave laborers. Concerning this systematic eradication of the ethnic composition of Eastern Europe, Himmler concluded: "However cruel and tragic each individual case may be, this method is still the mildest and best, if one rejects the Bolshevik [Communist] method of physical extermination of a people out of inner conviction as un-German and impossible." Hitler judged Himmler's proposals "very good and correct." Within weeks, this notion of expelling the Jews overseas was cemented in the form of the **MADAGASCAR PLAN**, which Hitler discussed with Italy's leader Benito Mussolini in late June. For a short time, the Madagascar Plan was the centerpiece of Nazi Jewish policy. Then, the plan became impossible to carry out, as the Germans were defeated in the Battle of Britain in September 1940.

The Lublin Reservation project and the Madagascar Plan were important stages in the evolution of Nazi Jewish policy. Shortly before the war, a Foreign Office circular had noted, in reference to the large Jewish populations in Poland, Hungary, and Romania: "Even for Germany the Jewish question will not be solved when the last Jew has left German soil." Germany now had direct control over much of Europe and a growing list of unequal alliances with countries that were not directly occupied. The Nazis considered the "Jewish question" no longer a German issue, but a European issue. They believed that German domination of the continent obligated them to solve this problem in a fundamental way. The removal of the Jews altogether—once Hitler's prescription for Germany—was now the unquestioned center of the Nazis' commitment throughout Europe. Clearly, with schemes such as the Lublin and Madagascar programs, the Nazis had already become used to the idea of an enormous loss of life among the Jews.

This changing mentality among the Nazis was reflected in their increasing references to a "final solution to the Jewish question." In June 1940, Heydrich referred to the Madagascar Plan as a "territorial final solution." Beginning in September 1940, Eichmann's staff routinely referred to "the doubtless imminent final solution to the Jewish question" when refusing to permit Jewish emigration from any country in Europe other than Germany. They wanted Germany to be the first *judenrein* ("cleansed of Jews," or "Jew-free") nation in Europe. By 1940, therefore, even before mass murder became the goal of Nazi Jewish policy, the Nazis were already thinking about the "Jewish question" in a way that was both "final" and trans-European.

From Expulsion to Extermination

Large-scale, systematic mass murder as a way of dealing with "problems" was becoming commonplace in Nazi Germany. It was already accepted that Poland was to be "de-nationalized" through the systematic liquidation of the Polish intelligentsia. At the same time, Hitler initiated the killing of Germans who were mentally ill or had genetic diseases. They were deemed "unworthy of life" and were put to death. This was referred to as the **EUTHANASIA PROGRAM**, but it was a forced program. It had nothing to do with any voluntary request of the victims to be released from their suffering. In its technology—which included the use of carbon monoxide in enclosed spaces (*see* **GAS CHAMBERS/VANS**)—and bureaucratic system of operation, this murder program suggested the mass murder of the Jews that was soon to follow.

Germany's preparations to invade the Soviet Union in the spring of 1941 sped up the movement toward the mass murder of European Jewry. The invasion promised to increase the conditions of the vicious circle in which the Germans had entrapped themselves. Each new military success increased the number of Jews under their control, whom they were committed to get rid of through a "final solution" of one kind or another. With the formation of the Operational Squads, systematic mass murder as a method of solving the Nazis' "Jewish question" began.

Even then, though, the evolution to the "Final Solution" was not yet complete. The Operational Squads were targeted against Jews in the newly occupied territories only. The squads moved into their tasks gradually, as their commanders tested the limits of their men and of army cooperation, as well as the helpfulness of local people. Only in late July or early August 1941 did all the mobile killing units begin the systematic mass murder of all Jews in the Soviet territories, including women and children.

At this point, Hitler was at the height of his success. The German army had torn through Soviet defenses and encircled huge numbers of Soviet troops. It had destroyed most of the Soviet air force and rampaged through two-thirds of the distance to Moscow. Victory seemed within reach, and Hitler expected to have all of Europe at his feet. In the excitement over the conquest of Poland, he had approved plans for a massive population reorganization on Polish territory, including the expulsion of Jews to the Lublin Reservation. With victory over France, he had approved the Madagascar Plan. Now, with the expected victory over the Soviet Union, the last barriers fell away. Precisely when and how instructions were given is not known, but Göring, Himmler, and Heydrich now knew what Hitler expected of them. On July 31, 1941, Heydrich visited Göring and had him sign an authorization to prepare and submit "an overall plan of the organizational, functional, and material measures to be taken in preparing for the implementation of the aspired final solution of the Jewish question."

During 1940, the Nazis began to realize that the answer to the "Jewish question" would have to be found outside European territory. Each new military success increased the number of Jews under their control, and they were committed to get rid of them through a "final solution" of one kind or another. The Third Reich could never be free of Jews as long as Jews lived in any part of German-controlled Europe.

Strategy for Mass Murder

If the notion of the "Final Solution" was now clear to the leading Nazis, the means of accomplishing it were not. The Operational Squads had run across many problems. The most important were the lack of secrecy, the psychological impact on the killers, and the inadequacy of the killing methods in relation to the number of intended victims. The firing-squad method had not worked well in the Soviet Union. It was even less suitable for murdering the rest of European Jewry. The Nazis thus chose to become pioneers of mass murder in an uncharted land. The past offered no suitable landmarks; but in the fall of 1941, new killing techniques were developed.

The physical setting of the **CONCENTRATION CAMPS**, the killing methods of euthanasia, and the deportation techniques of the population-resettlement programs were combined to create a system of **EXTERMINATION CAMPS**. In relative secrecy, a small number of workers using assembly-line techniques could kill millions of victims in these camps. The prisoners would be brought trainload by trainload, day after day, to these factories of death. The bureaucratic organization that coordinated the process would be separated from direct contact with the killing process, but still accepting of the idea that the Jews had to be removed one way or another. It would perform on a business-as-usual basis all the many tasks necessary to uproot millions of people and ship to their death. The German population in general, accepting the notion of the Jew as an enemy of the state, looked on with indifference.

Implementing the "Final Solution"

In the fall of 1941, steps were taken to turn the idea of a "final solution to the Jewish question" into reality. The deportation of the German Jews began in mid-October. The first gassing experiment was conducted in **AUSCHWITZ** in early September. Construction of two extermination camps at **BEŁŻEC** and **CHEŁMNO** was started in late October or early November. The first mass murder of German Jews took place in **KOVNO** and **RIGA** about a month later. The first extermination camp, at Chełmno, began full-time operations in early December.

The last step in turning the idea of the "Final Solution" into reality was the **WANNSEE CONFERENCE** of January 20, 1942. At this conference, Reinhard Heydrich and his "Jewish expert," Adolf Eichmann, met with the secretaries of the state ministries. Most of those attending were already aware that Jews were being killed, but here the full scope of the mass murder program was revealed—the goal was to get rid of every Jew in Europe. Heydrich requested the support of the state secretaries. He was pleasantly surprised by their enthusiasm for the project.

The "Final Solution" was first developed as a program to be carried out following Germany's expected victory over the Soviet Union, but it endured through Germany's changing fortunes of war. In 1942, with victory postponed, the Nazis claimed that the "Final Solution" had to be completed during the war to avoid an outcry from abroad. In 1944, with their fortunes in decline, they rushed to finish their gruesome task—to achieve a victory in their racial war that a military defeat could not undo. Nazi Jewish policy was shaped by a number of factors and evolved toward the "Final Solution" in fits and starts over many years. But in the end, it was the most important legacy, indeed the epitome, of Adolf Hitler and the Nazis.

SEE ALSO **GENOCIDE; RACISM; SPRACHREGELUNG.**

SUGGESTED RESOURCES

Breitman, Richard. *The Architect of Genocide: Himmler and the Final Solution.* New York: Knopf, 1991.

Browning, Christopher R. *The Path to Genocide: Essays on Launching the Final Solution.* New York: Cambridge University Press, 1992.

Friedlander, Henry. *The Origins of Nazi Genocide: From Euthanasia to the Final Solution.* Chapel Hill: University of North Carolina Press, 1995.

Public Opinion Under Nazism. Oxford: Basil Blackwell, 1996.

Rice, Earle. *The Final Solution.* San Diego: Lucent Books, 1998.

Forced Labor

The Nazis relied on the use of forced labor to build and operate concentration and extermination camps, and to maintain a steady flow of workers for factories and other industries that supported the war effort. Some of these laborers were voluntarily "recruited," and later deported, from occupied countries within the Reich. Others were Jews whose slave labor in the ghettos and labor camps of **POLAND** also contributed to the Nazi war machine and to their own extermination at the hands of their Nazi oppressors.

Imported Workers

Laborers from Germany's satellites or occupied territories who were brought to work in the Reich were called *Fremdarbeiter*, literally, "foreign workers." The idea of importing workers for forced labor was conceived in **BERLIN** even before the attack on Poland in September 1939. The idea was first put into practice in **AUSTRIA**, after the Anschluss—the Nazi-driven unification of Austria and Germany—in March 1938. Some 100,000 Austrian civilians, including 10,000 engineers, were taken to work in Germany.

The German authorities in charge of employment policy worked out a detailed program for drafting workers from German occupied territories. The plan included harsh methods of recruitment for use in Poland and the occupied Soviet areas. Far more lenient methods were used in the other countries under German occupation or in the satellite countries.

The first contingents of forced laborers were needed to replace the millions of Germans who had left the work force to be drafted into the army, and to eliminate the need to impose emergency labor drafts on Germans themselves. As the war dragged on with no end in sight, foreign workers were needed to meet the growing needs of the armaments industry and the economy in general.

Initially, the Germans tried to persuade people in the occupied countries to volunteer for work in Germany. Those who were ready to do so, mostly the unemployed and refugees who were in dire economic straits, were promised all sorts of material benefits by the Germans.

Mandatory Forced Labor

Immediately after the outbreak of the war, the Germans put **PRISONERS OF WAR** (POWs) to work to support the German economy, deliberately ignoring international law forbidding this practice. As early as the autumn of 1939, 340,000 Polish POWs were working for the Third Reich.

In the spring of 1940, the Germans introduced compulsory measures in the **GENERALGOUVERNEMENT**, including conscriptions—forced enlistments—of work-

Female prisoners perform forced labor in a factory owned by the AGFA camera company.

G erman victories in the first phase of World War II and the occupation of many lands which followed provided plenty of potential workers to exploit for Nazi purposes.

ers, the seizure of those who hadn't been exempted from such conscription, and the withholding of food rations from those who refused to work. In August 1942, a decree was enacted that implemented a policy of *Zwangsverpflichtung*, or forced labor, in all occupied countries and POW camps. In western European countries, the local authorities sometimes helped the Germans recruit workers. This was done in exchange for the release of POWs by the Germans or for a change in the status of POWs to that of foreign workers in Germany.

By 1942, the German drive to recruit foreign workers had become a sophisticated and brutal manhunt, one that met with growing opposition and was an important element in the rise of organized resistance movements in Nazi-occupied Europe. Although millions of people were conscripted for work in Germany between 1942 and 1944, reports of poor working conditions and brutal treatment, combined with growing signs of an impending German defeat, made it increasingly difficult to find enough workers to meet growing German demands. The German retreat in the east and the shrinking area under Nazi control also reduced the number of workers available to meet German economic needs.

Living Conditions for Foreign Workers

The majority of foreign laborers were brought from Poland and the **SOVIET UNION**. The rest were drafted in **FRANCE**, Czechoslovakia, the **NETHERLANDS**, **BELGIUM**, and Norway. Among the satellite countries and Germany's allies, **ITALY** was the only one to provide foreign workers in significant numbers. The percentage of foreign workers employed by the German economy never came up to German expectations, but it grew progressively. By late 1944, the number of foreign laborers (including POWs) reached approximately nine million. One of every five workers in Germany was a foreigner, and one of every four tanks and every fourth aircraft manufactured in Germany was produced by foreign workers.

The people responsible for maintaining work force and production were well aware that living conditions, wages, and general treatment of foreign workers all had a direct bearing on recruitment difficulties and production problems. However, in most instances, the actual supervision of the laborers was in the hands of the police—the *Sicherheitspolizei* (Security Police or Sipo) and the Foreign Workers section of the **GESTAPO**—and they were guided by racist principles, partisan considerations, and a xenophobic fear and hatred of strangers and foreigners, not by general principles of human resource management.

The treatment of laborers from eastern Europe differed sharply from that of the laborers from western Europe in terms of living and working conditions. Poles and Russians, who were from the east, were regarded as inferior—in racist terms, they were *Untermenschen*, or "subhumans"—and, as a rule, they were put on hard physical labor and subjected to harsh control, humiliation, and severe penalties. They had to wear an identifying sign on their clothes, *P* for Poles and *Ost* (east) for the Russians. They were not permitted to leave their lodgings after working hours; to use public transportation; to attend cultural events or visit places of entertainment or restaurants frequented by Germans; or even to participate in the same church services as Germans. The pay they received for their work was especially low. Germans were warned not to have any social contact with Poles or Russians and, above all, to abide by racial purity, that is, to shun sexual intercourse with them. Germans who violated racial purity standards were charged with *Rassenschande* (race defilement), which carried the sentence of death.

Although they, too, complained of being treated like slaves, conditions for foreign workers from the west were much better. Their employers, especially the farmers who had foreigners working for them, often disregarded the strict rules on the treatment of foreign laborers laid down by the Nazi party, especially since these laborers were indispensable to them. Additionally, as Nazi defeats increased the need for more laborers, the Germans had to consider improving the treatment of foreign workers. Eventually, some changes were implemented.

Racist considerations precluded the sending of Jews to Germany as foreign workers. The few Jews who did infiltrate the ranks of workers coming to Germany from various countries made every effort to avoid being identified as Jews. Masses of Jews who were working as forced laborers in the occupied countries or as prisoners in concentration camps were taken away from their places of work and deported to the extermination camps. And, at a time when Germany was suffering from a severe shortage of manpower, millions of Russian POWs were dying of starvation, ill treatment, and deliberate murder.

Jews as Forced Laborers

Jews of occupied Poland were drafted for forced labor from the beginning of World War II until its end. As soon as the German army entered Poland in September 1939, Jews were forced to clear roadblocks and debris and to pave roads. German military forces played an active role in forcibly recruiting Jews for such work, seizing them at random on the streets or dragging them out of their homes, and maltreating them while they were at work. Often the only purpose for subjecting Jews to forced labor was to degrade them. In such cases, Jews were compelled to carry out physical exercise or hard physical tasks that had no practical purpose at all, and were subjected to beatings and to harassment such as the cutting off of their beards.

Not surprisingly, promised benefits rarely materialized, and the Nazis came to the conclusion that voluntary efforts would never provide the number of foreign workers needed for the building of the Third Reich.

A child laborer works at a machine in a Kovno ghetto workshop.

The Nazi policies of racism and mass killings were detrimental to the Reich's total war effort.

On October 26, 1939, compulsory labor laws were announced for the GENER-ALGOUVERNEMENT—regions of eastern Europe occupied by German forces. The law applied to Jewish males aged 14 to 60. Subsequently, the law was extended to apply also to women and to children between 12 and 14. In the period from October to December 1939, compulsory labor was also introduced by locally issued decrees for Jews living in those parts of Poland incorporated into the Reich.

By mid-January 1940, Governor-General Hans FRANK ordered full implementation of the law of October 26, 1939. The decrees required compulsory labor, by all Jews—men and women alike—from the ages of fourteen to sixty, whether or not they had employment of their own. The compulsory service was scheduled to extend over two years, but it could be prolonged "in case the desired re-educational goal had not been achieved in that period." So as to put the laws into practice, the Germans ordered all Jews aged 14 to 60 to register; this process was to be enforced by the Jewish Councils (*see* JUDENRAT). In addition, Jews were forced into temporary labor assignments, such as removing snow, loading goods that the Nazis had confiscated from Jews, and building walls around areas earmarked as ghettos, where Jews were required to live.

Labor Camps and Ghettos

As time went on, special labor camps were put up for Jews, who were personally drafted to work in them. They were housed in barracks and they worked under very harsh conditions. In the Lublin district, twenty-nine such camps were in operation by July 1940. In August of that year, 20,000 Jews between 19 and 35 were ordered to report to labor camps. Many chose to disregard the call-up, despite the heavy risks involved, because of the intolerable conditions of life and work in the camps. The inmates were exposed to humiliation, beatings, and being pursued by vicious dogs. Frequently the men on forced labor had no living quarters assigned to them and had to sleep under the open sky; they also did not receive even minimal

food rations. Those working on outdoor projects sometimes had to stand in water during their work. Many people perished in the camps; others were completely exhausted when they returned home from the camps and were permanently disabled. Out of 6,000 men from the **Warsaw** ghetto sent to the labor camps, 1,000 were no longer fit for work within two weeks. In certain ghettos, such as **Łódź**, the entire population was on forced labor and the ghettos themselves were turned into labor camps.

In addition, many Jews also worked in German factories in Poland and in ghetto workshops, especially in the months preceding the liquidation of the ghettos. At the end of 1940 more than 700,000 people were on forced labor in Poland. That number dropped to 500,000 in 1942 and a little over 100,000 in mid-1943. Reasons for the decrease include the high mortality rate in the ghettos and the Nazi destruction of the Jewish population. Conditions of work in places other than labor camps differed from one to the other; all had in common a ten- to twelve-hour workday and the total absence of social benefits and vacations.

Pay for Forced Labor

Forced laborers were paid little or nothing for their work. The rule concerning Jews was that their pay had to be lower than that of other nationalities. Even when minimum wages were paid, substantial deductions were made for various purposes, as determined by the Germans. In **Białystok**, for example, the deductions amounted to 50 percent of the total, and for the work on the Frankfurt-Posen highway, as much as 80 percent was deducted from the pay. Where wages were paid, they were also so low that the recipients could not buy any extra food on the black market, which meant that they starved like all the others. In these ways, the German policy on forced labor by Jews, and on the wages for such labor, contributed directly to the physical destruction of the Jews.

The End of Forced Labor

After most of the Jews had been killed, those remaining in the ghettos were forced to keep on working in various ways. Some labored in the workshops; some sorted out the possessions of murdered Jews for use by Germans; and some worked in other institutions and factories, serving the needs of the Reich. Factories that employed Jews had to pay substantial sums to the Security Police. In turn, the Jews had to pay bribes in order to obtain employment, which they sought to do by any means in the belief that this would save them from deportation to the **EXTERMINATION CAMPS**.

In mid-1942 and in April and May of 1943, some of the Jews in the Generalgouvernement ghettos were taken to labor camps at **Trawniki** and Poniatowa, where they were put to work in various workshops. In November 1943, the Germans murdered forty thousand Jews in these camps (*see* **Erntefest**). In Łódź, forced labor was kept up longer than anywhere else, until the ghetto was liquidated in August 1944.

See also **CONCENTRATION CAMPS, EXTERMINATION CAMPS, RACISM.**

Forced laborers were paid little or nothing for their work. The rule concerning Jews was that their pay had to be lower than that of other nationalities.

SUGGESTED RESOURCES

Axelrod, Toby. *In the Camps: Teens Who Survived the Nazi Concentration Camps.* New York: Rosen Pub. Group, 1999.

Birnbaum, Jacob. *I Kept My Promise: My Story of Holocaust Survival.* Lexington, MA: Jason R. Taylor Associates, 1995.

Browning, Christopher R. *Nazi Policy, Jewish Workers, German Killers.* New York: Cambridge University Press, 2000.

Ferencz, Benjamin B. *Less than Slaves: Jewish Forced Labor and the Quest for Compensation.* Cambridge: Harvard University Press, 1979.

Voices of the Shoah: Remembrances of the Holocaust [sound recording]. Rhino Records, 2000.

France

From the 1870s until 1940, France was governed as a republic; this period in France's history is, in fact, designated as the Third Republic. The country had never had a constitution, but it was governed by constitutional laws. In June 1940, France was defeated by the German army and an armistice (peace agreement) was signed with **GERMANY**. Under this agreement, France was divided into two areas: the occupied zone, which fell under direct German occupation, and the unoccupied zone, where the French National Assembly took up new headquarters in the spa town of Vichy, in the south of France. The occupied zone, which included **PARIS**, encompassed the entire Atlantic and English Channel coasts and contained the more fertile regions in western, northern, and eastern France. The Vichy regime, or simply Vichy, as it is sometimes called, was in name, at least, the government in charge of the whole country; the Vichy leaders generally maintained cooperative relations with the Nazi occupation forces.

France During the Vichy Regime and Nazi Occupation

Following the armistice with Germany in 1939, the National Assembly voted to suspend the constitutional laws by which France had been governed. Marshal Philippe Pétain was granted full powers as head of state by the National Assembly. Minister of State Pierre **LAVAL** worked diligently to bring Pétain and Adolf **HITLER** together. Their eventual meeting at Montoire from October 22 to 24, 1940, proved that Vichy's "national revolution" included a policy of collaboration with Germany. France, under the "new order," was to become part of the New Europe under Hitler's direction.

Since the Third Republic and its liberal principles no longer existed, the Vichy regime embarked on a policy of returning the country to the ideals of prerevolutionary France. The regime replaced the French revolutionary principles of "liberty, equality, and fraternity" with the more nationalistic principles of "work, family, and homeland." In this effort, the Vichy government clearly reflected French public opinion. After being defeated by Germany, the French were ready for a period of national renewal. Pétain's nationalistic call for a "new order" inspired by work, family and homeland was resoundingly welcomed by almost all elements of French society, including the Catholic church, which welcomed Pétain's efforts to bring France back to what the it regarded as pure Christian principles. As part of its "new order," the Vichy methodically began to curb the influence of "foreigners" in the country, encouraging the harassment of Jews and various refugee groups.

Despite the general approval of efforts to revitalize French national pride, support for the Vichy regime was not universal. Beginning in the summer of 1941, after Germany invaded the **SOVIET UNION**, French Communists and Socialists became increasingly dissatisfied with Vichy. This failed to change the Vichy goal of cooper-

> After the economic and political uncertainties of the prewar period, the French were ready for a period of national renewal. As part of its "new order," the Vichy began to curb the influence of "foreigners" in the country, encouraging the harassment of Jews and various refugee groups.

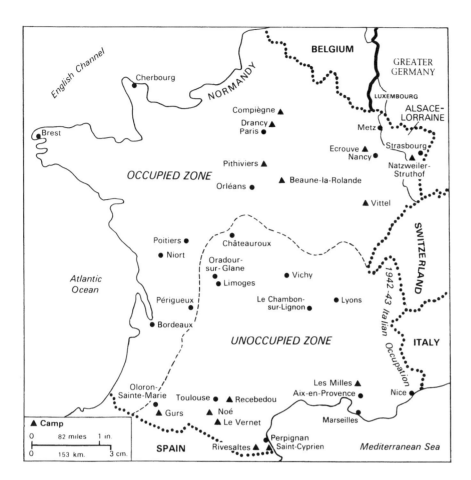

Vichy France and Occupied France.

ating with Nazi Germany. Indeed, the Vichy agreed to enact intensified **ANTI-JEW-ISH LEGISLATION** in the occupied zone. French officials were instructed to grant the German occupying forces all necessary assistance in making mass roundups of Jews in the summer of 1942. This was not well received. More and more French citizens protested against their government, among them leading figures in the Catholic and Protestant churches. Resistance activity, spurred on by increasing German repression and Vichy concessions, grew considerably.

By early November 1942 the Vichy zone had been occupied by the German and Italian forces. Although it was relatively peaceful, the German occupation had a negative effect on living conditions in France. The French people were increasingly taxed by the armistice agreement as occupation costs rose to approximately 500 million francs a day. In addition, France's food and raw materials were siphoned off for the war effort, causing shortages and economic hardships. More troubling was the growing number of French workers sent to Germany; by 1943 at least 700,000 had been deported for **FORCED LABOR**. Nevertheless, Laval did not reconsider his course of action. Convinced that Germany would prevail in the war, he believed it was in the long-term interest of France to continue to support the Third Reich.

The Italian occupation ended with the fall of Italy's fascist dictator Benito Mussolini, in 1943. The Allied landing in Normandy on June 6, 1944, signaled the end of the German occupation. The liberation of France came two months later. As the leader of the Free French movement Charles de Gaulle marched triumphantly into Paris, Pétain, Laval, and other Vichy officials fled to Germany. They would later be returned to Paris and tried for treason.

An antisemitic propoganda poster used by the Nazis to fuel antisemitic sentiment in France.

Jews in France

There is evidence that Jews have lived in France since the first century A.D. In 1306, 100,000 Jews were expelled from the country, although France had been a center of Jewish learning for nearly two centuries. Over several centuries, Jews returned to the region, and by the eve of the French Revolution (1789), the Jewish community in France numbered 40,000. The largest concentration was in Alsace-Lorraine. Jewish integration into French society had proceeded more or less smoothly, although there were occasional anti-Jewish episodes. Throughout the nineteenth century many Jews migrated to Paris, making it the center of Jewish life in France. In the period between the world wars, immigrants from eastern Europe also flocked to Paris, while thousands of Jewish refugees from Germany sought refuge in the city in the 1930s. At the onset of World War II, two-thirds of French Jews lived in Paris. Based on their countries of origin, there were many philosophical, social, and political differences among them.

ETAT FRANÇAIS

Ville de VICHY

ARRÊTÉ MUNICIPAL

RECENSEMENT des ISRAELITES

Nous, Maire de la Ville de Vichy, Officier de la Légion d'Honneur,
Vu la loi du 2 Juin 1941 remplaçant la loi du 3 Octobre 1940, portant statut des Juifs,
Vu la loi du 2 Juin 1941, prescrivant le recensement des Juifs,
Vu les instructions Préfectorales du 21 Juillet 1941,
Vu la loi du 5 Avril 1884,

ARRÊTONS :

ARTICLE PREMIER. — Toutes personnes françaises ou étrangères, quel que soit leur âge, qui sont juives au regard de la loi du 2 Juin 1941, portant statut des Juifs et se trouvant en résidence à Vichy, devront se faire recenser à l'ECOLE JULES-FERRY, face à la Justice de Paix, **AVANT LE 31 JUILLET 1941.**

ARTICLE DEUX. — Les intéressés devront se présenter dans le délai de rigueur fixé ci-dessus, au bureau de recensement qui leur délivrera les imprimés réglementaires de déclaration individuelle à remplir.

ARTICLE TROIS. — Il est rappelé, conformément à la loi, que toute infraction à ces dispositions sera punie d'un emprisonnement de un mois à un an et d'une amende de 100 à 10.000 francs ou de l'une de ces deux peines seulement, sans préjudice du droit, pour le Préfet, de prononcer l'internement dans un camp spécial, même si l'intéressé est Français.

ARTICLE QUATRE. — M. le Directeur de la Police d'Etat et les Agents placés sous ses ordres sont chargés, chacun en ce qui le concerne, de l'exécution du présent arrêté.

Fait à Vichy, en l'Hôtel de Ville, le 24 Juillet 1941.

Le Maire : **P.-V. LEGER.**

IMP. VIDAL & MARTIN

VILLE DE VICHY - SERVICE DU RATIONNEMENT

Distribution des Titres d'Alimentation

A sign announcing the conscription of Jews in Vichy, France, 1941.

In the 1930s France began to reassess its open-door policy toward Jewish immigrants. There was general pressure to put a stop to Jewish immigration and to annul Jewish rights. Though stringent restrictions against refugees were gradually introduced and internment camps were set up for them, Jews retained their civil rights until the fall of France and the establishment of the Vichy regime.

In the summer of 1940, when France fell to German control, about 350,000 Jews lived in the country, more than half of whom were not French citizens. Among these were tens of thousands of Jewish refugees from **BELGIUM**, the **NETHERLANDS**, and Luxembourg, some of whom had fled Germany several years earlier. Persecution of these Jews began almost immediately.

Deportations and Persecution

The deportation of French Jews to camps in eastern Europe from 1942 to 1944 was the culmination of two years of aggressive persecution. Jews had been subjected to anti-Jewish laws, economic isolation, imprisonment, harassment, and registration with the local police.

Compared with other nations occupied by the Nazis, France retained an unusual amount of autonomy. Throughout the entire period of the deportations of Jews, France had a French government, based in Vichy; a head of state (Marshal Pétain); an administration at least nominally responsible for the whole of the country; and a powerful police force.

The Germans needed and received a great deal of assistance from the French to carry out their plans against the Jews. After the war, defenders of Vichy claimed that the work of this government limited the number of Jewish deportees from France. However, close examination of the German record, as well as research on the role of Vichy and its agencies, tells a different story.

The deportation of the Jews to camps in eastern Europe from 1942 to 1944 was the culmination of two years of aggressive legislation and persecution. Jews were subjected to anti-Jewish laws, economic isolation, imprisonment, and registration with the local police. In October 1940, the Vichy government issued the comprehensive **JEWISH LAW** (*Statut Des Juifs*) in October 1940. It also established a central agency for coordinating anti-Jewish legislation and activity, the General Office for Jewish Affairs.

The Vichy leadership believed that the Germans would be grateful to the French for pursuing their own anti-Jewish policy, and would respond by giving them more autonomy. At the same time, the French were anxious to see that any property confiscated from the Jews did not fall into the hands of the Germans. Therefore, the Vichy regime launched an extensive program of **ARYANIZATION**—conversion of Jewish assets to non-Jewish ownership-in July 1941. The objective was to keep formerly Jewish property in France. In practice, "Aryanization" simply meant the confiscation of Jewish possessions by the state. It developed into a vast property transfer, involving some 42,000 Jewish businesses, buildings, and other properties.

Without personal or business assets, and barred from working in their professions, thousands of Jews were turned into penniless refugees in France. Foreign Jews were particularly vulnerable, and were especially victimized by both the Germans and Vichy. Thousands were forced into labor camps or interned, often in conditions that approached the Nazi **CONCENTRATION CAMPS** of the 1930s. The first victims of the Holocaust in France died in these camps; their number eventually reached about 3000.

After the **WANNSEE CONFERENCE** of January 1942, at which they received tacit support for their pursuit of a Jew-free Europe, the Nazis prepared to remove Jews from France and other western European countries. At the end of April, Pierre Laval became head of the French government under Marshal Pétain. On June 11, German officials decided to make regular deportations of Jews from France, Belgium, and the Netherlands. Demands for cooperation were made to the Vichy government. After deliberations, Laval and the French cabinet agreed to help.

Throughout the summer and fall of 1942, Jews were rounded up in both the occupied and unoccupied zones. Most of the work was done by the **FRENCH POLICE**. On July 16 and 17, in one of their most cruel operations, they rounded up 12,884 Jews in Paris. Some 7,000 of them—families with small children—were crowded for days in the Vélodrome d'Hiver sports arena with no food, water, or sanitary facilities. Elsewhere, parents were torn from their children, and the victims were packed into cattle cars and shipped to the transit camp at **DRANCY**, just outside Paris. In all, 42,500 Jews were sent eastward from France in 1942, perhaps one-third of them from the Vichy zone.

The **DEPORTATIONS** of the summer and fall of 1942 stirred the first serious opposition to Vichy. The roundups of Jews could scarcely be concealed, and the people bitterly disapproved of the separation of families. A split developed in the Catholic church, which had been solidly behind Pétain. Highly placed clergymen now made their first open protest against the anti-Jewish activity of the regime.

Further difficulties arose as the deportations gradually moved beyond Jewish immigrants to include French Jews as well. The Vichy regime had agreed to deport foreign Jews from both zones, but the authorities were soon pressured to send more Jews in order to fill the Nazis' deportation quotas. Even Laval dragged his feet; in August 1943 he refused to strip French Jews of their citizenship in order to facilitate their deportation. Despite these occasional protests and difficulties, the deportations continued. The last convoys left France in the summer of 1944.

Thousands of Jews were assisted by a small number of sympathetic French people, often at great risk to the rescuers. Many were French Protestants, themselves a somewhat harassed minority in France. Help and sanctuary also came from the Quakers, the American Jewish **JOINT DISTRIBUTION COMMITTEE** (known as the Joint), the YMCA, the Catholic Témoignage Chrétien, and Jewish resistance networks. An outstanding example of rescue work took place at the Protestant village of **LE CHAMBON-SUR-LIGNON**, which developed a kind of underground railway, smuggling several thousand Jews to safety.

In all, over 77,000 Jews from France were either killed in concentration camps in **POLAND** or died while in detention. Approximately 70,000 went to **AUSCHWITZ**, and the rest to other camps—**MAJDANEK** and **SOBIBÓR**, and a few dozen to **BUCHENWALD** in August 1944.

The **"FINAL SOLUTION"** in France was a Nazi project from beginning to end. Few of the French advocated the killing of Jews, and only a small number of extremists in Paris ever carried antisemitism to the murderous dimensions of Hitler and his associates.

There is no evidence, however, that Vichy authorities attempted in a concerted way to limit the deportations. Most of the officials at Vichy shared in the widespread anti-Jewish mood of 1940. The plight of the Jews was of secondary consideration; preserving as much French autonomy as possible under Nazi occupation was the primary interest, and that required a high level of collaboration with the Nazis. Recent research, therefore, rejects the theory the Vichy regime pursued a consciously plotted strategy to save as many Jews as possible.

Jewish Responses to Persecution

When the Germans invaded France in May 1940, more than 100,000 Jews fled to the unoccupied region in the south, among them Jewish leaders and rabbis. After the armistice was signed on June 22 and the French leadership called on Frenchmen to return to the north, as many as 30,000 Jews are reported to have returned to the occupied zone. During the initial months of confusion after the armistice, another 30,000 Jews crossed the southern French border in the hope of finding refuge abroad.

The process of reorganizing the Jewish community slowly began in the fall of 1940. Jews had varied and contradictory opinions about the possibility of Jewish life under Nazi occupation and Vichy rule; the native Jews and those who had emigrated from eastern Europe had rarely agreed on issues before the Nazi occupation, and this did not change in the face of Nazi control. By January 1941, Jewish leaders of both groups had been pressured, by the SS officials in charge of Jewish affairs, to create an umbrella organization known as the Coordinating Committee of Jewish

> "**I**n the course of the first two years of the Occupation, Le Chambon became the safest place for Jews in Europe."
>
> **Philip Hallie, *Lest Innocent Blood Be Shed: The Story of the Village of Le Chambon and How Goodness Happened There* (New York: Harper Torchbooks), 1994, p. 129.**

Thousands of Jews were assisted by a small number of sympathetic French people, often at great risk to the rescuers.

Welfare Societies. The Jewish leadership was concerned about the growing poverty within the Jewish community. But not all Jews felt that the Coordinating Committee was a good idea. Many sensed that working on the committee involved cooperation with the Germans on some level. Immigrant Jews, in particular, were not in favor of this. They stopped participating on the committee, thereby worsening relations within the community.

The contrasting attitudes between immigrant and native Jews with regard to the Coordinating Committee were reflected in the emergence of resistance activity. Far more Jewish immigrants than native Jews had gravitated toward resistance groups during the first 18 months of the occupation; they feared even the slightest association with the Germans. The more established sectors of the native community preferred to wait and count on the French authorities for support.

In the south of France, where massive migration had increased the Jewish population to approximately 150,000, the needs of the Jewish community were also urgent. Jews had flocked to the major cities—Lyons, Marseilles, Toulouse—and to hundreds of smaller ones. Former leaders of the Jewish community resettled in Lyons and Marseilles and gradually began to map out plans for relief. In the south, too, conflicts and lack of trust characterized relations between native and immigrant Jews.

Despite the flood of antisemitic legislation initiated by the Vichy regime, most Jews in the region trusted the Vichy leadership, and took a "wait and see" attitude rather than engaging in resistance activity. Individual and community attention centered on coping with the daily difficulties of life. As the war progressed, however, and Nazi intentions against the Jews became more apparent, opposition within the community grew.

The deportations that began in March 1942 jolted the community, sending Jews into a frenzied search for refuge from the Nazis and the French police. Jews began to seek hiding places in thousands of French villages and rural communities, aided by the local population. Thousands more attempted to cross over the border to Switzerland. More than 27,000 Jews were caught and deported by Germans that summer. Countless families were separated, and many were left homeless. These events accelerated Jewish resistance tendencies in both the north and the south.

Encouraged by French protests and humanitarian actions, Jewish relief groups encouraged Jews to resist the authorities. Some Jewish organizations turned to illegal activity—removing Jewish children to Christian homes and monasteries, forging identification papers and documents, aiding Jews in hiding and in crossing the border to Spain and Switzerland. These activities antagonized the Jews who still preferred to operate within the law.

French Jewry's predicament deteriorated still further in the wake of the German occupation of the south in November 1942. Some 2000 foreign and native Jews were seized in a large-scale roundup in Marseilles at the end of January 1943. More roundups followed in Lyons and other southern cities. As many as 30,000 Jews fled to the Italian occupied zone by September 1943. With the Italian defeat and subsequent German takeover of these regions, however, this was no longer a safe harbor. Thousands of Jews were rounded up by the German net; thousands of others avoided arrest by immediately going into hiding.

Jews who remained under German occupation, in the north and south, experienced varying conditions during this period. Parisian Jews enjoyed some relief after the traumatic days of July 1942. They did not experience another major roundup, but many left the city to hide in small villages and hamlets. By mid-1944, only

15,000 Jews lived openly in the capital. Many of them continued to receive relief in one form or another from Jewish organizations. In the German-occupied south, where Gestapo efforts to increase deportations were supported by the French militia, Jews were often on the run. In 1944, Jewish leaders set aside their ideological differences in order coordinate resistance activity among the Jewish groups.

Reconstruction of French Jewry

After the Holocaust, French Jewry confronted the massive task of rebuilding Jewish culture and community. Parisian Jewry was weakened seriously by the loss of approximately 50,000 members. Throughout France, Jews mourned the complete disappearance of hundreds of small communities. In addition, many large settlements were reduced to a mere handful of Jewish families.

However, in comparison with other European Jewish communities, the situation of French Jewry was far from hopeless. French Jews had experienced the Holocaust, but they had survived in large enough numbers to reassert themselves after the war. The unending stream of Jewish survivors fleeing **DISPLACED PERSONS'** camps and emerging from hiding—more than 35,000 in the first three years after the war—meant that France would soon contain the largest Jewish community on the Continent.

The Jewish community in post-war France faced many challenges, but three consumed most of its energy and interest: the restoration of stolen Jewish property; the care and feeding of refugees; and the plight of children who had lost their parents. Despite intense efforts, French Jewry had only limited success in reclaiming the businesses and other property of deportees. More successful were the activities of the Jewish Committee for Social Action and Reconstruction, which was able to feed and house nearly three-quarters of the 40,000 Holocaust survivors who sought refuge in France. Thanks to the efforts of relief and advocacy organizations for children, nearly 100 institutions were created to care for orphaned children and to reintegrate them into the community. While the French Jewish community was able to provide foster parents for orphans, however, it had little success in recovering Jewish children adopted by non-Jews during the war.

During the post-war years of 1940s and 1950s, the Jews of France managed to create new institutions and rehabilitate the tens of thousands of broken men and women who returned from the Nazi **EXTERMINATION CAMPS** and emerged from hiding. Nonetheless, the differences that created division in the pre-war years re-emerged. In addition to negotiating these renewed tensions, the Jews of France had to come to terms with the painful reality that the majority of the French people, as well as its government, had not actively opposed the Nazi's intended destruction of the Jews. French Jewry in the 1940s and early 1950s lacked confidence in its future. Though far from dead, the French Jewish community seemed to be marking time, waiting, as it had done in the past, for a fresh infusion of immigrants. This in fact took place, beginning in the mid-1950s, with the influx of Jews from North Africa.

A divided community at the outset of the war, French Jewry found itself both weakened and reoriented by the war's end. The Jewish community had lost around 78,000 Jews and harbored thousands of broken families in its midst. But the trend in 1944 toward organizational unity would serve the community well in the very difficult period of reconstruction to come.

SUGGESTED READING

Josephs, Jeremy. *Swastika Over Paris.* New York: Arcade, 1989.

Klarsfeld, Serge. *French Children of the Holocaust: A Memorial.* New York: New York University Press, 1996.

Lazare, Lucien. *Rescue as Resistance: How Jewish Organizations Fought the Holocaust in France.* New York: Columbia University Press, 1996.

Lewendel, Isaac. *Not the Germans Alone: A Son's Search for the Truth of Vichy.* Evanston, IL: Northwestern University Press, 1999.

Weisberg, Richard H. *Vichy Law and the Holocaust in France.* New York: New York University Press, 1996.

Frank, Anne

> "Never have we heard one word of the burden which we certainly must be to them, never has one of them complained of all the trouble we give....They put on the brightest possible faces, bring flowers and presents for birthdays.... although others may show heroism in the war or against the Germans, our helpers display heroism in their cheerfulness and affection."
>
> **Anne Frank, writing in her diary about those who helped her family remain hidden.**

Anne Frank's Family

Anne Frank's father, Otto Heinrich Frank (1889–1980), was born in Frankfurt, **GERMANY**. He grew up in a liberal Jewish environment, attended high school, and trained for a while at Macy's department store in New York City. During World War I, Frank was a reserve officer in the German army. After the war, he started his own business, with mixed success. In 1925, Frank married Edith Holländer, the daughter of factory owners in Aachen. The couple had two daughters, Margot Betti (born February 16, 1926) and Annelies Marie (born June 12, 1929), who was called Anne.

Soon after the Nazis came to power in January 1933 and the first anti-Jewish measures were announced, the Frank family decided to leave Germany. Otto Frank went to Amsterdam. He knew the city well from frequent visits and had several good friends there. After he found an apartment, the rest of his family joined him. Frank set up a company, Opekta, that made and distributed pectin for use in home-made jams and jellies. In 1938, Frank started a second company, Pectacon, with Hermann van Pels, who had recently fled to Amsterdam from Osnabrück in Germany with his wife Auguste and son Peter. Pectacon specialized in the preparation of spices for sausage making.

Anne and Margot Frank quickly adapted themselves to their new life. They learned Dutch and attended the local Montessori school. The Franks joined the liberal Jewish congregation of Amsterdam. Their relatively carefree existence came to an end on May 10, 1940, when the Germans invaded and occupied the Netherlands. The invasion was soon followed by anti-Jewish measures. In October of that year, a law was passed that required all Jewish-owned businesses to be registered. With the help of non-Jewish friends and colleagues, both of Otto Frank's companies, Opekta and Pectacon, were "Aryanized" on paper—that is, the ownership was transferred from Jewish to non-Jewish control, and the businesses continued. Another law stipulated that Jewish children could attend only Jewish schools, so Anne and Margot switched to the Jewish Lyceum.

Meanwhile, Otto Frank had begun preparations to go into hiding, if this proved necessary. Little by little, the family's possessions were brought to the vacant annex of Frank's office at Prinsengracht 263. Four employees were informed of his plans—Victor Kugler, Johannes Kleiman, Elli Voskuijl, and Miep Gies (born Hermine Santrouschitz)—and they agreed to help the Frank family. Miep had worked with Otto Frank for years and had become his closest associate. Born in Vienna, she was one of the many thousands of Austrian children who were taken into Dutch foster homes to improve their health after World War I. Miep had stayed on, and in 1941 she married Jan Gies.

The Franks' plans to go into hiding went into high gear on July 5, 1942, when Margot received a registered letter from the Nazi **CENTRAL OFFICE FOR JEWISH EMIGRATION** (Zentralstelle Für Jüdische Auswanderung). Margot, then sixteen

Otto Frank with daughters Margot (left) and Anne (front).

years old, was ordered to register for what the letter called "labor expansion measures." After consultation with the van Pels family, the Franks decided to go into hiding immediately. They moved into the annex the next day, followed a week later by the van Pels family and their fifteen-year-old son Peter. On November 16, 1942, they were joined by an eighth *onderduiker* (literally, "one who dives under"), the dentist Fritz Pfeffer, who had fled from Berlin in 1938. These eight people were to spend two years living in a few cramped rooms fashioned from a warehouse attic. Since food and clothing had become scarce and could be bought only with coupons, which Jews in hiding could not obtain, the four helpers in the office managed somehow to buy enough supplies to feed and clothe eight additional people, often at great risk to their own lives.

Eight people spent more than two years in a few cramped attic rooms. Only one survived what followed.

The Jews Are Betrayed

On August 4, 1944, the **SD** (*Sicherheitsdienst*; Security Service) in Amsterdam received an anonymous phone call—it has never been established from whom—with information about Jews in hiding at Prinsengracht 263. A police van immediately drove to the Prinsengracht, and the eight Jews were found and arrested. A

policeman named Silberbauer demanded money and jewelry; in order to hide these, he emptied an attaché case full of papers, which he threw on the floor. Among these papers was Anne Frank's diary. Also arrested were Kleiman and Kugler, two of the employees who had assisted the families. After the police left, Miep Gies and Elli Voskuijl went back to the annex to pick up many personal items, such as photographs, books, and other papers. They retrieved Anne's diary pages and put them away until Anne's return. A few days later, all of the furniture and clothing was hauled away from the annex, a customary procedure after an arrest. During the arrests, Miep Gies had realized that Silberbauer, like herself, came from Vienna. This may have been why he did not arrest her, although he made it clear that he suspected her of having helped the Jews. The next day, Miep sought him out to see if there was a way that the prisoners could be set free, but Silberbauer indicated that there was nothing he could do. Kugler and Kleiman were taken to the concentration camp in Amersfoort in the **NETHERLANDS**. Kleiman suffered a hemorrhage of the stomach, and was sent home in September 1944 through the intervention of the Red Cross. Kugler was able to escape while being transported in March 1945; he remained in hiding until the liberation of the Netherlands in May of that year.

After the Annex

The Jewish prisoners arrived at the **WESTERBORK** transit camp on August 8, 1944. Every week, a full trainload of prisoners left from there for the extermination camps. On September 3, the last transport to leave Westerbork for **AUSCHWITZ** departed. According to the meticulously kept transport lists, there were 1,011 people on board, among them the Franks, the van Pels family, and Pfeffer. When they arrived at Auschwitz-Birkenau, 549 of the prisoners were gassed immediately. Hermann van Pels was one of these. Edith Frank, her daughters Margot and Anne, and Auguste van Pels were interned in the women's block. Pfeffer was the next to die. He is listed in the death book of the **NEUENGAMME** camp on December 20, 1944. Edith Frank perished at Auschwitz-Birkenau on January 6, 1945. It has not been established where and when Auguste van Pels died, but it is assumed that it was at the end of March or early April, somewhere in Germany or Czechoslovakia. Peter van Pels was one of the many thousands of prisoners who were put on **DEATH MARCHES** because of the advancing Russian army. He died shortly before the liberation in May 1945 in the **MAUTHAUSEN** camp in Austria.

Anne and Margot were sent to **BERGEN-BELSEN** at the end of October 1944. This camp filled up with thousands of prisoners from other camps that were being vacated as the Russians advanced. Housing, food, and medicine were totally inadequate, and many prisoners weakened from hunger and the cold. A typhus epidemic took many victims. Margot died of typhus around the beginning of March; Anne, who believed that both her parents had perished, died a few days later, also of typhus. Two sisters from Amsterdam who had been with the Frank sisters in both Westerbork and Auschwitz later stated that they had carried Anne's body from the sick barrack. She was buried in one of the mass graves at Bergen-Belsen. Otto Frank was the only survivor of the eight who hid in the attic. The Soviet army liberated Auschwitz on January 27, 1945, and Frank returned to Amsterdam the following June. After Anne's death had been confirmed, Miep Gies returned to Otto Frank the papers that she had kept.

Anne's Diary

On June 12, 1942, her thirteenth birthday, Anne received a red-checked diary from her father. That same day, Anne wrote on the first page: "I hope I shall be able

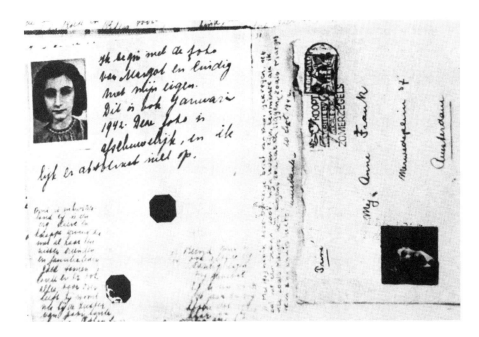

to confide in you completely, as I have never been able to do in anyone before, and I hope that you will be a great support and comfort to me."

In letters to an imaginary friend, Anne painted a picture of herself and her personal development in the context of the problems and fears of eight Jews trying to hide from deportation, unknowingly writing what would become one of the most famous accounts of life in hiding from Nazi persecutors. The frightening news about the developments on the outside reached those in hiding through the radio and through their helpers. Still, those in hiding tried to lead a normal life. For Anne as well as Margot and Peter, this meant doing homework with the help of their old schoolbooks and new books borrowed from the library by Miep and Elli.

Fear of discovery created enormous pressure on those in hiding. During the day, they could not move around or use the bathroom because not everyone in the office below was aware of their presence. The close quarters and constant tensions were often too much for Anne. On October 29, 1943, she wrote:

> I wander from one room to another, downstairs and up again, feeling like a song-bird whose wings have been brutally clipped and who is beating itself in utter darkness against the bars of its cage. "Go outside, laugh, and take a breath of fresh air," a voice cries within me, but I don't even feel a response any more; I go and lie on the divan and sleep, to make the time move quickly, and the stillness and the terrible fear, because there is no way of killing them.

Anne described conflicts with her mother, her special relationship with her father, her sexual development, and her efforts to improve her character. She fell in love with Peter but later wrote about her disappointment in him.

Anne's diary is also a monument to the helpers who struggled to obtain food and clothing and provided spiritual support for two years:

> Our helpers are a very good example. They have pulled us through up till now and we hope they will bring us safely to dry land. Otherwise, they will have to share the same fate as the many others who are being searched for. Never have we heard one word of the burden which we certainly must be to them, never has one of them complained of all the trouble we give.

They all come upstairs every day, talk to the men about business and politics, to the women about food and wartime difficulties, and about newspapers and books with the children. They put on the brightest possible faces, bring flowers and presents for birthdays and bank holidays, are always ready to help and do all they can. That is something we must never forget; although others may show heroism in the war or against the Germans, our helpers display heroism in their cheerfulness and affection.

On March 28, 1944, Anne heard a British radio report about a plan to gather diaries and letters about the war. "Of course, they all made a rush at my diary immediately," she wrote the following day. "Just imagine how interesting it would be if I were to publish a romance of the 'Secret Annex.' The title alone would be enough to make people think it was a detective story." On May 11, she wrote:

> Now, about something else: you've known for a long time that my greatest wish is to become a journalist some day and later a famous writer. Whether these leanings towards greatness (of insanity?) will ever materialize remains to be seen, but I certainly have the subjects in my mind. In any case, I want to publish a book entitled *Het Achterhuis* [The Annex] after the war. Whether I shall succeed or not, I cannot say, but my diary will be a great help.

Anne prepared a list of pseudonyms for possible publication: Van Pels became Van Daan, Pfeffer became Dussel, and so on.

Anne observed herself and her environment, made plans for the future, commented and criticized, and did not spare herself in that regard. In the high-pressure situation of the annex, she changed from a shy young girl to a young woman. Superficial comments about girlfriends and admirers made place for philosophical statements about herself and the world around her. One of the last entries in the diary is from July 15, 1944:

> That's the difficulty in these times: ideals, dreams, and cherished hopes rise within us, only to meet the horrible truth and be shattered. It's really a wonder that I haven't dropped all my ideals because they seem so absurd and impossible to carry out. Yet, I keep them, because in spite of everything I still believe that people are really good at heart. I simply can't build up my hopes on a foundation consisting of confusion, misery, and death. I see the world gradually being turned into a wilderness, I hear the ever-approaching thunder, which will destroy us too, I can feel the sufferings of millions, and yet, if I look up into the heavens, I think that it will all come right, that this cruelty too will end, and that peace and tranquillity will return again. In the meantime, I must uphold my ideals, for perhaps the time will come when I shall be able to carry them out. Yours, Anne.

Apart from the diary, Miep also saved two other works that Anne created: a book of stories, "Stories and Adventures from the Annex," and the "Book of Beautiful Phrases," in which Anne had copied quotations that had pleased her.

When Otto Frank showed some of the passages from Anne's diary to some friends, they persuaded him to find a publisher. The historian Jan Romein published an article in which he related his emotions on reading parts of the diary. Shortly thereafter, the publisher Contact approached Otto Frank and *The Annex* appeared in June 1947.

For many people, Anne's diary is their introduction to the Nazi persecution of the Jews. In 1950, it appeared in Germany and France, and in 1952 in the United States and England. For the American edition, Eleanor Roosevelt wrote in the preface: "This is a remarkable book. Written by a young girl—and the young are not

ANNE FRANK'S DIARY STILL GETS HEADLINES

The influence of Anne Frank's diary is such that those who try to deny the Nazis' crimes also denounce the diary as a fraud. In order to counter such efforts, in 1986 the Rijksinstituut for Oorlogsdocumentatie (Netherlands State Institute for War Documentation) in Amsterdam published an annotated edition of both versions of Anne's diary, the earlier edition with passages deleted by her father, because he deemed them too personal, and a later, complete version. Several pieces from her "Story Book" were also added to the diary. The English translation of the annotated diary appeared in 1989.

In 1998, Cor Suijk, a Holocaust survivor and friend of the Frank family, revealed that even after the "complete" diary was published in 1989, five unpublished pages were still in his possession. Asserting that the pages had been given to him by Otto Frank before his death in 1980, Suijk released excerpts of the missing information, including unflattering descriptions of Otto and Edith Frank's marriage, to an Amsterdam newspaper. At the time of his announcement, Suijk indicated that the pages would only be published in their entirety in exchange for increased financial support for his Holocaust awareness work in the United States, through the Anne Frank Center USA in New York. Suijk's control of the pages, as well as their authenticity, have remained controversial issues among Holocaust scholars and publishers.

afraid of telling the truth—it is one of the wisest and most moving commentaries on war and its impact on human beings that I have ever read."

The diary has been published in more than 50 editions; the total number of copies printed amounts to more than 25 million in 55 languages. Dramatic presentations have also reached a large public. The stage version by Albert Hackett and Frances Goodrich, *The Diary of Anne Frank*, premiered on Broadway on October 5, 1955, and received the Pulitzer prize for the best play of the year. The film version followed in 1959. In 1996, Jon Blair produced the film *Anne Frank Remembered*, which won an Academy Award for Best Documentary Film.

After Otto Frank's death, the rest of Anne's papers went to the Netherlands State Institute for War Documentation. The diary itself is on loan to the Anne Frank House and is on display there. The copyright is owned by the independent Anne Frank Foundation in Basel.

Anne's wish—"I want to live on, even after my death"—has become a reality. Throughout the world, she has become a symbol of the millions of victims of the Holocaust.

The Anne Frank House

After the publication of *The Annex*, many visitors found their way to the house at Prinsengracht 263, which was still being used as an office. In 1957, there

The house in Amsterdam where Anne Frank and her family hid from the Nazis for two years. It is now the site of a museum.

were plans to raze the house to make room for a new building, but public outcry prevented this action. The owner of the building then donated the house to the newly established Anne Frank Foundation on condition that the building be open to visitors.

The museum opened its doors in 1960. It was Otto Frank's wish that the museum not become a memorial to Anne but instead contribute to an understanding of prejudice and discrimination. For that reason, a primary goal of the museum is to educate visitors about the destructiveness of **ANTISEMITISM** and **RACISM**. The Anne Frank Foundation maintains a documentation center on antisemitism and racist groups in Western Europe and the United States. It produces teaching aids and organizes traveling exhibits in various languages. The foundation also has an office in New York City.

SUGGESTED RESOURCES

Anne Frank Remembered [videorecording]. Columbia TriStar Home Video, 1996.

Frank, Anne. *Anne Frank: The Diary of a Young Girl.* New York: Bantam Books, 1993.

Gies, Miep. *Anne Frank Remembered: The Story of the Woman Who Helped to Hide the Frank Family.* New York: Simon and Schuster, 1987.

Muller, Melissa. *Anne Frank: The Biography.* Translated by Rita and Robert Kimber. New York: Henry Holt, 1998.

Rol, Ruud van der. *Anne Frank, Beyond the Diary: A Photographic Remembrance.* New York: Viking, 1993.

Frank, Hans

(1900–1946)

Hans Frank was a lawyer and Nazi official who served as the governor-general of **POLAND** from 1939 to 1945. Frank graduated from a Munich *Gymnasium* (high school) in 1918. He displayed his commitment to militant nationalist and right-wing politics by joining the *Epp Freikorps* (a paramilitary group commanded by Ritter von Epp) in 1919 while he was pursuing the study of law at the universities of Kiel and Munich. In 1923 he joined the Storm Troopers (*Sturmabteilung*; SA) and **NAZI PARTY**, and took part in Hitler's ill-fated **Beer-Hall Putsch** in Munich. He fled briefly to **AUSTRIA**, then returned to **GERMANY** to finish his doctorate at the University of Kiel in 1924.

Beer-Hall Putsch
A failed attempt at a government take-over in Bavaria on November 8, 1923.

In 1926, Frank left the Nazi party in protest against Hitler's renunciation of German claims over the South Tyrol, only to rejoin a year later. His career in the party then flourished as he became attorney to various party members, most prominently defending Hitler in his many libel cases and serving as defense counsel in the 1930 Leipzig trial of three Nazi army officers. He also handled the very delicate matter of researching Hitler's family tree for possible Jewish ancestors.

After Hitler took power, Frank's usefulness rapidly diminished. A middle-class intellectual who was never admitted to the inner circle of Nazi leaders, Frank remained oblivious to Hitler's open aversion to law, lawyers, and any procedures that threatened to curtail his own freedom of action. He was appointed to numerous "official" posts that had little power during 1933 and 1934. From 1934 to 1941 he was president of the Academy for German Law, with the self-assigned task of reformulating German law on the basis of National Socialist principles.

When Germany conquered Poland in September 1939, the eastern third of the country was occupied by the **SOVIET UNION** (in accordance with the secret terms of the Nazi-Soviet Pact), the western third was annexed to the Third Reich, and the central region became a German-occupied territory known as the **GENERALGOUVERNEMENT**. Hans Frank, the legal expert of the Nazi party and Hitler's personal lawyer, was appointed governor-general. From that point on, Frank generally played a major role in implementing Nazi racial policies in eastern Europe.

As leader of the Generalgouvernement, Frank wanted to build up a strong power base for himself while retaining Hitler's favor. However, Hitler's practice of presiding over a chaotic system of "institutional Darwinism"—leaving his various subordinates to engage in a constant internal struggle for power and jurisdiction and keeping for himself the role of indispensable arbiter and pacesetter—was incompatible with Frank's passionate vision of logic, order, and "unity of administration."

Hans Frank in Nazi uniform.

Hans Frank (l) and General Field Marshal Wilhelm reviewing troops, October 1940.

In his desire to build up his own power base, Frank preferred a policy of economic stabilization, better treatment of the Poles, and an integration of the Polish people into the Third Reich. However, in an effort to remain in Hitler's good graces, and so as not to be upstaged by his rival, Heinrich **HIMMLER**, Frank often veered suddenly to support policies of radical brutality and destructiveness toward the Poles. In one shift of policy, he alternately opposed and supported the influx of Poles and Jews expelled from the "incorporated territories." On the one hand he approved the self-sufficiency of ghetto economies and encouraged the rational use of ghetto labor, while on the other, he supported the starvation and then mass murder of the Jews.

Ultimately, Frank's loyalty to Hitler and his own ambition could not be reconciled. He saw himself as the head of the model "crusader kingdom" in Germany's expansion to the east, while Hitler saw the Generalgouvernement as the racial dumping ground, the slave-labor reservoir, and finally the slaughter yard of the Third Reich. Since Himmler's views more closely approximated those of Hitler, Frank's defeat was inevitable. On March 5, 1942, Frank was summoned before a tribunal consisting of Himmler, Hans Heinrich Lammers, and Martin **BORMANN**. He was stripped of all jurisdiction over racial and police matters in the Generalgouvernement, yet he retained his now-powerless position as governor-general.

Perhaps hoping to force Hitler to relieve him from this humiliating position, Frank delivered a series of lectures at four German universities in the summer of

1942, denouncing the emasculation of German justice by the police state. He also sent Hitler a long memorandum criticizing **SS** policies in Poland. "You should not slaughter the cow you want to milk," he concluded. Hitler relieved Frank of all his party positions and forbade him to speak publicly within the Reich, but refused to accept his numerous letters of resignation. Thus Frank remained as governor-general until he fled as Russian troops approached. He took with him the many volumes of his official diary that have since become a major source for historians of the Third Reich and an important document for the Nuremberg Military Tribunals. Frank was tried among the major war criminals in the Nuremberg Trial, and hanged at Nuremberg.

SUGGESTED RESOURCES

"Hans Frank." *A Teacher's Guide to the Holocaust.* [Online] http://fcit.coedu.usf.edu/holocaust/resource/document/DocFrank.htm (accessed on August 22, 2000).

"Individual Responsibility of Defendants: Hans Frank," in *Nazi Conspiracy and Aggression* (vol. II). USGPO, 1946. [Online] http://www.ess.uwe.ac.uk/genocide/Frank.htm (accessed on August 22, 2000).

French Police

After **FRANCE** was defeated by **GERMANY** in 1940, the northern part of the country was occupied by Germany, and the southern part was governed by the Vichy administration, which was a German ally. The entire French Police force, including the section serving in the German-occupied zone, functioned under the authority of the Vichy government. About 130,000 policemen served in the French police force, 30,000 of them in **PARIS**. They included special branches such as intelligence, which gathered information about the enemy, and squads for suppressing the anti-German Resistance activists.

In contrast to this large French police force, the German force numbered at most around 3,000 police. Their performance was hampered by their inability to speak French and their unfamiliarity with the terrain in which they were stationed. As a result, the Germans assigned to the French police the tasks of maintaining public order, preventing subversive activities, suppressing crime, and implementing the German anti-Jewish policy.

On July 16 and 17, 1942, 13,000 Jews were arrested in Paris, among them 4,000 children, as well as old people and the handicapped and ill. They were concentrated mainly in the Vélodrome d'Hiver, a closed structure in which even basic amenities had not been prepared. There were, for example, no toilet facilities. The arrests were made by 9,000 French policemen who were brought in for this operation. More than 10,000 Jews who were supposed to be arrested managed to leave their homes in time to escape; some of them had been warned by humane police officials.

In July 1942 Carl Albrecht **OBERG**, a leader of the German police and **SS** in France, and René Bousquet, chief of the Vichy police, signed an agreement. It spelled out the authority of the French police and the quantities of weapons and equipment they would be allowed. Until the summer of 1943, the Oberg-Bousquet agreement was easily enforced, and the French police cooperated with the Germans. The French police force confiscated the Jews' property and businesses, conducted mass arrests, and made sure that the Jews wore the yellow Jewish badge (*see*

BADGE, JEWISH) and that their identity cards were stamped with the word *Juif* ("Jew"). The police force was also responsible for the construction and operation of the CONCENTRATION CAMPS, and the French police provided armed guards to escort the trains transporting deported Jews to the German border. In the camps supervised by the French police, negligence, corruption, unsanitary conditions, and poor medical services were common. A special police section in Paris was active in the destruction of underground Communist partisan (guerilla) units, which included a large number of Jews.

In the summer of 1943, thousands of young Frenchmen were notified that they would be recruited for FORCED LABOR in Germany. In protest, groups of PARTISANS were organized throughout the country. While attacking the occupation police force, they did not inflict as much damage on the French police. As a result, the French police gradually stopped arresting Jews, and the French administration in the DRANCY concentration camp was replaced by the GESTAPO (German secret police).

In 1944, Joseph Darnand, head of the French fascist militia, was appointed chief of police in place of Bousquet. From then on the operations against the Jews were performed by the brutal militia forces, which carried out their tasks against the Jews of France efficiently, and without mercy.

SUGGESTED RESOURCES

Lewendel, Isaac. *Not the Germans Alone: A Son's Search for the Truth of Vichy.* Evanston, IL: Northwestern University Press, 1999.

Weisberg, Richard H. *Vichy Law and the Holocaust in France.* New York: New York University Press, 1996.

Freudiger, Fülöp

(1900–1976)

Fülöp Freudiger was an Hungarian Jewish leader born in BUDAPEST to a well-to-do family that had been elevated to the nobility by Emperor Franz Josef. Freudiger succeeded his father, Abraham, as the head of the Orthodox Jewish community of Budapest in 1939. As a founder and leading figure of the Orthodox Relief and Rescue Committee of Budapest in 1943 and 1944, he helped many of the foreign Jewish refugees who were illegally in HUNGARY.

After the German occupation of the country on March 19, 1944, he was appointed to the Central Jewish Council (Központi Zsidó Tanács), the JUDENRAT of Budapest. With the help of Rabbi Michael Dov Weissmandelof Bratislava, Freudiger was able to establish a close relationship with Dieter WISLICENY of the SPECIAL COMMANDO (Eichmann Sonderkommando) shortly after the Germans occupied Hungary. He also received from Weissmandel a copy of the AUSCHWITZ Protocols (a report by two Auschwitz escapees), and distributed information about the mass killings taking place at Auschwitz to Jewish and non-Jewish leaders in Hungary. By bribing Wisliceny, Freudiger succeeded in rescuing eighty prominent Orthodox Jews from various ghettos in Hungary.

With Wisliceny's aid, he and his family escaped to Romania, on August 9, 1944. Freudiger later settled in Israel, where his role in the Central Jewish Council (Judenrat) and his escape were subjects of controversy. He served as a prosecution witness in the Eichmann Trial in 1961.

SUGGESTED RESOURCES

"Affidavit of Dieter Wisliceny," in *Nazi Conspiracy and Aggression.*, vol. VIII. USGPO, 1946. [Online] http://www.ess.uwe.ac.uk/genocide/Wisliceny.htm (accessed on August 30, 2000)

Handler, Andrew, ed. *Young People Speak: Surviving the Holocaust in Hungary.* New York: Franklin Watts, 1993.

Gas Chambers/Vans

The use of lethal gas was a Nazi method for "efficient" mass murder. Both mobile and stationary gas chambers were used for this purpose by the Nazis. The first recorded instance of mass murder by gas took place in December 1939, when an **SS SPECIAL COMMANDO** (*Sonderkommando*) unit used carbon monoxide to kill Polish mental patients. The following month, Viktor Brack, head of the **EUTHANASIA PROGRAM**, decided to use pure carbon monoxide in his euthanasia institutions, since it had already been tested successfully.

After the **"FINAL SOLUTION"** was set in motion in the summer of 1941, gassing was introduced as a method for the mass murder of Jews. The method was launched in December 1941 at **CHEŁMNO**. Mobile vans had been built and equipped for this specific purpose—a project that the **REICH SECURITY MAIN OFFICE** (*Reichssicherheitshauptamt*; RSHA) had been working on since September of that year. Unlike the method used for the euthanasia murders, the exhaust gas from the trucks was piped into the closed van. Depending on the size of the truck, 40 to 60 people could be gassed at a time. A total of 20 such mobile gas chambers were built. Most of them were used by the four **OPERATIONAL SQUADS** (*Einsatzgruppen*) deployed on Soviet soil.

Gas Vans

On June 2, 1942, a Nazi report noted that the vans were an effective tool in the extermination of Jews:

"Since December 1941...97,000 persons have been processed with the help of three vans, without a single disruption."

Fifteen gas vans were in regular operation in German-occupied Soviet territory. They were also used elsewhere, although documentary evidence detailing locations and dates is scarce. It is known that gas vans were employed to kill Jews in Yugoslavia and at the **LUBLIN** and **MAJDANEK** camps. The gas vans were used to empty prisons or to assist in the liquidation of the ghettos.

After several months of operation, the vans developed operational problems due to technical deficiencies. There were also frequent breakdowns in transit, due to the condition of Soviet roads, and the SS men assigned to unload the vans began to experience severe mental stress. Ultimately, although about 700,000 people were murdered through their use, the gas vans did not meet Nazi expectations as effective instruments for the trouble-free killing of masses of people. For that purpose, stationary gas chambers proved more efficient.

Gas Chambers

The first stationary gas chambers were put up at the **BEŁŻEC** camp, in February 1942. There were several trial gassings with carbon monoxide cylinders and exhaust

"I have had the vans ... disguised as housetrailers.... [They] had become so well known that not only the authorities but the civilian population referred to them as the 'Death Vans' as soon as one appeared."

—From an SS report on the use of gas vans in Kiev, May 1942

Photograph of the rear side of a gas chamber, black furnace at right, taken at Majdanek after the camp was liberated in 1944.

T he Nazis sought to camouflage the killing operation until the victims were just steps away from their deaths. In Treblinka, not only were the gas chambers designed to appear as shower rooms, but the camp featured flower beds, as well. In an attempt to create what on the surface appeared to be a pleasant environment, they practiced complete deception.

gas. The exhaust gas was chosen as the better alternative, since it was cheaper and did not require special supplies. The next month, regular killings began at Bełżec, by means of three gas chambers in a single wooden barrack. **SOBIBÓR** camp was next, in May. But here, the installation was a brick building, with concrete foundations, that contained the gas chambers. **TREBLINKA** was the third and last of the **AKTION (OPERATION) REINHARD EXTERMINATION CAMPS** in the **GENERALGOUVERNEMENT**.

In the summer and fall of 1942, the capacity of the extermination camps was greatly increased. The existing gas chambers were enlarged, and new ones were added. In the ten gas chambers of Treblinka, 2,500 people could be put to death in a single gassing round, lasting an hour. The victims were forced to enter with their arms raised so that as many people as possible could be squeezed into the chambers. Babies and small children were thrown on top of the human mass. The tighter the chambers were packed, and the warmer the temperature inside the chamber, the faster the victims suffocated. All the gas chambers in the extermination camps were disguised as shower rooms to fool the victims.

Each of the Aktion Reinhard killing centers operated in approximately the same way. When a transport arrived at the well-camouflaged station, the prisoners were evaluated in a *Selektion*, which determined whether they would die immediately or after they had performed useful work for the camp administration. A few of the victims were selected to form a special command; these prisoners would later perform the task of removing and burying the bodies of the dead. A handful of victims with special skills were chosen to work in the repair shops that serviced the camp SS staff and their Ukrainian helpers. The vast majority went through an assembly-line procedure, moving along the various camp stations, at which they surrendered any valuables left in their possession, undressed, and had their hair cut off. This procession ended in the gas chambers. Men were separated from women and children, in part to keep up the pretense that the prisoners would actually take showers and be disinfected, and in part to minimize resistance. Once the victims were dead, the members of the special command removed their bodies from the gas chambers and buried them. (Later on, the bodies were cremated, instead of buried.)

After a time, the men of the special command were killed as well. They were replaced by new prisoners from later transports.

From Carbon Monoxide to Zyklon B

In their search for a more efficient means of extermination, the Nazis experimented with other forms of poison gas, and also with electrocution. When electrocution was found to be impractical, gassing experiments with **ZYKLON B** took place at **AUSCHWITZ**. The experiments were performed on Soviet **PRISONERS OF WAR**, in preparation for the mass murder of Jews in the adjoining Birkenau camp. Zyklon B proved far better than diesel-exhaust gas, and Auschwitz camp commandant Rudolf **HÖSS** decided to use it exclusively. A crystalline form of hydrogen cyanide, Zyklon B turned to gas immediately upon contact with oxygen, giving off deadly fumes that killed everyone in the gas chamber. Depending on weather conditions, especially temperature and humidity, the murder operation in the Auschwitz-Birkenau gas chambers took from 20 to 30 minutes. According to Höss: "In all the years, I knew of not a single case where anyone came out of the chambers alive."

The gassing facilities at Auschwitz were repeatedly enlarged, to keep up with the thousands of people sent there to die. After an inspection of the Auschwitz-Birkenau facilities in the summer of 1942 by SS head Heinrich **HIMMLER**, the decision was made to build more efficient crematoria. The ovens were connected to the gas chambers in Birkenau. The use of the new combined gas chambers and crematoria considerably speeded up the murder process in Auschwitz, which soon became Nazi Germany's main killing center.

In Majdanek, mass murder by gassing was introduced in September 1942 with the use of carbon monoxide cylinders. Zyklon B was used instead, beginning in the spring of 1943. Some of the major **CONCENTRATION CAMPS** also had gas chambers, even if they were not operated mainly as mass extermination sites. One each was in operation in **MAUTHAUSEN** (beginning in the fall of 1941), **NEUENGAMME** (September 1942), **SACHSENHAUSEN** (March 1943), **STUTTHOF** (June 1944), and **RAVENSBRÜCK** (January 1945). All of them used Zyklon B.

SUGGESTED RESOURCES

Borowski, Tadeusz. *This Way for the Gas, Ladies and Gentlemen.* New York: Viking Press, 1967. Reprint, New York: Penguin, 1992.

Müller, Filip. *Eyewitness Auschwitz: Three Years in the Gas Chambers.* New York: Stein and Day, 1979. Reprint, Chicago: Ivan R. Dee, 1999.

Shtetl [videorecording]. WGBH Video, 1996.

GEHEIME STAATSPOLIZEI. SEE GESTAPO.

Generalgouvernement

The Generalgouvernement was an administrative unit established by the Germans on October 26, 1939. Made up of the occupied regions of **POLAND** that had not been incorporated into the Reich, this was an area with a total population of twelve million. The full official designation was Generalgouvernement für die

Generalgouvernement, January 1940.

Wehrmacht
Regular combined German armed forces.

Besetzten Polnischen Gebiete (General Government for the Occupied Areas of Poland), and it was only in July 1940 that the shortened name came into use. The Germans had used this name previously, when they occupied Poland in World War I and set up an administration there, also called the Generalgouvernement.

The Generalgouvernement area was divided into four districts, **KRAKÓW**, **WARSAW**, Radom, and **LUBLIN**, which in turn were split into subdistricts. The administrative center was Kraków. In the summer of 1941, following the German attack on the **SOVIET UNION**, Galicia became the fifth district, adding between three million and four million to the population. The Nazis permitted only a few Polish institutions to function; among them were the bank that issued the country's currency, the Polish Police, and the Central Relief Committee. All of them operated under the strict supervision of the occupation authorities. Heading the Generalgouvernement was the governor-general, Hans **FRANK**. As of May 1940, Frank operated through the Generalgouvernement administration, headed by Josef Bühler. The **SS** and police were headed first by a high-ranking SS officer, Friedrich **KRÜGER**, and then by Wilhelm **KOPPE**.

Destruction of Polish Culture

The occupation authorities believed that the task of the Polish population of the Generalgouvernement was to obey the Germans and work for them. At first the Poles were regarded as a reservoir of manpower, to be exploited for the needs of the Reich. Later, the Germans considered a number of projects, such as the establishment of colonies, "Germanization," expulsion of the population of **ZAMOŚĆ**, and identification of those Poles who were of German origin.

The Nazis used extreme terrorization to gain the obedience of the Polish population. For every German killed by the underground, 50 to 100 Poles were executed. Of exceptional cruelty were two terror actions that the Germans carried out. The first was Special Action Kraków in November 1939, in which 183 staff members of schools and colleges in Kraków were arrested while attending a meeting with the German police. They were deported to **SACHSENHAUSEN**, from which many never returned. The other action took place in **LVOV**, where 38 Polish professors were executed shortly after the **Wehrmacht** entered the city.

The Germans destroyed Polish cultural and scientific institutions, and instituted a large-scale program of plundering artistic and archeological treasures. In the economic sphere, the Poles were left only with small industries and work on the land. Heavy food quotas were levied on the villages, and trade in foodstuffs was prohibited, so that urban Poles were restricted to the starvation diet provided by the food rations. As a result, the Poles engaged in widespread food smuggling.

The Ukrainians in the Generalgouvernement were intended by the Germans to provide a counterweight to the Poles. The Ukrainians in the Generalgouvernement received certain concessions not extended to Ukrainians in their native land, which had also come under Nazi control. Their living conditions even improved, in comparison with the prewar situation.

The Jewish people of the Generalgouvernement, numbering 1.8 million, were the victims of the same discriminatory decrees imposed on Jews elsewhere. Their property was confiscated, and they were drafted for forced labor. From early 1940, the Jews were imprisoned in ghettos, where they suffered from severe shortages and were isolated from the rest of the world. In the spring of 1942 the Germans began deporting the Jews from the ghettos to **EXTERMINATION CAMPS** in the Lublin district, and by 1944 all the ghettos in the Generalgouvernement were liquidated. By

early August 1944 a part of the Generalgouvernement—the area between the Vistula and Bug rivers—was liberated by Soviet forces and the Polish National Liberation Council had been formed, with its center in Lublin. The rest of the Generalgouvernement was set free in January 1945, by the Soviet Army.

SEE ALSO **AKTION (OPERATION) REINHARD.**

SUGGESTED RESOURCES

Altshuler, David A. *Hitler's War Against the Jews—The Holocaust: A Young Reader' Version of the War Against the Jews 1933–1945 by Lucy S. Dawidowicz.* New York: Behrman House, 1978.

Ayer, Eleanor H. *In the Ghettos: Teens Who Survived the Ghettos of the Holocaust.* New York: Rosen Pub. Group, 1999.

Roland, Charles G. *Courage Under Siege: Starvation, Disease, and Death in the Warsaw Ghetto.* New York: Oxford University Press, 1992.

Shoah [videorecording]. New Yorker Video, 1999.

Generalplan Ost

Generalplan Ost (General Plan East) was the Nazis' long-range plan for expelling millions of people—Jews and non-Jews alike—from the central area of eastern Europe and settling it with Germans. Versions of the plan were drawn up by at least two separate departments of the Reich, which functioned independently of one another.

In July 1941, Professor Konrad Meyer-Hetling, head of the planning section in the Reich Commissariat for the Strengthening of German Nationhood, submitted proposals for the settlement of Polish territories that had been incorporated into the Reich (German empire). Describing these proposals as "preliminary suggestions for *Generalplan Ost*," he addressed them to Heinrich **HIMMLER**, who headed the Reich Commissariat. The final version of the plan was presented by Meyer-Hetling in an exhibition called "Planning and Construction in the East." The plan was published in book form in 1942.

The earliest mention of the Reich's plans for eastward expansion was made by Reinhard **HEYDRICH** in a speech he made in Prague in October 1941, after his appointment as Reich Protector of **BOHEMIA AND MORAVIA** (which had been part of Czechoslovakia). Heydrich predicted that Germany would take over eastern Europe in stages. Negative remarks about this plan were made in a memorandum drawn up by Erhard Wetzel, one of the German officials in charge of racial policy. In February 1942, Wetzel identified a section of the **REICH SECURITY MAIN OFFICE** (RSHA) as the source of *Generalplan Ost*, rather than Meyer-Hetling's planning section. Wetzel knew that the RSHA was working on an overall plan for the territories in the east, which included the eventual settlement of 31 million people in that region. Adolf **HITLER** hoped that within ten years, four million Germans would be settled in the east. The number would increase to ten million within twenty years.

Wetzel's memorandum—presented as an expert opinion—was highly critical of the RSHA's plans and questioned the expertise of the plan's author. In his opinion, the figure given by the RSHA for the current population of the eastern territories was too low, and the estimate of the number of people who would be available for

Generalplan Ost was a variation of the overall Nazi plan to claim and utilize European territory for Aryan purposes.

When Generalplan Ost was first conceived, the population of the areas to be resettled by Germans was estimated at 45 million, and the number of Jews among them at 5 million to 6 million. Of the 45 million, 31 million were classified as "racially undesirable" and were to be expelled to western Siberia. A small number were to be put to work in the administration of the vast expanses of Russia.

settlement in the east was too optimistic. He also questioned whether the RSHA's analysis of the racial makeup of those living in the territories was scientifically accurate. Finally, he expressed reservations about the proposal that Poles be resettled in western Siberia; he thought this would be against the interests of the Reich. Despite these doubts, however, Wetzel's memorandum supported the aim of *Generalplan Ost*, which was to transform central-eastern Europe into a German colony.

The Plan

Generalplan Ost was considered a reflection of Himmler's views, and it was to be implemented after the war over a period of 30 years. The first ten million settlers in the east were to come from German territories and non-German countries in Europe with German populations. The territories designated for resettlement were the occupied areas of **POLAND**, the Baltic states, **BELORUSSIA**, the Soviet districts of Zhitomir and **KAMENETS-PODOLSKI**, a part of the Vinnitsa district of the **UKRAINE**, the Leningrad district, the Crimea, and parts of the Dnieper River basin.

According to *Generalplan Ost* as drawn up by the RSHA, about 80 percent of the population of Poland, 64 percent of the population of the western Ukraine, and 75 percent of the population of Belorussia would be expelled and resettled. The rest of the local population was to stay in place; most to be Germanized, or forced to adopt German customs. Himmler stated that they would "either be absorbed or killed." The RSHA version of *Generalplan Ost* was an elaboration of Hitler's idea of expelling and resettling elsewhere the population of Polish territories that were incorporated into the Reich.

On Himmler's orders, the Reich Commissariat for the Strengthening of German Nationhood began active preparations for *Generalplan Ost* in late January of 1942. With Meyer-Hetling in charge, the Commissariat established the legal and economic principles on which the future reconstruction of the east was to be based, and included the settlement of the Crimean peninsula. The project was to be completed within 25 years after the end of the war.

Priority would be given to agricultural settlement. The urban population would be kept at a minimum, especially in the north. Meyer-Hetling estimated the costs of the project at 45.7 billion reichsmarks. The funds would come from various sources, including special taxes levied on the conquered countries.

Himmler responded immediately to the plan when it was presented to him, demanding that the length of time allowed for its implementation be reduced from 25 years to 20. In September 1942 Himmler mentioned the establishment of settlement bases as far east as the Don and the Volga rivers in Russia.

In 1942 Meyer-Hetling presented to Himmler a detailed plan, including a financial estimate. Again Himmler gave the subject his immediate attention. This time he demanded that the area to be colonized include the **GENERALGOUVERNEMENT**, the Baltic states, Belorussia, the Crimea (including **KHERSON**), and the Leningrad district. On Himmler's orders, Meyer-Hetling hastily revised and completed the plan, which now became the Master Plan for the colonization of the east. In its new version, the area earmarked for settlement by Germans was larger than in the RSHA's version of *Generalplan Ost*.

In early 1943, the RSHA arranged for a meeting about Meyer-Hetling's plan. The area in which the plan was to be carried out now comprised 270 thousand square miles, an increase from 225 thousand square miles to plan for in 1938. Among the subjects that came up at the meeting was the transfer of the existing population in the area earmarked for German settlement: six million to seven million people were to be moved from the Polish area incorporated into the Reich; ten million from the Generalgouvernement; three million from the Baltic states; six million to seven million from the western Ukraine; and five million to six million from Belorussia.

The Jews were singled out for "total removal," by which the Nazis meant extermination. In the first decade of the plan's operation, the "racially undesirable" population was to be removed, presumably to be followed, in the second decade, by the "politically undesirables." The Protectorate of Bohemia and Moravia was not included in the immediate plans of resettlement. After the battle of Stalingrad, Himmler rapidly lost interest in having a definitive version of the plan drawn up. In addition, following his proclamation of total war, Hitler ordered a halt on the planning of all postwar projects, including this one.

The work on *Generalplan Ost* and the Master Plan coincided with the period when massacres in eastern Europe were at their height. Millions of Soviet prisoners of war and millions of Jews were being murdered. In 1941 and 1942 several million people were killed in Poland and in the occupied areas of the **SOVIET UNION**. During that period, one million Poles and two million Ukrainians were sent to the Reich to work in **FORCED LABOR**. Another two million Poles were Germanized. German authorities had also begun settling Germans in several of the areas designated for that purpose in *Generalplan Ost*. They were encountering some resistance in that operation and running into difficulties caused by the military situation. About 30,000 Germans from **LITHUANIA** who had been waiting to be resettled in the Polish territories of the Reich were sent to the southwestern part of Lithuania instead. Between November 1942 and August 1943, Poles living in the southeastern part of the **LUBLIN** district (the so-called **ZAMOŚĆ** region) were expelled from their homes and replaced by Germans.

Germany was able to carry out, almost in full, the **"FINAL SOLUTION"**—the murder of the Jews, whom the Nazis regarded as their main racial enemy. This operation cost the lives of millions of people. *Generalplan Ost* demonstrates that there were other racist plans that provided for the expulsion of many peoples, especially Slavs. These plans had only begun, with full implementation planned for after the Germans had won the war.

SUGGESTED RESOURCES

"Hitler's War: Hitler's Plans for Eastern Europe." *Holocaust Awareness.* [Online] http://www.dac.neu.edu/holocaust/Hitlers_War.htm (accessed on August 23, 2000).

Scheffler, Wolfgang. "The Forgotten Part of the 'Final Solution': The Liquidation of the Ghettos," in *Simon Wiesenthal Center Annual,* vol. 2 (1997). [Online] http://motlc.wiesenthal.com/resources/books/annual2/chap02.html (accessed on August 23, 2000).

Genocide

Genocide, from the Greek word *genos*, meaning "race," and the Latin word *caedes*, meaning "killing," refers to the liquidation—complete elimination or annihilation—of a people. The term "genocide" was first introduced by Raphael Lemkin, a Jewish legal scholar, who used it at a 1933 conference of fellow jurists in Madrid, Spain. Lemkin further defined and analyzed it in books that he wrote during World War II. On December 9, 1948, the United Nations General Assembly adopted a

convention for "the prevention of genocide and the punishment of the organizers thereof."

The term is now widely used in legislation, international conventions, legal judgments, and scientific and general literature. It is generally applied to the murder of human beings by reason of their belonging to a specific racial, ethnic, or religious group, unrelated to any individual crime on the part of such persons, the intention of the murderer or murderers being to cause grievous harm and destroy the specific group.

Lemkin pointed out that the crime of genocide need not mean the immediate and total destruction of the group. It may also consist of a series of planned actions designed to destroy basic components of the group's existence, such as its national consciousness, its language and culture, its economic infrastructures, and the freedom of the individual.

The United Nations Genocide Convention specifically mentions the following actions, which, when carried out against a national, ethnic, racial, or religious group in order to destroy that group, in full or in part, meet the definition of genocide:

1. Killing persons belonging to the group

2. Causing grievous bodily or spiritual harm to members of the group

3. Deliberately enforcing upon the group living conditions that could lead to its complete or partial extermination

4. Enforcing measures designed to prevent births among the group

5. Forcibly removing children from the group and transferring them to another group

As indicated by this list of crimes, a close link exists between these actions and many of the crimes dealt with by the International Military Tribunal (IMT) at Nuremberg that were defined as "CRIMES AGAINST HUMANITY." These crimes included murder, cruel treatment, and persecution on racial and ethnic grounds that were not directed against individuals or groups of individuals as such, but rather had the purpose of destroying the very existence of the group or groups to which the victims belonged. The IMT did not seek to determine the guilt of the accused brought before it for the crime of genocide, since that crime was not listed in the London Agreement under which the IMT was established. However, the charge of genocide was included in the Subsequent Nuremberg Proceedings and in several of the trials of Nazi criminals held in **POLAND**. (See **TRIALS OF THE WAR CRIMINALS**). Among these were the trial of Amon Goeth, the liquidator of the Kraków and Tarnów ghettos and a commandant of the **PŁASZÓW** camp; and the case of Rudolf **HÖSS**, the commandant of **AUSCHWITZ**-Birkenau. A Polish court announced its verdict against Arthur Greiser, the former German administrator in the Warthegau region of Poland, on July 9, 1946. The court defined several of the crimes committed by Greiser against the Polish people as "genocide." These included:

1. Placing Poles in a special unlawful category with regard to rights of possession, employment, education, and the use of their native tongue, and applying a special criminal code to them

2. Religious persecution, having the characteristics of genocide, of the local population, by mass murder and the imprisonment of Polish clergy (including bishops) in concentration camps; reduction of the availability of religious facilities to a bare minimum; and destruction of churches, cemeteries, and church-owned buildings

3. Genocide-like actions against cultural and educational treasures and institutions

4. Humiliating the Polish people by treating them as second-rate citizens, and differentiating between the Germans as the "master race" and the Poles as the "servant race"

The Polish court also determined that Greiser had ordered or cooperated in actions designed to cause criminal harm to the lives, well-being, and property of thousands of Polish residents of the occupied area and had made it his objective to carry out a total genocide-like attack on the rights of small and medium-sized ethnic populations, on their national identity and culture, and on their very existence.

The government of Israel joined the Convention on the Prevention and Punishment of Genocide, and on the basis of that convention enacted, in 1950, the Genocide Prevention and Punishment Law 5710-1950. The definition of genocide in that law follows that of the United Nations Genocide Convention. Israeli legislation also used that definition in another law, the Nazis and Nazi Collaborators (Punishment) Law 5710-1950. That law was first used against a Nazi criminal in the trial of Adolf **EICHMANN**. It contains the definitions of crimes against humanity and war crimes as laid down in the London Agreement on the establishment of the International Military Tribunal, and it also contains the definition of "crimes against the Jewish people." The latter is defined as applying to any one of the following actions, carried out with the intent of exterminating the Jewish people, totally or partially:

1. Killing Jews

2. Causing grievous bodily or mental harm to Jews

3. Placing Jews in living conditions calculated to bring about their physical destruction

4. Imposing measures intended to prevent births among Jews

5. Forcibly transferring Jewish children to another national or religious group

6. Destroying or desecrating Jewish religious or cultural assets or values

7. Inciting hatred of Jews

Like the Polish definition in the Greiser case, and in other cases, the Israeli law mentions the concept of cultural genocide, but in the main it refers to the special form of crimes against humanity as contained in the **NUREMBERG LAWS**, and particularly to the specific form in which genocide was in fact carried out, especially against the Jewish people. The crime against the Jewish people was a crime against that people only, since it was committed against Jews only. Nevertheless, in formal legal, as well as in social, terms, and in its political and moral aspects, the crimes against the Jewish people were also crimes against the principles of humanity and an offense against the whole of mankind, by seeking to remove from its midst one of its component parts.

The experts on the subject all agree that genocide is a component of the Holocaust. However, historians point out that the Nazi crime against the Jewish people was unique and extended far beyond genocide, by virtue of the planning that it entailed, the task forces allocated to it, the killing installations set up for it, and the way the Jews were rounded up and brought to extermination sites by force and by stealth. Above all, the Nazi crime exceeded the boundaries of genocide in its charge against Jews as a whole of being a gang of conspirators and pests whose physical destruction must be carried out for the sake of society's rehabilitation and the future of mankind.

On November 4, 1988, President Ronald Reagan signed legislation that made the United States the 98th nation to ratify the United Nations Genocide Convention.

SEE ALSO **"FINAL SOLUTION"; RACISM.**

SUGGESTED RESOURCES

Benz, Wolfgang. *The Holocaust: A German Historian Examines the Genocide.* New York: Columbia University Press, 1999.

Breitman, Richard. *The Architect of Genocide: Himmler and the Final Solution.* New York: Knopf, 1991.

Friedlander, Henry. *The Origins of Nazi Genocide: From Euthanasia to the Final Solution.* Chapel Hill: University of North Carolina Press, 1995.

Genocide [videorecording]. Simon Wiesenthal Center, 1981.

Lifton, Robert Jay. *The Nazi Doctors: Medical Killing and the Psychology of Genocide.* New York: Basic Books, 1986.

Gens, Jacob

(1905–1943)

Jacob Gens was head of the JUDENRAT (Jewish Council) in the VILNA ghetto. Gens was born in Illovieciai, a village in the Šiauliai district of LITHUANIA. In 1919, when Lithuania was fighting for its independence, he volunteered for the Lithuanian army and was sent to an officers' training course. He graduated as a second lieutenant, and was sent to the front to join the fight against Poles. He served in the army until 1924. He then enrolled in Kovno University, earning his living as a teacher of Lithuanian and of physical education in the Jewish schools of Ukmerge and Jurbarkas. Three years later, he became an accountant in the Ministry of Justice in KOVNO. He completed his university studies in law and economics in 1935. In the late 1930s, as an officer in the reserves, he was sent to the staff officers' course and promoted to captain.

In July 1940, when Lithuania became a Soviet republic, Gens was dismissed from his post. Gens feared that he was in danger of being arrested in a campaign that was being waged against anti-Soviet elements, and he moved to Vilna. A Lithuanian friend helped him obtain work as an accountant in the municipal health department.

When the Germans occupied Vilna in late June 1941, his Lithuanian friend, who headed the health department, appointed Gens director of the Jewish hospital. At the beginning of September, when a ghetto was set up in Vilna, Anatol Fried, chairman of the Judenrat, who had become acquainted with Gens while a patient in the Jewish hospital, appointed Gens commander of the ghetto police. Gens set up the police force, organized it, and made it into an orderly and disciplined body. The Jewish police were assigned a role in the Nazi *Aktionen* (operations) that were conducted in the ghetto from September to December 1941, in which tens of thousands of Jews were murdered. According to most of the evidence available, Gens, within the framework of his job, did his best to help the Jews. He became the predominant personality in the ghetto and its provisional governor. His direct contact with the German authorities, bypassing the Judenrat, added to his prestige among the Jews in the ghetto. Gens involved himself in employment and cultural activities as well as other aspects of ghetto life.

Jacob Gens.

In July 1942 the Germans dismissed the existing Judenrat and appointed Gens head of the ghetto administration and sole representative of the ghetto (*Ghettovorsteher*), thereby making his position official. Gens promoted the idea of "work for life," meaning that the survival of the ghetto Jews depended on their work and productivity. He believed that efforts had to be made to gain time and keep the ghetto in existence until Germany was defeated in the war, and that this could be achieved by working for the Germans. He constantly sought to increase the number of Jews in such positions. In the last few months of the ghetto's existence, 14,000 people out of the total ghetto population of 20,000 were employed inside or outside the ghetto. On one occasion, Gens was ordered by the Germans to send the Vilna ghetto police to the Oshmiany ghetto, to carry out a *Selektion* and to hand over 1,500 children and women who were not employed. Instead, Gens delivered to the Germans 406 persons who were chronically ill or old. He justified this action to the Jews by claiming that if the Germans and the Lithuanians had done the selecting, they would have taken the children and the women, whom he wanted to keep alive for the sake of the future of the Jewish people.

Gens's attitude toward the ghetto underground was ambivalent. On the one hand, he maintained contact with the underground leaders and declared that when the day of the ghetto's liquidation arrived, he would join them in an uprising; but on the other hand, when the underground's activities endangered the continued existence of the ghetto, he opposed it, and he complied with a German demand to hand over to them the underground commander, Yitzhak Wittenberg.

The process of liquidating the ghetto had been set in motion in August and September 1943, and Gens knew that his life was in danger. His Lithuanian wife and his daughter were both in Vilna, where they lived outside the ghetto. He had several offers from his Lithuanian relatives and friends to leave the ghetto and take refuge with them, but he refused, believing that in his role he was engaged in a mission on behalf of the Jewish people. On September 14, 1943, nine days before the final liquidation of the ghetto, Gens was summoned to the Gestapo. The previous day, he had been warned that the Germans were planning to kill him, and had been urged to flee. He refused, believing that his escape would mean disaster for the Jews who remained in the ghetto.

Gens reported to the Gestapo on September 14, and at 6:00 P.M. he was shot to death in the Gestapo courtyard. News of his death reached the ghetto at once, and the Jews who were still alive mourned his passing. Gens' belief that if the ghetto were productive its Jews would be saved proved baseless; but under the terrible conditions prevailing at the time, he did his best, as he understood it, to save as many as possible.

SUGGESTED RESOURCES

Dawidowicz, Lucy S. *From That Place and Time: A Memoir, 1938–1947.* New York: W. W. Norton, 1989.

Tushnet, Leonard. *The Pavement of Hell.* New York: St. Martin's Press, 1972.

Germany

Jews in Germany

The first Jews came to Germany in Roman times, settling in the cities along the Rhine. From the tenth century on, records show a continuous history of Jews.

Germany, February 1938.

By the late Middle Ages the Jewish population of Germany was united. The German Jewish community became one of the centers of spiritual creativity among European Jewry, and the cradle of the Yiddish language. Jews gained prominence in commerce. However, there was widespread persecution of Jews over the centuries and, in various parts of Germany, entire Jewish communities were destroyed. Some of the worst persecutions took place during the Crusades (especially in 1096) and during the period of the Black Death (1348–49), when bubonic plague killed millions of Europeans. From the fifteenth century, and especially during the Protestant Reformation, Jews lost ground. They were expelled from most of the large German cities. Some stayed in Germany, moving to small communities; others moved to the newly emerging centers of Jewish population in eastern Europe.

Throughout the nineteenth century, Jews struggled for social and political emancipation. They reached that goal when Germany was unified in 1871. Jews in Europe were revitalized by a number of developments in the nineteenth century, including the rise in modern scholarly study of Judaism and Jewish history; the growth of new religious movements in Judaism; the rapid urbanization of the Jews; and the integration of Jews into modern society and economic life. Jews contributed to cultural life, social and political philosophy, the economy, and even political life in Germany.

Antisemitism

However, many Germans opposed these developments. By the 1870s they had organized politically to promote ANTISEMITISM—which in its modern form also included RACISM as a basic ingredient. Antisemitic political parties won support.

Although its influence waned toward the end of the nineteenth century, anti-semitism continued to flourish in economic, social, and academic organizations. It penetrated the major political parties and became a factor in the struggle between the national conservative and democratic socialist camps over the future political character of German society.

In response, German Jews in imperial Germany established political organizations for the defense of the Jews' civil rights, including the CENTRAL UNION OF GERMAN CITIZENS OF JEWISH FAITH (Centralverein Deutscher Staatsbürger Jüdischen Glaubens). Also in the 1890s, the German Zionist Organization was formed and its leaders became influential in the World Zionist Organization. The Zionist movement was centered on the goal of creating a Jewish homeland in the Middle East.

During and after World War I, as imperial Germany collapsed and was replaced by the democratic regime of the Weimar Republic (1918–33), there was unprecedented integration of Jews in every sphere of life, including the theater, music, visual arts, philosophy, and science. Among the 38 Nobel prize winners in Germany up to 1938, nine were Jews. Jews were active in political and public life and held major posts in the democratic and socialist parties. Not surprisingly, anti-semitism in politics and private organizations also increased during this period.

By the early 1920s, Jews were being blamed in many circles for Germany's defeat in World War I and for the economic and social crises that struck the Weimar Republic after the war, climaxing in the terrible inflation of 1922 and 1923. Antisemites criticized the presence of Jews from eastern Europe who had immigrated to Germany before, during, and after the war.

The most radical among the antisemitic movements and political parties was the relatively small National Socialist party, which had been founded in Bavaria in 1919. Its platform boldly called for the abolition of civil rights for Jews and the elimination of Jews from various spheres of life. The propaganda speeches and publications of the party's leaders, especially those of Adolf HITLER, presented a radical antisemitic ideology that did not stop short of demands for the "total elimination of the Jews" and called for the "extermination" of the Jews *mit Stumpf und Stiel* ("root and branch"). When the German economy and republic stabilized in 1924, anti-semitic parties temporarily lost strength and their membership in the Reichstag (Parliament) dropped from 40 to 14.

Weimar Republic Years (1918–33)

In 1925, according to census figures, there were 564,379 Jews living in Germany, representing 0.9 percent of the total population. About 377,000 lived in six large cities that also had the largest Jewish communities: BERLIN, Frankfurt, Hamburg, Breslau, Leipzig, and Cologne. Approximately 90,000 Jews lived in the smaller cities. The remaining 97,000 lived in over a thousand towns and villages with a population of less than 10,000. Most Jews belonged to the middle class and were self-employed, in various branches of business and in the professions. Jews had become assimilated, as shown by the growing number of mixed marriages, secessions from the organized Jewish community, and conversions to Christianity.

Despite assimilation, the activities of Jewish political, religious, and social organizations were maintained and even expanded during the Weimar era. New political and social organizations were added to the Centralverein, the Zionist Federation, the Orthodox and Liberal organizations, and the German Jews' Aid Society, which already existed. The major new organizations were the Reich Union of Jewish

The most radical among the antisemitic movements and political parties in the early 1920s was the relatively small National Socialist party. Its platform called for the elimination of Jews from various spheres of life.

The Nazis turned the "Jewish question" into a major issue in their struggle against the democratic regime.

Frontline Soldiers; left- and right-wing Zionist parties such as the Jewish People's Party; youth and sports organizations; and student groups.

Religious and general Jewish studies taught in the rabbinical seminaries in Berlin and Breslau were broadened and intensified. The influx of Jewish scholars and intellectuals from eastern Europe, coupled with the revival of Jewish consciousness among the established Jewish population, had turned Germany into a great center of modern Jewish scholarship and culture. The Jewish population began to take an increased interest in Jewish learning and adult Jewish education centers thrived. Jewish periodicals and Jewish publishing houses played an important role in Jewish life.

In the final years of the Weimar Republic, as Germany was hard hit by the global economic crisis, the National Socialist party gained power. In 1928, the Nazis had won only 3 percent of the vote. However, in September 1930, in the first elections that took place during the economic crisis, their share jumped to 18 percent, and in July 1932 to 37 percent of the vote. With 230 members in the Reichstag, the Nazis became the largest party.

As the Weimar era drew to a close, antisemitism profoundly affected Jewish life. It was a major part of the **NAZI PARTY**'s violent struggle for power, and its effects went beyond the desecration of synagogues and Jewish cemeteries, and personal attacks on individual Jews. The Nazis turned the "Jewish question" into a major issue in their struggle against the democratic regime. As a result, not only was their position in German society impaired, the Jews themselves underwent a crisis of Jewish consciousness and began to reexamine their Jewish identity.

From 1933 to 1938

In January 1933, on the eve of Hitler's rise to power, the Jewish population of Germany numbered 522,000 Jews by religion. However, the Nazis used racial criteria to define, identify, and persecute Jews through legislation and violence; by their racial definition, the number of Jews in Germany was 566,000.

On January 30, President Paul von Hindenberg appointed Adolf Hitler Reich chancellor (prime minister). Immediately, Hitler's National Socialist (Nazi) party and its paramilitary organizations—primarily the SA (Sturmabteilung; Storm Troopers) and the **SS**—began to seize, by violence where necessary, all government and public institutions. Their goal was to transform Germany into a totalitarian state under the control of the National Socialist Party. They terrorized opponents of National Socialism, targeting members of opposing political parties, intellectuals, and especially Jews. As their major target, Jews were subjected to public humiliation and arrested. Jewish public officials and persons in positions of authority were forced to quit their jobs, especially at the universities and the law courts. The Nazis made plans to seize Jewish property and boycott all Jewish businesses and services. The anti-Jewish boycott of April 1, 1933 marked the first time the new regime openly took discriminatory action against a part of the country's citizens. This event deeply shocked Germany's Jews and evoked a sharply hostile reaction from world public opinion.

The boycott was halted after one day, but anti-Jewish laws were enacted. These laws began abolishing equal rights for Jews, reversing a principle established by the German constitution in 1871. The Enabling Law, passed on March 24, 1933, had given the government absolute dictatorial powers. This emergency law was used to abolish democratic freedoms for all citizens, along with Germany's independent political parties and organizations. This process of "Nazification" led to the reorganization

of all spheres of public and official life, including control of the media and all forms of publication, and a wide-ranging purge of civil and public service agencies.

The Nazis enforced anti-Jewish policy by means of laws, decrees, administrative terror and "spontaneous" acts of terror. The regime encouraged general hostility toward Jews by the population. The early anti-Jewish laws included the Law for the Restoration of the Professional Civil Service. The racist basis of that law, expressed by the "Aryan paragraph," became the foundation for all anti-Jewish legislation passed before the enactment of the **Nuremberg Laws** in the fall of 1935. Other laws restricted the practice of law and medicine by Jews and limited the number of Jews in educational institutions, in cultural life and journalism. Only Jews who had served as frontline soldiers in World War I were excepted from these laws.

Nazi legislation formalized the ideology of discrimination against the Jews and put policy into action. At the same time, it served as a means of restraining "spontaneous" terror and stabilizing the status of the Jews in Germany. Some officials advocated such "stabilization," fearing that Germany's international standing and efforts to restore the economy would be adversely affected by the appearance of unrestrained Nazi action against the Jews. This "restraint" would not last indefinitely.

The regime terrorized its opponents by arresting and imprisoning them in **CONCENTRATION CAMPS**. Jews made up a high percentage of the detainees and were singled out for particularly cruel treatment, which often resulted in death. Thousands of Jews fled from Germany. A census taken in June 1933 shows that during the first six months of that year, about 26,000 Jews "by race" had left the country. By the end of 1933, 63,000 Jews had emigrated.

The German people did not uniformly support the regime's policy against the Jews, and while there was broad agreement on the need to find a "solution" to the "Jewish question," there were also reservations about using violence. There were also individual cases of solidarity with the Jews. However, the leadership of institutions such as the Protestant and Catholic churches, made few public protests. Their objections referred primarily to the thousands of Christians of Jewish origin who were affected by the racist legislation.

Jews also reacted differently on an individual and organizational level. Their social and political status had suffered a tremendous blow, but their existing organizational network was scarcely touched—indeed, new organizations developed. Their forced separation and isolation from the general society did not diminish the continuing existence of the Jews' own institutions, but individuals and families were devastated by the uncertainties brought on by the Nazi regime.

Nonetheless, the organizational structure of German Jewry adapted to changing conditions. In 1932 Jewish organizations throughout Germany had begun to form a national federation; it made its first public appearance in the Third Reich in May 1933. In September of that year, a truly representative and comprehensive national organization was established, which was called the Reich Representation of German Jews, under the leadership of Rabbi Leo Baeck and Otto **Hirsch**.

The Reich Representation of German Jews intended to represent the Jews of Germany in interactions with German authorities and with Jews in other countries. The new organization assumed leadership of the Jewish population and coordinated a wide range of new activities. It expanded educational opportunities for youth and adults, especially through the work of the Jewish Center for Adult Education, which dealt with vocational training and retraining, welfare operations, economic assistance, employment assistance, and preparing for emigration. The group assumed responsibility for communication with the authorities on matters pertaining to Jew-

A dolf Hitler readily acknowledged that the Nazi Party had used Germany's democratic, representative form of government as a means to achieve its goal of establishing a totalitarian regime that would eradicate principles of democracy from Germany.

ish security. On several occasions, as when the Nazi newspaper *Der Stürmer* (The Attacker) published a special issue on the blood libel—the accusation that Jews kill gentiles to obtain their blood for Jewish rituals—the Reich Representation of German Jews reacted with public protests.

Despite the emergence of umbrella organizations, different political and religious factions still competed for influence and representation within German Jewry. The main split was between the mainstream Jews and the Zionist movement. The mainstream focused on the struggle for Jewish existence and the preservation of Jewish rights in Germany. The Zionists' primary goal was to prepare the Jews for a new life in the national home in Palestine. The Zionist movement was gaining popularity, particularly among Jewish youth.

The authorities, mainly the **GESTAPO** and the **SD** (*Sicherheitsdienst*; Secret Service), closely watched all public activities by Jews and restrained mainstream activities that encouraged German Jews to stay in the Reich. The Zionist movement was generally able to carry on with little interference. Despite National Socialism's sharp opposition to the establishment of a separate Jewish state, the Nazis believed the work of the Zionists would hasten the emigration of Jews from Germany.

In June 1934, Hitler staged a killing spree in which the top officials of the SA and a number of opposition leaders were executed. This purge strengthened the conservative and antisemitic elements in the government. It also shifted the balance of power to agencies like the SS. Heinrich **HIMMLER**, chief of the SS and the Gestapo, seized control over all police forces in the Reich. The Nazis created special sections in the Gestapo and SD to deal with the "Jewish question."

A new drive of violence against the Jews was launched in 1935. It was orchestrated by Joseph **GOEBBELS** and Julius **STREICHER**, who organized massive rallies and published propaganda designed to incite hostility against the Jews of Germany. Persons accused of having committed "race defilement," that is, sexual intercourse between Jews and "Aryans," were denounced and publicly humiliated. Various German regions passed local anti-Jewish legislation, forbidding Jews to display the German flag, for example, and outlawing marriages between Jews and Aryans. More and more Jews left the provinces, where they suffered the most, to take up residence in the large cities.

The terror campaign peaked in the summer of 1935 and was one of the factors leading to the enactment of the **NUREMBERG LAWS** in September. Designed to restore "law and order" while meeting the demands of radical party members for implementation of the original antisemitic planks in the Nazi platform, the Nuremberg Laws were constitutional laws. They included the Reich Citizenship Law and the Law for the Protection of German Blood and German Honor, and contained the Nazi's new definition of the term "Jew," based on race. This definition was the basis for all subsequent anti-Jewish legislation until 1943, when a final decree was enacted denying Jews the protection of the courts.

Secret government and party reports revealed that the German population had mixed reactions to the Nuremberg Laws. Hitler had described the laws as a possible framework for the continued existence of the Jews in Germany, so some people regarded them as a solution of sorts, providing for racial, social, and cultural segregation of the Jews from the German people. Other individual Germans objected to the wide-ranging discrimination on ethical, religious, or intellectual grounds; some made their criticism known. Yet a third group, consisting mainly of radical Nazi party members, found the Nuremberg Laws too moderate and called for a more far-reaching solution of the "Jewish question," including violence. The church leadership took no public stand on the laws, despite the fact that the laws also affected thousands of converts.

On an individual basis, Jews were tremendously troubled. There were many suicides and emigration increased as Jews saw the foundations of their existence collapsing.

Front page of the *Badische Presse* newspaper of 16 September, 1935, in Karlsruhe, Germany and a Jewish identification card. The headline reads "The Nuremburg Laws."

The SD's Section for Jewish Affairs was also reorganized in 1935, with Herbert Hagen as section chief and Adolf **EICHMANN** as his deputy. This section would ultimately seek complete control of Jewish affairs in the Reich and beyond its borders.

In 1936, when the Olympic games were held in Berlin, there was a temporary relaxation in public anti-Jewish activity. The Jews had managed to create a pattern of life that could be maintained even under a racist totalitarian regime. However, a new and sweeping antisemitic policy was being formulated. Hitler's secret memorandum on the Four-Year Plan, which he wrote in August 1936, contained an ideological and political section in which he called for an all-out war against Judaism as a driving motive in Germany's future foreign policy and its preparations for the war against the **SOVIET UNION** that was sure to come within four years. In late 1936 and early 1937 the SD's Jewish section drafted a document that spelled out the practical details of this policy, which called for further isolation of Jews from the econo-

In the area of cultural activities, the Cultural Society of German Jews was founded in July 1933. Its goals were to find employment for the many newly-unemployed Jewish artists and intellectuals and to serve as the cultural center for the Jewish population.

In 1936, when the Olympic games were held in Berlin, there was a temporary relaxation in public anti-Jewish activity. However, Hitler's new and sweeping antisemitic policy was being formulated as part of his Four-Year Plan.

my and the use of officially organized terror to pressure Jews to leave Germany. This policy was implemented on an informal basis in the second half of 1937, mainly by **ARYANIZATION** (*Arisierung*)—the usually forced conversion of Jewish business enterprises to non-Jewish ownership.

In 1937, there were signs of opposition to the Nazi regime from various sectors of German society, including the churches. Pope Pius XI issued the German-language encyclical *Mit brennender Sorge* (With Burning Concern), which was distributed all over Germany. The encyclical denounced Nazi neo-paganism and the cult of racism, but it did not explicitly condemn the persecution of the Jews. In response, the regime staged numerous show trials of clergy, who were imprisoned in concentration camps. Secret official reports showed that disapproval of and outright opposition to the regime, even within the ranks of the military, were becoming a threat to its stability. Consequently, Hitler introduced drastic changes in the top echelons of the army and the ministries of war and foreign affairs. These foreshadowed radical changes in both internal and foreign affairs.

In March 1938, Germany "annexed" **AUSTRIA** in what was called the *Anschluss*. In September, the Sudetenland (a portion of Czechoslovakia) was annexed. These were both part of Hitler's new plan for Europe. His plan also included the creation of the Protectorate of **BOHEMIA AND MORAVIA** out of the occupied western part of Czechoslovakia in March 1939, and, finally, the invasion of **POLAND** in September 1939, which marked the beginning of World War II. On January 30, 1939, Hitler declared: "If international-finance Jewry in Europe and elsewhere once again succeeds in dragging the nations into a world war, its outcome will not be the Bolshevization of the globe ... but the annihilation of the Jewish race in Europe."

In 1938 the Third Reich further radicalized its anti-Jewish policy, which was applied in the newly acquired territories. There were new laws and decrees, mass arrests of Jews, and a variety of "spontaneous" and official terror actions. On March 28, 1938, a law was passed that abolished the legally recognized status of the Jewish communities. On April 26, a new decree ordered the registration of Jewish property, and on June 15, 1,500 Jews were imprisoned in concentration camps. Other anti-Jewish laws passed at this time forbade Jews to practice medicine (June 25); ordered male Jews to assume the name Israel, and female Jews, the name Sarah (August 17); forbade Jews to practice law (September 27); and stipulated that the passports of Jews be marked with a capital *J*, standing for *Jude* (October 5).

On October 28, 1938, 15,000 to 17,000 Jews of Polish nationality were expelled from Germany. The Polish government refused to admit them into Poland. They were trapped in the no-man's-land between the two countries. People all over the world heard about their bitter fate. On November 7, Herschel Grynszpan, a Jewish youth whose parents were among the expelled Jews, shot Ernst vom Rath, a German diplomat in Paris. The Nazis used this act as the pretext for an organized pogrom against the Jews, which took place November 9 and 10 in every part of Germany and in the areas it had annexed that year (Austria and the Sudetenland). In this pogrom, which came to be called **KRISTALLNACHT**, or "Night of Broken Glass" (so named from the shattering of the windows of Jewish enterprises), hundreds of synagogues and thousands of Jewish businesses were burned down, destroyed, or damaged. Some 30,000 Jews were put into concentration camps, and almost one hundred Jews were murdered.

After this pogrom, the Nazi regime imposed a collective fine of one billion marks on the Jews and enacted a new series of harsh laws and regulations. Jews were eliminated from the German economy (November 12); Jewish pupils were expelled from public schools (also on November 12); Jews were restricted from most public

German men walk past the broken window of a Jewish-owned business in Berlin, Germany on November 10, 1938, following the Kristallnacht pogrom of the night before.

places (November 28); and all Jewish newspapers and periodicals were ordered shut down (there were 65 newspapers and periodicals and 42 organizational bulletins with a total monthly circulation of 956,000). All Jewish organizations were dissolved, leaving only the Reich Representation of German Jews, the Cultural Society of German Jews, and, temporarily, the Palestine Office of the Zionist organization. The only paper permitted to be published was the *Jüdisches Nachrichtenblatt*, the semi-official newspaper of the Reich Representation.

German public reaction to the Kristallnacht pogrom, like that to the Nuremberg Laws, was diverse. The disapproval voiced focused primarily on the damage caused to German property and the German economy, and only in small degree on the moral aspect of the terror directed against the Jews and the destruction of their property. Once again the church leadership did not take a public stand, although a few individual clerics denounced the riots. The underground German Communist party condemned the pogrom in its newspaper.

From 1938 to 1945

Before the end of November 1938 the Reich Representation for German Jews resumed its activities, helping Jews to emigrate from Germany and obtaining the release of concentration camp prisoners. In February 1939 a new organization was formed with representatives from all over Germany. The new Reich Association of Jews in Germany, would focus on emigration, Jewish education, and welfare. At the time, the German authorities supported the present authoritative, centralist Jewish organization. On July 4, 1939, a law was passed granting recognition to the Reich Association of Jews in Germany. However, the government required that all Jews by race, as defined in the Nuremberg Laws, must belong to the new organization. It was further put under the supervision of the Ministry of the Interior, and, therefore, under the control of the SS.

In 1938 and 1939, emigration of Jews from Germany reached new heights—49,000 in 1938 and 68,000 in 1939—despite increasing difficulties. Emigration

In addition to laws, decrees, and government-sanctioned violence directed toward the Jews in 1938, there were "spontaneous" and "unofficial" acts of persecution, including the destruction of Jewish property, the expulsion of Jews from smaller population centers, and the desecration and destruction of synagogues, among them the main synagogues at Munich and at Nuremberg.

Cities that participated in the Kristallnacht pogrom of November 9, 1938.

© Martin Gilbert 1982

The outbreak of the war set off a new round of anti-Jewish decrees and regulations affecting nearly every sphere of life for Jews living in Germany.

obstacles included new restrictions on entry in many countries, restrictions on immigration to Palestine, and the failure of the **EVIAN CONFERENCE**. The Reich Association of Jews in Germany continued to support Jewish emigration even after the war broke out, routing emigrants through neutral Spain and Portugal to the Western Hemisphere; through the Soviet Union to East Asia; and through **ITALY** and the Balkan states to Palestine by means of **ALIYA BET** ("illegal" immigration). In October 1941, however, all Jewish emigration was prohibited.

Economically, Jews were suffering greatly, and the Reich Association for Jews in Germany faced enormous social welfare problems. The German Jews had been deprived of their jobs, the average age of the Jews remaining in Germany was quite high, and money was needed to help impoverished Jews who could not afford to pay their own emigration costs. The main source of funds came from a progressive tax imposed on Jews who still had property in their possession, including Jews who were about to emigrate. The Reich Association also continued to receive financial assistance from American Jewish welfare agencies, until America's entry into the war in December 1941.

As more countries became involved in the war, the Germans expanded their policy of Jewish persecution, applying it in occupied and annexed countries. Jewish persecution differed from one country to another, but its ultimate aim was the same everywhere—the **"FINAL SOLUTION"** of the "Jewish question." In Germany itself the outbreak of the war set off a new round of anti-Jewish decrees and regulations affecting nearly every sphere of the Jews' life. One decree prohibited Jews from leaving their homes after dark and placed certain sections of cities out of bounds to them. Another reduced their allocation of rationed foods and restricted their purchases to certain shops and certain times of day. Other decrees, by the dozen, ordered the Jews to hand over their jewelry, radios, cameras, electrical appliances, and any other valuables in their possession. In September 1941 all Jews aged six and above were ordered to wear the *Judenstern* (the Jewish star;

Germany, November 1942.

see **BADGE, JEWISH**), and Jews were no longer permitted to use public transportation. In contrast to the situation in most other countries of Europe, no ghettos were created in Germany; the isolating of the Jews was achieved by imposing residential restrictions that forced them out of their homes and concentrated them in "Jewish buildings." Jews who were declared "fit for work" were put on forced labor, and the Nazis continued to arrest individual Jews and send them to concentration camps. The persecution of the Jews through myriad decrees and regulations was formally ended, in July 1943, by a superseding decree that denied Jews any protection of the law and placed them under the exclusive jurisdiction of the security services and the police.

The first deportations of Jews from Germany took place in February 1940 (*see* **NISKO AND LUBLIN PLAN**). These deportations ended in the spring, but that summer, after the victory over **FRANCE**, the Nazis decided to deport the Jews to Madagascar (*see* **MADAGASCAR PLAN**). In October 1940, in one night, all the Jews of Baden, the Palatinate, and the Saar district—7,500 persons—were deported to France, most of them to the **GURS** camp, and from there to **EXTERMINATION CAMPS**

In the fall of 1941, the operational squads began killing masses of Jews in German-occupied Soviet territory. The first phase of the total annihilation of the Jews of Europe had begun.

in the east. In October 1941 the systematic deportation of masses of Jews from Germany was launched.

Beginning in the fall of 1941, the procedure for the mass deportations usually consisted of rounding up Jews and taking them to special assembly points in the large cities. Lists of deportation candidates were compiled by the Gestapo. In many places the local Jewish community was ordered to distribute the deportation orders to its members.

In the fall of 1941, the OPERATIONAL SQUADS (*Einsatzgruppen*) were killing masses of Jews in the German-occupied Soviet territory. The first phase of the total annihilation of the Jews of Europe had begun. Some of the deportees from Germany were killed upon their arrival in the ghettos (as in Riga and Minsk). In 1942 and 1943, German Jews were deported by the tens of thousands directly to extermination camps, mainly to AUSCHWITZ. Some 42,000 Jews from Germany, mostly elderly people and those with "privileged status," were sent to the THERESIENSTADT ghetto; the majority either perished there or were deported to the extermination camps. Even before the systematic mass annihilation started, several hundred Jews were murdered between 1939 and 1941 inside Germany, through the EUTHANASIA PROGRAM.

Despite the progressive radicalization of the Nazi policy on the Jews, the Association for Jews in Germany continued to function throughout the war. It faced unprecedented challenges, especially with the onset of the mass deportations in 1940. Most of the Jewish population in Germany lacked the basic necessities of life. The association had to provide emergency housing for the thousands of Jews who had been evicted, and particularly for those evacuated from medical institutions and old-age homes. Until the summer of 1942, when the Jewish school system closed down, on orders issued by the Gestapo, schools were provided by the association. The association also continued to support the agricultural training farms of the Zionist movements. These establishments, too, were gradually closed down in 1942 and 1943, during the mass deportations.

Germans and "The Final Solution"

The Nazi extermination of the Jews should be seen as part of a larger concept. The Nazis intended to restructure the face of Europe by exterminating and subjugating entire sectors of the population and by uprooting millions of people from their homes, mainly in eastern Europe (*see* GENERALPLAN OST). During the war, in addition to the Jews, the Nazis also murdered GYPSIES, the chronically and mentally ill in Germany itself, Soviet prisoners of war, and intellectual and political elites in Poland and in the Soviet Union.

The attitudes of the German people regarding the "solution of the Jewish question" remained fairly constant throughout the war years. The growing isolation of the Jews during the war, prior to their deportation, was due in part to an absence of concern on the part of the German population about what was happening to the Jews. But even at that stage, particularly before the start of the mass deportations, there was pressure by some nationalist groups for a more extreme anti-Jewish attitude in Germany, along the lines of the policy that had been introduced in Poland by this time. These Germans wanted further restrictions on the Jews in day-to-day life. They wanted them to wear the Jewish badge, and they called for the expulsion and liquidation of the Jews.

Others, however, had reservations about the treatment of the Jews, especially with respect to the introduction of the yellow badge and the first deportations to the east. Their concerns were heightened after reports about the mass murder of

Jews in eastern Europe began filtering back to the population. These reservations were expressed primarily in the educated circles of the middle class, among religious Germans, and in the lower ranks of the clergy. As throughout the Holocaust, the church leadership did not protest.

After the German defeat at Stalingrad and the massive air raids on German cities in 1943, Germans were more likely to express strong disapproval in response to continuing reports of the mass murders of Jews. It is also clear that thousands of Germans risked their lives and the lives of their families to extend help to Jews, thus saving some of the Jews who had gone into hiding. On the whole, however, it appears that the majority of the German people maintained a passive attitude toward the fate of the Jews.

Conclusion

Of the 566,000 Jews (as defined by race) who lived in Germany when Hitler came to power, some 200,000 fell victim to the Nazi extermination policy and another 300,000 were saved, mostly by emigrating from the country. The actual number of Jewish emigrants from Germany between 1933 and 1945 was 346,000. This figure includes 98,000 who escaped to European countries conquered later by the Nazis; of these, an estimated 70,000 were deported during the Nazi occupation, along with Jews from those local populations. Around 5,000 of these deportees survived the war. Approximately 137,000 Jews were deported directly from Germany, of whom about 9,000 survived. The number of German Jews who died includes several thousand Jews who were murdered in the euthanasia program or who committed suicide. In addition to the 20,000 Jews surviving the war in Germany (15,000 in the open, mostly **MISCHLINGE** (Part Jews), and 3,000 to 5,000 who went into hiding), another 5,000 survived in the Theresienstadt ghetto and 4,000 in other concentration camps.

In 1933, Rabbi Leo Baeck said, "The Third Reich has put an end to a thousand years of Jewish history in Germany." These prophetic words proved true to an unimaginably tragic extent.

SEE ALSO **TRIALS OF THE WAR CRIMINALS, YOUTH MOVEMENTS.**

SUGGESTED RESOURCES

Bar-On, Dan. *Legacy of Silence: Encounters with Children of the Third Reich.* Cambridge: Harvard University Press, 1989.

Feldman, George. *Understanding the Holocaust.* Detroit: UXL, 1998.

Friedländer, Saul. *Nazi Germany and the Jews.* New York: HarperCollins Publishers, 1997.

Goldhagen, Daniel Jonah. *Hitler's Willing Executioners: Ordinary Germans and the Holocaust.* New York: Knopf, 1997.

Kaplan, Marion A. *Between Dignity and Despair: Jewish Life in Nazi Germany.* New York: Oxford University Press, 1998.

Gestapo

"Gestapo" is a shortened form of the German words "Geheime Staatspolizei," meaning Secret State Police. They were the secret state police, first of Prussia, and later the Third Reich. The Gestapo became the Nazis' main tool of oppression and destruction.

Members of the Gestapo arresting suspects in Berlin during World War II.

The Prussian Gestapo (1933–44)

The Gestapo originated in the political department of the police headquarters in Berlin during the Weimar Republic. At that time, the department served the government as a domestic intelligence agency. The political police became a semi-official federal bureau of investigation during the 1920s. When Adolf **HITLER** became the chancellor of Germany, Hermann Göring was made the interior minister of Prussia, and also head of the Prussian political police. Göring appointed Rudolf Diels its first executive director.

Diels transformed the organization into the police-intelligence tool of a totalitarian dictatorship. He helped purge "politically unreliable elements" and Jewish officials. He also established a semi-independent headquarters, the Gestapa (Geheimes Staatspolizeiamt), comprised of low-level but experienced Prussian bureaucrats.

Under Hitler's leadership, the government passed the emergency regulations of February 28, 1933, which gave the Gestapa complete freedom to impose "protective custody" upon anyone, to prevent undesirable political activities, and to wiretap political suspects and follow all their activities. The torture and execution of prisoners without regular legal proceedings remained illegal, but it often took place in makeshift SA (Sturmabteilung; Storm Troopers) and **SS** bunkers and **CONCENTRATION CAMPS** already in existence.

On April 11, 1933, the Gestapa was separated entirely from the overall police structure. The First Gestapo Law, of April 26, 1933, officially gave Diels the

authority of an independent state political-police commissioner. However, Diels' power was reduced as the SA and SS steadily gained more control.

The Second Gestapo Law, of November 30, 1933, made Göring head of the political police and Diels directly responsible to him. The secret police now became officially known as the Gestapo. Free to act without fear of legal or administrative lawsuits, the Gestapo assumed direct control over its field branches. Specially trained, ruthless bureaucrats produced regular intelligence reports on political and ideological "enemies of the Reich." In 1934, a Jewish Section was established in the Gestapa.

The Gestapo under Himmler and Heydrich

Under Heinrich **HIMMLER** and Reinhard **HEYDRICH**, the Gestapo played an important role in the unification of the SS and the police. First, Himmler established SS control over the political police and concentration camps in Bavaria in early 1933. Later he imposed this model on all the German states, including Prussia, where as Göring's deputy he took over the Gestapo on April 20, 1934. He made Heydrich its director. Later in the year, Himmler was made the chief of all the political police in Germany.

Although all German concentration camps came under the control of the SS, the Gestapo had the power to send its victims to them. Moreover, through a "political section" in the camps' headquarters, the Gestapo could order that prisoners be released, tortured, or executed. Similar treatment awaited its victims in its own basements. To circumvent the criminal code that forbade torture and murder, the Gestapo adopted methods, tested in the **DACHAU** concentration camp, of fabricating natural causes of death or informing the inmates' families that the prisoners had been "shot while trying to escape."

In June 1936 Himmler officially became the chief of all the German police; he now controlled both the concentration camps and the police. Himmler reorganized the police system, with Hitler's consent, so that he gained complete independence from the state and the Reich bureaucracy. He set up two main branches of the police force, the Order Police, or Orpo, and the Security Police, or Sipo. The Orpo was the "regular" police and included the Protection Police—the uniformed officers, the rural police, the firefighting police, and various technical and auxiliary services. Sipo was composed of the Gestapo and the Criminal Police. The Gestapo and the field units (now renamed Staatspolizeileitstellen; state regional headquarters) took over all the German political-police agencies. After Himmler's takeover, the Gestapo grew enormously with the recruitment of personnel lacking the traditional qualifications for public service.

From the time of Himmler's takeover until September 1939, when the **REICH SECURITY MAIN OFFICE** (*Reichssicherheitshauptamt*; RSHA) was established, the structure of the Gestapo stayed the same. Division I handled organization and finance, including legal matters. Its director between 1935 and 1939 was Dr. Werner **BEST**, an SS lawyer and **SD** (Security Service) executive. Division II, under Heydrich's direct control, was the main body of the Gestapo. Under Heinrich **MÜLLER**, Section II 1 was charged with fighting the "enemies" of the regime, which included the Communists, Social Democrats, the outlawed trade unions, monarchists, and anti-Nazi ultraconservatives. Special sections dealt with Austrian matters, Jews, other religious groups, Freemasons, and immigrants. Division III was the counterintelligence unit. Between November 1937 and October 1938, special Gestapo-SD units were trained to terrorize and Nazify foreign countries. After Adolf **EICHMANN** drove Jews from **AUSTRIA** later in 1938, Müller, with Eichmann as executive,

assumed control of the forced emigration of the Jews from all Nazi-controlled territories. Following **KRISTALLNACHT** (November 9–10, 1938), the Gestapo became the main instrument of the regime's anti-Jewish policies.

The Gestapo during World War II (1939–45)

In 1939 the Gestapo, as part of the Sipo, was fused with the SD to form the RSHA. Thus, young, ruthless, and fanatical SD agents such as Eichmann became Gestapo officers; the academics, lawyers, and old-style Prussian civil servants either were pushed aside or integrated themselves into the spirit and practices of the SS-infested civil service. With the creation of the RSHA, the Gestapo was expanded, with the border police now coming under its auspices. When the war began, the Gestapo took part in the enslavement of "inferior races," "pacifying" and subduing the occupied territories in the west, persecuting the Jews, and, finally, carrying out a major role in the **"FINAL SOLUTION."** Throughout this period, Müller was the head of the Gestapo and Eichmann was the head of the Jewish section.

The Gestapo's main tool remained the "protective custody" procedure, which allowed the agency to act freely against "enemies of the Reich." These activities were carried out on orders by Heydrich; by his successor, Ernst **KALTENBRUNNER**; by Müller; or by RSHA section chiefs such as Eichmann. The Gestapo did not even take the trouble to place Jews and **GYPSIES** in the category of "enemies of the Reich" but rather rounded them up, stole their property, deprived them of their citizenship, and finally deported them. The Gestapo could commit such acts with impunity. Its position above the law and its special political mission were spelled out in an RSHA decree of April 15, 1940: "The powers required by the Gestapo for the execution of all measures necessary to their task stem not from specific laws and ordinances, but from the overall mission allotted to the German police in general and the Gestapo in particular in connection with the reconstruction of the National Socialist State."

In the occupied territories, local Gestapo representatives harassed the Judenräte and took their members hostage, perfected a special jargon of deceit (*see* **SPRACHREGELUNG**), and supervised the phasing out of the ghettos. They also pressured satellite countries to deport their Jews. Eichmann's Jewish section and his field representatives generally arranged deportations to concentration and extermination camps. In particular, Eichmann maintained direct control over the special camp in **THERESIENSTADT** and the Special Commando that deported most of Hungarian Jewry to **AUSCHWITZ** in 1944.

Persecuting defenseless Jews and maintaining control through terror, the Gestapo relentlessly served Hitler and the goal of remaking the world in the Nazi image. Millions of Germans accepted the Gestapo in its initial phase, collaborated with it later, and supplied the military-organizational framework that made Gestapo atrocities possible.

SUGGESTED RESOURCES

Aubrac, Lucie. *Outwitting the Gestapo.* Lincoln: University of Nebraska Press, 1993.

Crankshaw, Edward. *Gestapo: Instrument of Tyranny.* New York: Viking Press, 1956. Reprint, New York: Da Capo Press, 1994.

Delarue, Jacques. *The Gestapo: A History of Horror.* New York: Paragon House, 1987.

Gellately, Robert. *The Gestapo and German Society: Enforcing Racial Policy, 1933–1945.* New York: Oxford University Press, 1990.

Getter, Matylda

(d. 1968)

Sister Matylda Getter was mother superior of the **WARSAW** branch of the Order of the Franciscan Sisters of the Family of Mary, a Polish religious order that carried on educational work, mainly among orphans, and cared for the sick in hospitals. In 1942, Sister Matylda decided to accept all the Jewish children fleeing from the Warsaw ghetto who were brought to her and to shelter them in the order's many locations, but especially in its branch at Pludy, about 7.5 miles (12 kilometers) outside Warsaw, on the right bank of the Vistula River.

It is estimated that Sister Matylda was instrumental in rescuing several hundred Jewish children from certain death, despite her own frailty as an elderly woman ill with cancer. Her principal aim was not to gain new souls for the church, but to rescue human lives. She was accused by some of unnecessarily endangering the lives of the many non-Jewish orphans in the order's homes by harboring Jewish children in their midst. Her reply was that by virtue of the Jewish children's presence, God would not allow any harm to befall the other children. Special precautions were taken to remove children who were too obviously Jewish-looking for temporary shelter elsewhere when Sister Matylda was alerted to possible Gestapo raids on the orphanages. When time proved too short for this, children with a more Jewish appearance would have their heads or faces partially bandaged, to look as though they had been injured. After the war, the children were released to their parents or relatives.

Sister Matylda Getter was posthumously recognized by Yad Vashem as **"RIGHTEOUS AMONG THE NATIONS."**

SUGGESTED RESOURCES

Bauminger, Arieh L. *The Righteous Among the Nations.* Tel Aviv: Am Oved, 1990.

A Teacher's Guide to the Holocaust: Rescuers. [Online] http://fcit.coedu.usf.edu/holocaust/people/rescuer.htm (accessed on August 24, 2000).

Glazman, Josef

(1913–1943)

Josef Glazman was a Jewish underground and partisan leader, born in the town of Alytus, in southern **LITHUANIA**. Glazman was given a nationalist and traditional upbringing and was active in the Betar Zionist youth movement. In 1937 he was appointed Betar leader for Lithuania, retaining the post until July 1940, when the Soviets dissolved all Jewish political movements in the country.

In the first phase of Soviet rule in Lithuania, from July 1940 to the end of June 1941, Glazman was one of the underground leaders of the Revisionist party. When the Germans occupied Lithuania, Glazman was in **VILNA**, where he was arrested and sent on forced labor in nearby Reise. In early November of 1941 Glazman returned to the Vilna ghetto, where he organized an underground group made up of Betar members. In order to aid his underground activities he joined the **JEWISH GHETTO POLICE**, and at the end of November 1941 he was appointed its deputy chief.

Josef Glazman.

Glazman was one of the founders of the **UNITED PARTISAN ORGANIZATION** (Fareynegte Partizaner Organizatsye, FPO) of the Vilna ghetto and participated in its founding meeting on January 21, 1942. He became the FPO's deputy commander, and was in charge of its intelligence section and commander of one of its two battalions. His official post as deputy chief of the Jewish ghetto police assisted the underground's operations. Glazman also took an active part in the ghetto's educational and cultural activities. In June 1942, when the ghetto administration was reorganized, Glazman left the police and was appointed head of the ghetto housing department within the **JUDENRAT** (Jewish Council).

Glazman's relations with Jacob **GENS** (chief of the ghetto police and, as of July 1942, ghetto head) were strained because of Glazman's underground activities and their differences over policy. At the end of October 1942, Glazman was arrested on Gens's orders and dismissed from his post. He was released in mid-December 1942 after being jailed for several weeks. In June 1943 he was again arrested and sent to

the Reise labor camp, also on Gens's orders. The FPO and ghetto police fought over his arrest.

A few weeks later, Glazman was returned to the ghetto. In July, Glazman left the ghetto, leading the first group of FPO members into the forest in order to establish a partisan base. On the way they fell into a German ambush and during the fight the group lost a third of its men. At the end of July, Glazman and his men reached the Naroch Forest, where he formed the Revenge (Nekama) Jewish partisan unit of the partisan brigade commanded by Fyodor Markov. At the end of September the Soviet command decided to dissolve the Jewish unit. As a result of this decision, the unit also lost most of its weapons. Glazman and a group of his comrades joined the Lithuanian partisan command.

At this time the Germans launched a determined drive against the partisans in the Naroch and Kozhany forests. Glazman and a group of 35 Jewish partisans tried to break through to the Rudninkai Forest in the south in order to join up with FPO members who had gone there from the Vilna ghetto. On October 7, 1943, a superior German force surrounded Glazman and his men. In the fierce struggle that followed he and his comrades were killed; only one member of the group, a young girl, was saved.

SUGGESTED RESOURCES

Partisans of Vilna [sound recording]. Chicago: Flying Fish, 1989.

Porter, Jack Nusan, ed. *Jewish Partisans: A Documentary of Jewish Resistance in the Soviet Union During World War II.* Washington, DC: University Press of America, 1982.

A Teacher's Guide to the Holocaust: Rescuers. [Online] http://fcit.coedu.usf.edu/holocaust/people/rescuer.htm (accessed on August 24, 2000).

Globocnik, Odilo

(1904–1945)

Odilo Globocnik was a senior **SS** commander and a principal participant in the extermination of Polish Jewry. Born in Trieste to an Austrian-Croat family of minor officials, Globocnik was a contractor by profession. He joined the **NAZI PARTY** in **AUSTRIA** in 1931 and the SS in 1934. His illegal activity on behalf of the party caused him to be imprisoned several times. Before the annexation of Austria to **GERMANY** in 1938, Globocnik was already active in the formation of Nazi factory cells in the provinces of Austria. In 1936 he was appointed provincial party leader in Carinthia. He earned rapid promotions in 1938: to colonel in March, and to state secretary and *Gauleiter* (district leader) of **VIENNA** in May. He lost this position in January 1939 because of financial wrongdoing, but was pardoned by Heinrich **HIMMLER**, and in November 1939 was appointed district SS and Police Leader for the **LUBLIN** district of **POLAND** and promoted to the level of major general in the SS.

In 1941 Himmler entrusted Globocnik with the planning and establishment of police- and SS-fortified strongholds in Poland, and he was made head of all death camps that year. In 1942, Globocnik was given the responsibility of implementing **AKTION (OPERATION) REINHARD**. He used the camps of **BEŁŻEC**, **SOBIBÓR**, **TREBLINKA**, and **MAJDANEK** to carry out a fourfold task: the exploitation of the Jewish work force, the extermination of Jews, the acquisition of the real

Odilo Globocnik.

estate of the murdered Jews, and the seizure of their valuables and movable property. More than two million Jews were killed during Aktion Reinhard, and property to valued at 178 million Reichsmarks was seized and turned over for the benefit of the Third Reich.

In August 1943, as a result of differences with other Nazi party and SS leaders, Globocnik was transferred to Trieste. He committed suicide in May 1945 after being taken captive by British troops at the end of the war.

SUGGESTED RESOURCES

The SS. Alexandria, VA: Time-Life Books, 1989.

A Teacher's Guide to the Holocaust: Perpetrators. [Online] http://fcit.coedu.usf.edu /holocaust/people/perps.htm (accessed on August 24, 2000).

Williamson, Gordon. *The SS: Hitler's Instrument of Terror.* Osceola, WI: Motorbooks International, 1994.

Goebbels, Joseph

Joseph Goebbels.

(1897–1945)

Joseph Goebbels, who would become the Nazis' chief propagandist, was born in Rheydt, in the Rhine district, into a poor and pious Catholic family. He studied at the University of Heidelberg and earned a doctorate in literature and philosophy. After failing in his attempts to become a writer, Goebbels discovered his talents as a propagandist and speaker for the **NAZI PARTY**, which he joined in 1924. Before long he became one of Adolf **HITLER**'s most ardent admirers and in 1926 was appointed *Gauleiter* (district leader) of Berlin, his assignment being to win over the capital for the party. In 1928 he was elected to the Reichstag (a house of the German Parliament). Two years later he was also appointed the party's chief of propaganda. He then ran the Nazis' stormy election campaigns from 1930 to 1933.

On March 13, 1933, soon after Hitler came to power, Goebbels was appointed minister of propaganda and public information. He imposed Nazification upon the country's artistic and cultural life, working through the branches of the ministry that reported to him. He controlled the media, and it was at his prompting that "un-German" books were burned on May 10, 1933. Goebbels was also one of the creators of the "Führer" myth, an important element in the Nazis' successful bid for the support of the masses.

By the time the Nazi regime was firmly established, Goebbels's position had weakened. Once the political forces that had opposed the Nazis were destroyed, Goebbels no longer had an "enemy" to fight (except for the Jewish "enemy"), and Hitler was angered by the frequent crises in Goebbels's marital life, fearing that they might cause damage to the party's image.

When the war broke out, Goebbels assumed a key role in psychological warfare, and when the situation on the fronts took a turn for the worse, he again played a central part in the leadership. Once again in Hitler's good graces, Goebbels was appointed to the task of propagandizing and mobilizing the population for the war effort.

Goebbels was the father of modern propaganda in a totalitarian state. The propaganda he spread was remarkably filled with defamations, libels, and lies; he was

convinced that people would believe the lies if only they were repeated often enough, and the bigger the lie, the better chance it had of being believed. Goebbels's propaganda always incited hate against some enemy. He was fanatic in his **ANTISEMITISM**, but his hatred of Jews was also based on the utilitarian value of exploiting antisemitism to further his propaganda aims.

Goebbels was relentless in depicting "the Jew" as the principal enemy of the German people. It was Goebbels who conceived the idea of the **KRISTALLNACHT** ("Night of the Broken Glass") pogroms in November 1938, and it was he who gave the event the name by which it continues to be known. Following these pogroms, he used his influence to drastically reduce organized Jewish activities and freedom of movement. Once the war began, he launched a concerted effort to greatly diminish living conditions for the Jews of Berlin. The first **DEPORTATIONS** of Berlin Jews, in October 1941, were carried out to fulfill an express promise that Goebbels had given to Hitler, to make Berlin *judenrein* ("cleansed of Jews") as soon as possible.

When Hitler committed suicide in the besieged capital, Goebbels refused to accept the position of Reich chancellor, to which he was appointed in Hitler's will. On May 1, 1945, Goebbels and his wife, Magda, dressed their six children, ages four to twelve, in white party outfits and then ordered an SS doctor to give them lethal injections. Goebbels and his wife then committed suicide by ordering an SS man to shoot them.

SUGGESTED RESOURCES

Goebbels, Joseph. *The Goebbels Diaries.* Garden City, NY: Doubleday, 1948. Reprint, New York: Penguin, 1983.

Heiber, Helmut. *Goebbels.* New York: Hawthorn Books, 1972. Reprint, New York: Da Capo Press, 1983.

Hitler's Henchmen [videorecording]. Windsong/La Mancha, 1991.

Reuth, Ralf Georg. *Goebbels.* New York: Harcourt Brace, 1993.

GORDONIA. SEE YOUTH MOVEMENTS.

Great Britain

World War II began with **GERMANY**'s invasion of **POLAND** in September 1939. At the time, although Britain's political and economic interests stretched around the world, from East Asia through India, the Middle East, the Mediterranean, and to the North Sea, Britain was unable to defend its huge empire on its own.

British politicians were aware of Britain's fundamental weakness. The huge human and material losses of World War I (1914–18) were still keenly felt, and until 1936 there was little public support for a serious military-rearmament program. Not surprisingly, British foreign policy attempted to soothe, or appease, potential enemies and worked to gain friends among neutral countries by meeting their demands. After the complete German takeover of Czechoslovakia, however (against the agreement reached at the Munich Conference of September 1938), Prime Minister Neville Chamberlain reversed his government's foreign policy based on appeasement. He decided to offer a mutual-defense pact to Poland in order to avoid German aggression against that country.

By May 1940, Britain was the only country in Europe still fighting Adolf Hitler. Despite their isolation and increasingly desperate situation, the British refused all negotiations with the Germans.

Unprepared for War

The British army was too weak and unprepared for war to present any meaningful threat to Germany. When war began in September 1939, there were only two fully trained divisions in the United Kingdom. Other British troops were spread out among the colonies, including almost 17,000 in Palestine. Still, Britain (together with its ally, **FRANCE**) declared war on Germany two days after Germany invaded Poland.

Poland quickly fell to the Germans and the months that followed were popularly called the "phony war." There were no more German advances until May 1940. Britain used this period to dramatically improve its military strength. Although the United States was technically neutral in the war, President Franklin D. Roosevelt promised that American supplies would be available to Great Britain. The British dominions—Canada, South Africa, Australia, and New Zealand—and India also declared war on Germany. However, they were too far away from the main theater of action in Europe to help much until the fighting spread to North and East Africa and to Asia.

Britain's most significant ally was France. The two countries' strategy was based on a combined use of their navies to prevent German control of the seas. This was essential, since Germany needed to import materials over water.

In May 1940, the Germans moved against **BELGIUM**, Luxembourg, and the **NETHERLANDS**. Germany also invaded France. Soon afterward, **ITALY** joined Germany as an Axis power and declared war on Great Britain. Britain was the only country in Europe still fighting Adolf **HITLER**, but the British refused all negotiations with the Germans. The successful evacuation of 200,000 British troops from France at Dunkirk (Dunquerke), in June 1940, allowed Britain to prepare for an expected German invasion of the British Isles. During this period of crisis, the government of Neville Chamberlain was replaced by a national coalition led by Winston Churchill. The new prime minister announced that Britain would continue fighting until the defeat of Germany.

Between August and October 1940, the Luftwaffe (the German air force) failed to defeat the British Royal Air Force in the prolonged Battle of Britain. Still, Britain's overall situation was bad. The fall of France to Germany had deprived Britain of the support of the French navy and troops. Italy's entry into the war complicated Britain's position in the Middle East, Africa, and India.

Great Britain's isolation was eased by the growing willingness of the United States to support the British war effort. In March 1941, the U.S. Congress passed the Lend-Lease Act, allowing the United States to supply Britain with weapons under a leasing arrangement. This acknowledged that an eventual British victory against Hitler was important to American security. The growing political alliance between the two powers was expressed in the Atlantic Charter of August 14, 1941.

After the German air force lost the Battle of Britain, Hitler abandoned his plan to invade the British Isles and turned his attention to the **SOVIET UNION**. On June 22, 1941, "Operation Barbarossa" began. German troops invaded the Soviet Union from the Baltic Sea south to Romania. Despite Prime Minister Churchill's strong anti-Communist beliefs, he immediately offered Soviet leader Joseph Stalin supplies and weapons. Hitler's decision to strike out to the East—to fight a war on two fronts—transformed the nature of World War II. It especially relieved the pressure on Britain and on British positions in the Middle East. The Japanese attack on Pearl Harbor on December 7, 1941, and the official declaration of a state of war between the United States and Japan (followed soon after by the German declaration of war

against the United States), meant that the war had become truly global. Britain was no longer alone.

An Allied Effort

By the beginning of 1942, a "grand alliance," led by Churchill, Roosevelt, and Stalin, had been formed. Several basic principles guided their joint, "Allied" effort against the Axis. First, the war against Germany was given priority over the war in the Pacific, despite the rapid advance of Japanese forces. With many German troops fighting on the Soviet front, Great Britain and the United States worked to open a second European front against the Germans as soon as possible.

Three remaining principles of the Allies' policy toward Germany eventually had major implications for the relief and rescue of European Jewry. First of all, a blockade of supplies to occupied Europe was recognized as an essential weapon against the German war effort. Secondly, it was agreed that there would be no negotiations with Hitler. This was to reassure Stalin that Britain and America would not join with the Germans in a joint effort to destroy the Soviet Union. Although there were contacts with the Germans by means of neutral states and the International Red Cross on various humanitarian issues, the principle of "no negotiations" prevented any serious consideration of German proposals for the ransom of Jews. Finally, the Allies agreed that they would fight until the unconditional surrender of Germany and the Axis.

The tide of war turned in late 1942. The German advance into Russia was halted at Stalingrad in October, and the German forces were defeated at El Alamein in November. These events marked the beginning of the eventual defeat of Nazi Germany.

War's Effects at Home

The impact of the war was far-reaching in Britain. As large numbers of men were enlisted in the army, women entered the workforce in unprecedented numbers. The important role played by organized labor in the war effort, and the central role of the Labour party in the coalition government, led to demands for social reform. The desire for change was reflected in the results of the elections held right after the end of the war in Europe. Despite Churchill's popularity as a war leader, his Conservative party lost the elections in July 1945 to the Labour party. The head of the Labour party, Clement Attlee, became prime minister. (Churchill later returned as prime minister, in 1951.)

World War II also transformed Britain's dependent empire. The mystique of British power and supremacy diminished as colonies in East Africa were occupied by Italian forces and in Asia by the Japanese. Even after the Japanese had been defeated, Britain was not able to reestablish its authority in a number of colonies. In other parts of the empire, political concessions were granted to nationalist forces to secure their support during the war effort. These changes led to the effective loss of the empire by the mid-1950s. The war marked the end of Britain's role as a great power.

Appeasement of Nazi Germany

Great Britain's policy toward Germany in the period between the two world wars, especially in the second half of the 1930s, was one of appeasement. "Appeasement" was originally a positive term, describing an effort to establish peace between antagonistic

The Allies—Great Britain, the United States and the Soviet Union—agreed to fight until the unconditional surrender of Germany.

World War II marked the
end of Great Britain's role as
a global empire.

countries. After World War II, however, the term acquired a negative sense, being linked, by association with British policy, with weakness in the face of aggression. An agreement with Hitler, signed by Prime Minister Neville Chamberlain at the Munich Conference in September 1938, came to be viewed as the lowest point of appeasement. It surrendered Czechoslovakia, a friendly and free country, to Nazi Germany, whether out of cowardice or foolish blindness concerning Hitler's true aims.

Britain's appeasement policy was adopted many years before the **NAZI PARTY**'s rise to power with its policy of aggression. It was a direct result of the peace agreements at the end of World War I, and in particular of the Treaty of Versailles. Even during the Versailles Conference, the harsh terms dictated to the Germans worried the British and Americans. They debated whether to aim for a peace treaty, in a spirit of appeasement, or to insist on harsh terms. The second option was chosen, which produced a sense of guilt and sympathy toward Germany among many of the politicians involved. Appeasement toward Germany was also historically in the national interests of Britain; maintaining peace through the post-war renewal of economic ties in Europe, especially with Germany, was necessary in restoring and maintaining international trade.

British politicians tended to see the Nazis' rise to power as a result of the harsh policy toward Germany. Their negative feelings about Nazism, however, did not change their appeasement policy. As German strength grew, Great Britain increased its efforts for good relations. Various proposals were made for the economic appeasement of Germany: the granting of colonies in Africa, trade agreements, and even military agreements. But Germany adopted a policy of presenting "done deals" that modified the terms of the peace treaty. For example, it abolished military restrictions and moved its army into the demilitarized Rhine region.

Up to 1937, Britain practiced a policy of "passive appeasement," simply accepting Hitler's aggressive actions. When Chamberlain became prime minister in May 1937, he started a policy of "active appeasement." He tried to prevent war through cooperation with Germany. Relations between Czechoslovakia and Germany deteriorated, however, and by mid-September 1938 the danger of war seemed imminent. Chamberlain went to meet with Hitler in Germany. Before the talks, the British government had decided to give autonomy to the Germans within Czechoslovakia. At the meeting, however, Hitler and Chamberlain immediately agreed on the annexation of areas of Czechoslovakia to Germany. The Munich Agreement was signed after two weeks of talks.

At that time, the attempt to appease Germany by putting pressure on an independent state (Czechoslovakia) was not seen in Britain as a weak or treacherous act, but as a bold step to save Europe from war. But when Hitler introduced new demands, doubts grew in Britain about the morality and the usefulness of this act of appeasement. In Parliament, Winston Churchill, a longtime critic of appeasement, harshly criticized the Munich Agreement. Both in Parliament and in the press, the agreement was attacked as a shameful giving-in that would encourage further acts of aggression from Hitler.

This was confirmed when Hitler violated his pledges and occupied all of Czechoslovakia in March 1939. Appeasement now appeared to be a complete failure. Chamberlain was obliged to change his policy. He guaranteed support to Poland and Romania, which were expected to be Hitler's next victims. Still, he did not abandon hope of salvaging peace by maintaining contact with leading figures in Germany. Even after Germany invaded Poland in September 1939, when he was forced to declare war on Germany, Chamberlain did so reluctantly, unconvinced of the need to fight.

Fascism in Great Britain

Beginning in 1923, a number of fascist organizations came and went in Britain. With the formation of the British Union of Fascists (BUF) by Sir Oswald Mosley in 1932, FASCISM in Britain took an important step forward. But the extremism of the fascist Nazi Germany lost the BUF some support, as did its involvement in political violence and its ANTISEMITISM. There were violent street clashes between fascists and anti-fascists. With the government's 1936 ban on the wearing of uniforms in public, growth of the BUF (whose hallmark was the wearing of a black shirt) was further hindered. Economic recovery in the course of the 1930s did not help the BUF's cause. Even so, Mosley's movement was active until World War II, and Mosley continued to attract large crowds at public meetings.

The outbreak of the war soon resulted in the restriction of fascist activity. In early 1940, leading members of the BUF, including Mosley, were interned under a law that allowed the government to hold people who had had associations with enemy powers. Arnold Leese, another prominent fascist, was among the other internees. By the end of the war, fascism in Britain had become associated with the excesses of Nazi Germany.

Jewish Refugees

Between 1933 and 1945, Great Britain was an important country of refuge for Jews fleeing Nazi-controlled Europe (see REFUGEES, 1933–45). For its size, Britain gave shelter to a significant number of Jews during the Holocaust. Britain had a liberal tradition of granting asylum to refugees, and it was the preferred country of immigration. Others sought temporary refuge there while waiting to emigrate elsewhere. A third group looked to Britain as the entry point for the territories in Britain's large dependent empire.

British immigration policy, however, like that of many countries, changed in response to events. The first wave of refugees arrived in Britain in the months after Hitler's rise to power in January 1933. Church groups, in particular the Quaker Society of Friends, were active on their behalf. The Parliament was sympathetic to these first victims of Nazism. Because Britain did not border on Germany, the number of refugees arriving there shortly after the Nazi seizure of power was small. In December 1933, there were only 3,000; and in April 1934, just 2,000. Would-be refugees met with many difficulties, mainly due to the immigration laws of 1919 (the Aliens Law), which remained in effect until 1938. The government made no distinction between refugees and other immigrants. It required financial guarantees on the refugees' behalf and pledges that they would remain in Great Britain only temporarily. The official attitude toward Jewish refugees was affected by the government's policy of non-intervention in Germany's internal matters. The humanitarian approach to the refugees, supported by groups outside the government, was seen as harming Britain's political and economic interests. But after Germany's annexation of Austria in March 1938 (the *Anschluss*), Great Britain became a haven for many refugees. The coordination of ways to help refugees reached its height in the year before World War II began, as did the rate of immigration. Among the non-Jewish public, there was a great deal of support for Jews who had escaped from Nazi Germany. However, many refugees discovered pockets of hostility, such as among the trade unions.

Aggressive German actions in 1938 (the *Anschluss* in March, the German occupation of the Sudetenland that October, and KRISTALLNACHT in November) brought British immigration policy under intense pressure. Pressured by pro-refugee groups and members of Parliament, and embarrassed by international response to the

Negative feelings about Nazism did not change the policy of appeasement. As German strength grew under Hitler, Great Britain increased its efforts to maintain good relations, until war on Germany was declared in September 1939.

Jewish refugee children arrive in Great Britain.

Britain's humanitarian approach to refugees, supported by agencies outside the government, was criticized as harmful to Britain's political and economic interests.

British campaign against Jewish immigration into Palestine, Britain made it easier for refugees to enter. But with the outbreak of war in September 1939, all immigration into Britain and the British Empire from enemy or enemy-controlled territory was banned. Jewish refugees continued to reach Britain after 1939, but in very small numbers. Later, as the tide of war turned, the restrictions on entry were partly lifted.

Eventually, more than 10,000 unaccompanied refugee children, most of them Jewish, reached Great Britain from Central Europe. (*See* **RESCUE OF CHILDREN**.) Until the outbreak of the war, more than 80,000 Jewish refugees reached Great Britain, and 55,000 remained there. In addition to 10,000 children, some 14,000 women entered the country as domestic help. In a special camp, Kitchener, in Richborough, Kent, 5,000 people who needed immediate shelter were housed during an 18-month period from the end of January 1939. The government gave them a group entrance visa and waived the normal regulations for passports and individual permits.

Jewish organizations in Great Britain were concerned about the refugee problem early on. Various groups guaranteed care and financial support. As the numbers of desperate refugees increased, however, thousands of applicants had to be turned away. In addition to generous contributions to support children and various refugee-aid organizations, British Jews gave personal bonds that enabled thousands

of refugees to enter Great Britain and guaranteed their support once they arrived. Many volunteers worked in relief organizations.

With the outbreak of war, refugee children were evacuated, along with British children, to the Midlands and Wales. The treatment of refugees at this time became worse. Following the outbreak of hostilities, all Germans and Austrians in Great Britain, including Jewish refugees, were defined as "enemy aliens." The war caused mass hysteria and open hostility toward the refugees. The government, with the full support of the public and the press, opened internment camps for aliens from Germany and Austria in the early summer of 1940. Within several weeks, about 30,000 were interned in camps—most of them Jewish refugees who unhesitatingly supported the Allies. Later in the summer of 1940, the government took an additional step that had great ramifications: It deported aliens from Great Britain.

Only after the scandals and disasters resulting from the **DEPORTATIONS** (such as the sinking of the ship *Arandora Star* carrying deportees, with great loss of life) did the injustice and the futility of the policy became evident. Shortly thereafter, the government changed its policy, canceling deportations and returning some of the deportees to Great Britain. Within a year, almost all of the internees were released and were integrated into British society. Thousands of them joined the British army in the war against the Nazis.

SUGGESTED RESOURCES

Bolchover, Richard. *British Jewry and the Holocaust.* New York: Cambridge University Press, 1993.

Bower, Tom. *The Pledge Betrayed: America and Britain and the Denazification of Postwar Germany.* Garden City, NY: Doubleday, 1982.

Breitman, Richard. *Official Secrets: What the Nazis Planned, What the British and Americans Knew.* New York: Hill and Wang, 1998.

Wasserstein, Bernard. *Britain and the Jews of Europe, 1939–1945.* New York: Oxford University Press, 1979. Reprint, New York: Leicester University Press, 1999.

Grodno

Grodno is a city in the western part of **BELORUSSIA** (now called Belarus). In the period between world wars, Grodno was part of **POLAND**; in September 1939 it was occupied by the Red Army and annexed to the **SOVIET UNION**. Grodno had one of the oldest and largest Lithuanian Jewish communities, with a Jewish population of 25,000 people. It took pride in its numerous social and cultural institutions and was a center of Zionism.

On the first day of their invasion of the Soviet Union, June 22, 1941, the Germans reached Grodno. As soon as they entered the city, they put all Jews aged 16 to 60 into forced labor. In July of that year, 80 Jews belonging to the intelligentsia were put to death. The Germans administratively transferred Grodno from Belorussia to the district of **BIAŁYSTOK**, and annexed it, in March 1942, to East Prussia.

On November 1, 1941, the Germans ordered the establishment of two ghettos, ghetto "A" for skilled workers and ghetto "B" for "nonproductive" Jews. The ghettos became the centers of educational, cultural, communal, and youth movement activities, with the participation of community leaders, educators, and members of Zionist **YOUTH MOVEMENTS**.

Because of its location, between **VILNA** and Białystok, Grodno became a center for the Jewish underground. It was one of the first places to hear reports of the large-scale massacres at **PONARY**. At the beginning of 1942 an underground movement was founded in the Grodno ghetto. Its membership base combined non-Zionist and Zionist youth movements, and the Communists. The pioneering Zionist movements wanted to fight inside the ghetto, whereas the Communists urged escaping from the ghetto into the forests to fight as **PARTISANS**—paramilitary groups organized for sabotage, revenge, and assassination attempts against the Nazi forces and sympathizers. Mordechai **TENENBAUM** twice went to Grodno trying to set up an underground that would encompass all the Jewish movements, from the revisionist Zionists to the Communists. He had some success, and some of the underground activists were transferred to the Białystok ghetto.

On November 22, 1942, 2,400 Jews from Grodno were taken to **AUSCHWITZ**. While this **DEPORTATION** was underway, Zerah Silberberg, one of the Zionist activists in the Białystok underground, went to Grodno to train the underground commanders and try to establish unity among the youth movements.

An additional 2,000 Jews were deported from Grodno at the end of November 1942; their destination was Kielbasin, a transit camp for later deportation to **EXTERMINATION CAMPS.** A second transport of Jews from Grodno to Kielbasin followed in early December. The underground had a plan to assassinate the German commander of ghetto "B," but failed to carry it out. Five members were sent to the forests; four died there and the one survivor returned to the ghetto, declaring that Jews without weapons could not survive in the forest. The determination to stay in the ghetto and fight gained in strength among the underground members, but some groups of Jews continued to escape into the forests. Several women members of the underground who had set up a workshop for forging documents were moved to Białystok on orders of the underground, to serve as liaison officers. Two underground members set an ambush one night for the commander of ghetto "B," but they were shot before they could draw their guns. Another assassination attempt, whose target was the commander of ghetto "A" and the superior of the commander of ghetto "B," Kurt Wiese, also failed.

In a deportation that came to an end on January 22, 1943, 10,500 Jews were taken to Auschwitz. Many of the deportees jumped off the trains, and some of these made their way to the Białystok ghetto. The last group of Jews to be deported from Grodno, numbering some 500 persons, was taken to Białystok. The flight to the forests, mostly on an individual basis, continued in the winter of 1943, the destination being the nearby forests of Nacha and Augustów. The non-Jewish partisan units did not accept these escapees, and hunger and cold forced some of them to return to the Grodno ghetto. A number of young people from Grodno who had gone to Białystok left that ghetto for the forest in August 1943 and operated in the areas under the name "White Furs," mainly taking revenge on local peasants who had collaborated with the Germans. The group finally managed to join a Soviet partisan unit, and fought with it up to the liberation.

Grodno was liberated by the Red Army on July 14, 1944. Approximately two hundred Jews were still alive, including partisans and persons who had survived or who came back to Grodno from other places in the Soviet Union.

SUGGESTED RESOURCES

Gitelman, Zvi, ed. *Bitter Legacy: Confronting the Holocaust in the USSR.* Bloomington: Indiana University Press, 1997.

Lost Jewish Worlds: the Communities of Grodno, Lida, Olkieniki, Vishay. Jerusalem: Yad Vashem, 1996.

Haika Grosman.

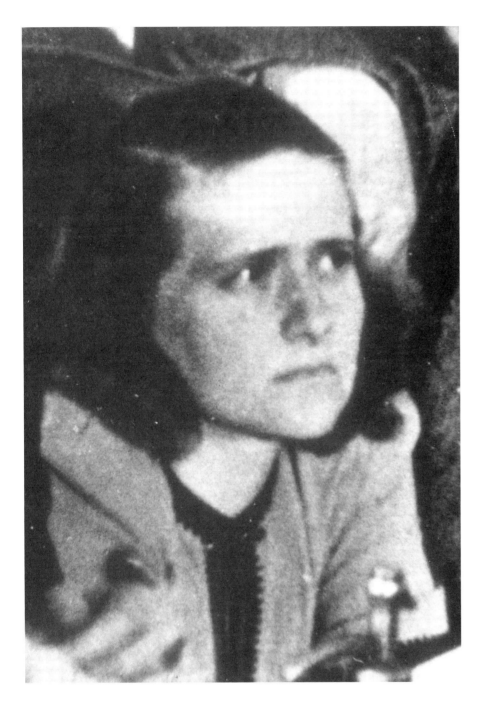

Grosman, Haika

(b. 1919)

Haika Grosman was an underground activist and partisan. Born in **BIAŁYSTOK**, Grosman became a member of the Zionist youth movement, Ha-Shomer ha-Tsa'ir, at an early age. At the outbreak of World War II she moved to **VILNA** to help organize members of the pioneering Zionist **YOUTH MOVEMENTS** in that city. Following the German invasion of the **SOVIET UNION** (June 22, 1941), Grosman returned to Białystok, where she became one of the organizers of the underground movement there.

Posing as a Polish woman, she went on many underground missions to various cities and ghettos, including the **WARSAW** ghetto. She belonged to the "Antifascist Białystok" cell and, along with five other young women who posed as Poles, she gave assistance to the Jewish underground and to the partisans who were then organizing themselves in the forests around the area. She participated in the Białystok ghetto revolt in August 1943, and became a member of a local Jewish partisan unit.

After liberation, Grosman served as the Ha-Shomer ha-Tsa'ir representative in the institutions set up by the remnants of the Jewish population in **POLAND**. She settled in Israel in 1948, joining Kibbutz Evron in western Galilee. Grosman became politically active in Israel and was a member of the Knesset (the Israeli parliament) from 1969 to 1981, and again from 1984. She is the author of *People of the Underground* (published in English as *The Underground Army*, 1988), which contains memoirs and chapters on the struggle of the Białystok Jews.

SUGGESTED RESOURCES

Partisans of Vilna [sound recording]. Chicago: Flying Fish, 1989.

Porter, Jack Nusan, ed. *Jewish Partisans: A Documentary of Jewish Resistance in the Soviet Union During World War II.* Washington, DC: University Press of America, 1982.

A Teacher's Guide to the Holocaust: Resisters. [Online] http://fcit.coedu.usf.edu/holocaust/people/resister.htm (accessed on August 24, 2000).

Gross-Rosen

Gross-Rosen was a **CONCENTRATION CAMP** established in the summer of 1940 as a satellite camp of **SACHSENHAUSEN**. It was located near the granite quarry of Gross-Rosen, in Lower Silesia, a region of German-occupied territory. On May 1, 1941, Gross-Rosen became an independent concentration camp; it remained in operation until mid-February 1945. At first, the camp prisoners were put to work in the quarry, which was owned by the SS German Earth and Stone Works. Prisoners also worked in the construction of the camp, which was accelerated in the summer of 1943. A large number of subcamps soon followed. The number of prisoners grew steadily, from 1,487 in 1941 to 6,780 in 1942. There were 15,400 prisoners in 1943, and 90,314 in 1944 (not allowing for the fact that many prisoners were counted twice). On the eve of the camp's liquidation, there were 97,414 inmates.

In its final stage, Gross-Rosen had a prison population of 78,000 (52,000 men and 26,000 women), representing 11 percent of all the prisoners then in Nazi concentration camps. A total of 125,000 prisoners of different nationalities passed through Gross-Rosen. It is estimated that 40,000 of them perished in the camp and in the evacuation transports.

Jews at Gross-Rosen

Jews were the largest group among the victims in Gross-Rosen. Beginning in late 1943, 57,000 Jews were brought there, including 26,000 women. The assignment of Jews to the camp, and their use as labor for the German war economy, resulted from a reorganization of the **SS** methods for exploiting Jews and from the evacuation of the **PŁASZÓW** and **AUSCHWITZ**-Birkenau camps. The Jews were distributed among satellite camps outside the main camp.

The first Jewish prisoners to arrive in Gross-Rosen were sent there from **DACHAU** and Sachsenhausen. In 1942, small groups of Jews, 100 in all, arrived from Poland's Radom district, from the prison in **TARNÓW**, and from Sachsenhausen and **BUCHENWALD**. They were housed in Block 4, which was run by German convicts. Among these convicts were several particularly brutal sadists and murderers.

The living and working conditions of the Jewish prisoners were extraordinarily harsh and inhumane. The work in the quarry and the construction of the camp were backbreaking. Prisoners were also used for special work assignments during what were supposed to be their hours for rest. The Jewish prisoners were not permitted to establish contact with one another; each prisoner was restricted to his or her own block. They were also denied medical attention. Before long, their health had deteriorated and they were completely exhausted. The death rate was high. Among the survivors, some were *Muselmänner* (*see* **MUSELMANN**)—inmates on the verge of death. In December 1941, 119 of these became victims of the **EUTHANASIA PROGRAM**. The high death rate continued in 1942. Prisoners classified as "disabled" were sent to Dachau. The last 37 Jewish prisoners were transferred to Auschwitz on October 16 of that year, in the course of an operation designed to remove Jews from all camps in Germany. For a period of twelve months, Gross-Rosen was *judenfrei* ("free of Jews")—a Nazi goal.

In October 1943, however, more Jewish prisoners were brought to Gross-Rosen, this time in larger groups and transports. The first such group consisted of 600 prisoners moved from the Markstadt labor camp to Fünfteichen, a new Gross-Rosen satellite camp. They were put to work there in Krupp factories. Another group of 600 Jewish prisoners was put at the disposal of **I. G. FARBEN**, to work in factories at Dyhernfurth, where poison gas was to be produced. More groups came in March 1944, beginning an uninterrupted flow of Jewish prisoners that continued until January 1945. Additional Gross-Rosen satellite camps were put up to accommodate them.

Most of the Jewish prisoners were from **POLAND** and **HUNGARY**, but others were from **BELGIUM**, **FRANCE**, Greece, Yugoslavia, Slovakia, and **ITALY**. The Jewish prisoners of Gross-Rosen were distributed among more than 50 satellite camps, called labor camps (*Arbeitslager*). Some of these satellite camps were put up when Gross-Rosen took over a number of forced-labor camps (*Zwangsarbeitslager*). A total of 28 such camps were taken over by Gross-Rosen. Of these, 20 were kept in operation as Gross-Rosen satellite camps. The prisoners from the remaining eight camps were transferred to existing satellite camps. Most of the camps were for men or women only.

A second group of completely new satellite camps for Jews was eventually put up. More transports of prisoners came in to meet increased demand for weapons, and, later, upon the partial evacuation of the Płaszów and Auschwitz camps. Especially notable among these camps were 12 that made up the "giant labor camp" (*Arbeitslager Riese*) complex, all for men. Established from April to June 1944, they were a labor reserve for the construction of Adolf **HITLER**'s underground home. These camps held 13,000 Jews, most of them from Hungary. The hard labor involved in building underground passages, roads, and so forth, together with the poor living conditions and total lack of hygiene, soon caused a large number of prisoners to become *Muselmänner*. As a result, 857 prisoners too weak to work were sent from these camps to Auschwitz, on September 29 and October 19, 1944. The death

Most of the Jewish prisoners in Gross-Rosen were from Poland and Hungary, but others were from Belgium, France, Greece, Yugoslavia, Slovakia, and Italy.

rate in the giant labor camp complex was exceptionally high. At least 3,068 prisoners died there.

In some other satellite camps for Jewish prisoners, the inmates worked in armaments and other factories. The women, distributed over 42 satellite camps, came mostly from Poland and Hungary. They arrived from Poland in late 1944, when Płaszów, Auschwitz-Birkenau, and the ŁÓDŹ ghetto were evacuated (the last via Auschwitz). They also came from Hungary in transports that first passed through Auschwitz-Birkenau. The prisoners in 13 of these camps worked in textile factories; in one camp, in the aircraft industry; and in another, in an armaments factory. The conditions in the women's camps were less harsh; out of 5,000 prisoners, 58 died—a relatively small number. Other satellite camps for women were put up at different times.

Before 1944, there were no large transfers of Jewish prisoners from Gross-Rosen to other concentration camps. Records show only the transfer of some 200 *Muselmänner* to Auschwitz and of 400 prisoners to Buchenwald. But there were frequent transfers from one satellite camp to another to meet current requirements of the war economy, and, at a later stage, as part of the gradual liquidation of Gross-Rosen.

Evacuation of Gross-Rosen

In the first phase of the evacuation—the last ten days of January 1945—the satellite camps on the eastern bank of the Oder River were liquidated. The men's satellite camps located there were moved to the main camp. Most of the prisoners in the women's camps were transferred to concentration camps deep inside Germany. The prisoners were evacuated by foot, in what came to be known as DEATH MARCHES, in the cold of winter and without food. Many prisoners perished on those marches, but no accurate estimate can be made of their number. The ultimate fate of many prisoners remains unknown.

The main camp, Gross-Rosen itself, was evacuated in early February 1945, and the remaining satellite camps after that. The prisoners in the main camp were evacuated by rail. But the condition of the cars that were used (they normally carried coal) and the lack of food caused the death of many people after a few days in transit. The prisoners of the satellite camps were evacuated on foot. Those of the Bunzlau camp, for example, were on the march from February 12 to March 26, 1945, with 260 dying en route.

During the evacuation of the Gross-Rosen camps, 3,500 Jews—mostly women—were moved to BERGEN-BELSEN. Some 5,565 were moved to Buchenwald; 489 to Dachau; 4,930 to Flossenbürg; 2,249 to MAUTHAUSEN; and 1,103 to DORA-MITTELBAU. The NEUENGAMME camp also took in a small number of women prisoners.

Including the transfers made in 1944, at least 19,500 Jewish prisoners were moved from Gross-Rosen to other camps in Germany. Those totaled 35 percent of the total number of Jewish prisoners in Gross-Rosen. The fate of the other 37,500 has not been established so far; some of them, no doubt, were included in the evacuation. The number of Jewish prisoners in the Gross-Rosen camp complex who did not survive is unknown, except in the case of the giant labor camp complex.

About half of the Jewish prisoners in the satellite camps are known to have been left behind. The surviving prisoners in these camps were liberated by Soviet troops on May 8 and 9, 1945. Twenty of the women's satellite camps were liberated; in 13 of them, 9,000 women survived. In Langenbielau, 1,400 surviving Jews were recorded upon liberation. In Brünnlitz, 800 had survived; and in Waldenburg, 600.

D uring World War II, Gross-Rosen grew from a small work camp occupied by 100 laborers housed in wooden barracks to a sprawling complex of 70 satellite camps housing between 80,000 and 90,000 prisoners who worked primarily in the German munitions industry, poison gas factories, and in the nearby quarry.

Even from these incomplete figures it is clear that a large proportion of the prisoners lived to see the Nazi regime's downfall. When the satellite camps were liberated, Jewish committees were formed in them. They took the prisoners under their care, especially the many who were sick. They obtained food and clothing and helped to return prisoners to their countries of origin.

SUGGESTED RESOURCES

Preissinger, Adrian. *Death Camps of the Soviets, 1945–1950: From Sachsenhausen to Buchenwald.* Ocean City, MD: Landpost Press, 1994.

Grüninger, Paul

Paul Gruninger (l) in police uniform, February 15, 1934.

(1891–1972)

As the local police commandant of the Saint Gall canton in Switzerland, on the Austrian frontier, Paul Grüninger was responsible for assisting thousands of Jewish refugees.

After **AUSTRIA**'s annexation by **GERMANY** in March 1938, the stream of Jewish refugees seeking to leave the Reich increased, and many sought to gain access to Switzerland. The Swiss government, however, closed its borders to Jewish refugees. Grüninger was instructed on August 18, 1938, to refuse entry to refugees fleeing Germany for racial reasons. Confronted by an unending wave of Jewish refugees at his border post, he defied his government's instructions and allowed all the Jews crossing the border at his checkpoint to enter the country. As a cover up, he predated official seals in the refugees' passports to indicate that their holders had entered the country prior to the August 1938 government ruling. Thus, from August through December 1938, when he was summarily suspended, Grüninger allowed some 3,600 persons (according to the state prosecutor's records) to illegally enter Switzerland.

Alerted by the German diplomatic staff in Bern, the Swiss government began investigating Grüninger's activities in January 1939, and charges were filed against him. Found guilty of insubordination, he was sentenced in 1941 to a stiff fine and the forfeiture of all retirement and severance payments. Grüninger was later denied access to other suitable positions in the government and the private sector, and he was never fully accepted or forgiven by the Swiss government. In 1971, he received recognition from Yad Vashem as one of the **"RIGHTEOUS AMONG THE NATIONS."**

SUGGESTED RESOURCES

Bauminger, Arieh L. *The Righteous Among the Nations.* Tel Aviv: Am Oved, 1990.

A Teacher's Guide to the Holocaust: Rescuers. [Online]
http://fcit.coedu.usf.edu/holocaust/people/rescuer.htm (accessed on August 24, 2000).

Gurs

Gurs was the first detention camp to be established in **FRANCE**, and one of the largest. The Gurs camp was 50 miles (80 kilometers) from the Spanish border and

Women prisoners stand behind a barbed-wire fence at the Gurs detention camp in Gurs, France, 1942.

10 miles (16 kilometers) from the town of Oloron-Sainte-Marie, on the plateau overlooking the lower Pyrenees.

The Gurs camp was set up in April 1939, coinciding with the collapse of the Spanish republic, and the first prisoners to be detained in it were Spanish soldiers who had fled to France in the wake of Francisco Franco's victory; among them were Jewish volunteers of the International Brigade. In early 1940 some 4,000 German and Austrian nationals—most of them Jews—were interned in Gurs, as were leaders of the French Communist party who had denounced the war against GERMANY. Between October 22 and 25, 1940, four months after France had surrendered, the German authorities—in violation of the armistice with France—deported to Gurs the entire Jewish population of Baden and the Palatinate, as well as Jews from some locations in Württemberg. Some 7,500 Jews were included in Aktion Bürckel, named after Josef Bürckel, the *Gauleiter* (district leader) of Alsace-Lorraine.

All the non-Jewish German nationals and pro-Nazis had been released from Gurs in mid-July 1940, shortly after the French defeat. The French Communists were set free at the end of October 1940; of the Jews, 2,000 were released in stages between November 1940 and August 1942, and emigrated overseas.

Conditions in the camp were very harsh: the sanitary arrangements were primitive, there was a shortage of water, and all the detainees suffered constantly from hunger. In the winter of 1940–41, 800 detainees died in epidemics of typhoid fever and dysentery that broke out in the camp. A total of 1,167 detainees were buried in the Gurs cemetery, as well as 20 who were non-Jewish Spaniards.

Despite the harsh conditions in the camp, many cultural activities took place and on a very high level—concerts, theater performances, lectures, and exhibitions. There were also courses of instruction in Hebrew, French, English, Jewish history, the Bible, and the Talmud, and thousands of prisoners attended religious ceremonies and prayer services on the holy days.

Around 6,000 Jewish prisoners were deported from Gurs to **Auschwitz**-Birkenau and **Sobibór** by way of the **Drancy** camp, the first transport leaving Gurs on August 6, 1942, and the last in the fall of 1943; by December 29, 1943, no more than 48 Jews were left. The camp was liberated in the summer of 1944. French poet Louis Aragon said of the Gurs camp: "Gurs is a strange sound, like a moan stuck in the throat."

SUGGESTED RESOURCES

Josephs, Jeremy. *Swastika over Paris.* New York: Arcade, 1989.

Weisberg, Richard H. *Vichy Law and the Holocaust in France.* New York: New York University Press, 1996.

Gypsies

Gypsies, who are also called Romani, have been living in Europe since the fifteenth century. They are a people who are bound by a common language and culture, and—until the twentieth century—by a nomadic way of life. The Gypsies were among the groups singled out by the Nazi regime for persecution.

While there are differences of opinion about their early history, most scholars assume that the Gypsies originated in India and were in Iran by the fourteenth century. By 1438, they had reached **Hungary**, and had entered Serbia and other Balkan countries in southern Europe. From there they spread into **Poland** and Russia, and by the sixteenth century, they reached Sweden, **Great Britain**, and Spain, where they settled in fairly large numbers. While some Gypsies became Muslims or Eastern Orthodox (Christians), most European Gypsies became Roman Catholics. They kept many of their pre-Christian beliefs alongside their new religion. The Gypsies' oral language has many dialects, and only in recent times has it become a written language.

Prejudice and animosity toward Gypsies was (and continues to be) widespread. Their professions were dictated by their wandering way of life and by the fact that in their adopted countries, most were not allowed to obtain land. They usually bought and sold horses and other animals, engaged in trades, were skilled at making things out of gold and silver, and played music. Fortune-telling, for which they gained a wide reputation, was usually a sideline. Gypsies were frequently accused of stealing and dishonesty, largely because of their nomadic lifestyle and foreign language. Like Jews, they became scapegoats and were the object of murderous official policies. For example, Prussian king Frederick William I decreed in 1725 that all Gypsies over 18 were at risk of being killed. In spite of all the prejudice against Gypsies, their music and poetry inspired famous artists, such as composer Franz Liszt. In many ways, Gypsies shared with Jews the dubious honor of being the quintessential strangers in an overwhelmingly settled Christian Europe.

When a modern industrial society developed in Europe, the Gypsies were out of place in the eyes of the authorities. In 1899 Bavaria, a state in southeastern **Germany**, established a special office in Munich for Gypsy affairs. It was the center for anti-Gypsy policies in Germany until the Nazi period. In February 1929, this Munich office became a Central Bureau for the Nazis, and had close ties to a similar office in Vienna. That same year, new laws allowed the police to coerce Gypsies into forced labor conditions, against their will. Similar regulations were in effect in other European countries.

A Gypsy (Roma) couple, sitting in an open area at the Belzec concentration camp.

The Gypsies occupied a special place in Nazi racist theories. The basic attitude of the Nazi regime was extremely hostile: The Nazis subscribed to old prejudices against Gypsies, and they idealized a "pure" Germanic society with a settled, peasant lifestyle. This ideal was the opposite of the Gypsies' way of life. In the eyes of the regime, the Gypsies were "asocials"—work-shy, alien individuals who did not fit into the new society that was to be built. One could not very well doubt the "Aryan" parentage of the closely knit Gypsy families, but to Germans they were also "people of different blood" (*Andersblütige*). According to a report submitted to Nazi leader Heinrich **HIMMLER** in 1941, there were some 28,000 Gypsies in Germany, and an additional 11,000 in Austria. Most of these Gypsies belonged to the Sinti and Lalleri tribes.

Anti-Gypsy Legislation

When the **NUREMBERG LAWS** were passed in September 1935, the interpreters of these decrees (which deprived Jews of many civil rights) applied them to Gypsies as well as Jews. In 1936, groups of Gypsies were delivered to the **DACHAU** camp as "asocials." At this time a racist theorist, Dr. Robert Ritter, was invited to set up a center that eventually was called the Research Office for Race Hygiene and Population Biology. Ritter was to examine the Gypsy population from the Nazis' racial perspective and propose solutions for what to do with them.

According to Ritter and his co-workers, an examination of some 20,000 Rom showed that over 90 percent should be considered **MISCHLINGE** (of mixed blood). This solved the problem of having to deal with an "Aryan" minority; the Nazis simply denied that the Gypsies were "Aryans." Ritter proposed that the Nazis prevent Gypsies from mixing with people of "German blood" and separate "pure" Gypsies from *Mischlinge* Gypsies. He also suggested performing sterilizations on the latter, and putting them in forced-labor camps. Both "pure" and *Mischlinge* Gypsies were considered "asocial." By making this assumption, the Nazis maintained an element of continuity with traditional European discriminatory thought. According to Himmler's decree of December 14, 1937, "preventive" arrests could be made of persons who, while not guilty of any criminal act, "endangered the communality by their asocial behavior." Administrative regulations implementing this decree, which were issued on April 4, 1938, specified that it was directed against "beggars, vagabonds (Gypsies), prostitutes ... without a permanent residence."

Memories of a Gypsy Holocaust Victim

At 15, Karoly Lendvai lost everyone. From his town of Szengai, 75 miles southwest of Budapest, he and his family were rounded up by Hungarian police and forced to walk 40 miles north to Komarom, to a notorious Csillag internment camp which was run by the Arrow Cross, the Hungarian fascists. Fifty years on, Karoly Lendvai's memory was undimmed.

"As we were marched through, others joined our group, more Gypsies and more gendarmes.... Some babies died along the way, and some would-be escapees were shot, left by the roadside. No one knows who they were.... We were in the camp about two weeks with hardly any food.... More people died as typhus broke out, and others were killed. The dead were thrown into a huge pit, covered with quicklime. "There were layers upon layers of dead. I do not know when the pit was finally filled because one day we were herded into cattle cars to be taken who knows where."

Lendvai was saved by an air raid. In the confusion of sirens and bombings he escaped into the woods "for about a year ... [and] I never saw the others again...." At 65, [Lendvai] still could not quite believe that all of this happened simply because Gypsies were Gypsies; but he knew that his family had all been murdered. Prisoners of the . . . internment camp were transported to Auschwitz.

"Rot you Jew-Gypsy!" Lendvai remembered an Arrow Guard screaming at him as he was being pushed onto a train. The curse still troubled him: "Why," he interrupted himself ... "why did he call me a Jew?"

Isabel Fonseca, **Bury Me Standing: The Gypsies and Their Journey** *(New York: Knopf) 1996, pp. 252–53.*

It soon became clear to the Nazis that this provision was too broad and could not be implemented. Another regulation went into effect on March 1, 1939, which clarified Himmler's policies and underlying ideas. To deal with what he labeled "the Gypsy plague," Himmler called for a separation between Gypsies and Germans, and between "pure" and *Mischlinge* Gypsies. The way of life of both categories of Gypsies would be regulated by the police.

Nazi racial policies became increasingly harsh, and after the Nazi conquest of Poland in September 1939, the fate of the German Gypsies became tied up with that of the Poles and Jews. At that time, Reinhard **HEYDRICH** issued instructions for the removal of 30,000 Gypsies from all of Germany to the **GENERALGOUVERNE-MENT**, along with the removal of Poles and Jews from the newly occupied western Polish territories. This order may have been designed to remove all *Mischlinge* Gypsies from Germany, but by April 1940, the Nazi governor of the Generalgouvernement, Hans **FRANK**, had received only 2,500 Gypsies, who came from the western territories. These Gypsies were mostly released in Poland.

Attitudes toward the Gypsies became more brutal as time went on. In the fall of 1941, 5,007 Austrian Gypsies of the Lalleri tribe were deported to the ŁÓDŹ ghetto. They were among those murdered in the CHEŁMNO extermination camp in early 1942. There were no known survivors. In addition, 3,000 Austrian Gypsies were placed in concentration camps.

Solutions for the "Gypsy Problem"

By early 1942, roughly two-thirds of the 28,607 German Gypsies had been classified by Ritter: 1,079 were defined as "pure," 6,992 as "more Gypsy than German," 2,976 as "half-breeds," 2,992 as "more German than Gypsy," and 2,652 as "Germans who behaved as Gypsies." Others were still being investigated. From the Nazi point of view, the "problem" of how to deal with the Gypsies could be solved with this intricate classification system. The result, according to Nazi logic, would be murder for some Gypies, and more regulations for others. "Pure" Gypsies would not be excluded from society (i.e., murdered). And so on October 13, 1942, Himmler issued a clarification concerning pure "Sinti Gypsies for whom in the future a certain freedom of movement is to be permitted." *Mischlinge*, "who are good *Mischlinge* in the Gypsy sense, are to be reintroduced into racially pure Sinti Gypsy clans." For these "pure" or relatively "pure" Gypsies, there would be appointed nine chiefs, who would supervise them. According to a document of January 11, 1943, over 14,000 Gypsies were to be included under this lifesaving provision. As for the others, Himmler issued a clear order on December 16, 1942, indicating that they were to be sent to AUSCHWITZ. Exceptions would be made for those who were "socially adapted," specifically, those who were former Wehrmacht (German army) soldiers or "war industry workers in important positions." For Gypsies in these exempted categories, sterilization was proposed.

Himmler's regulations were neater on paper than when put into practice. In reality, the distinctions between these groups of Gypsies were not that clear, and it is unlikely that German statistics on Gypsies and "Germans wandering about in the Gypsy manner" were very accurate. In addition, the documents regulating exceptions were not always followed faithfully. Auschwitz survivors have related stories of Gypsies—good Nazis and loyal Germans, some of officer rank—who were weeded out of German army units and sent to Auschwitz. Others were apparently not touched. It depended on the zeal of the local commander or the civilian party boss, and on his interpretation of the instructions. Nor were the Gypsies shipped to Auschwitz all German citizens; some were from the Balkans.

The first large transport of Gypsies arrived in Auschwitz on February 26, 1943. At the same time, a Gypsy family camp was established in Birkenau. The number of Gypsies in the Auschwitz "Gypsy camp" is believed to have been about 20,000. Living, or rather existing, in the most indescribable conditions, a great many of them died from starvation, epidemics, and "medical experiments," such as Josef MENGELE's experiments with twins. On August 2, 1944, 2,897 Gypsies were gassed as part of the destruction of the Gypsy family camp. Practically all the women and children were killed. Some of the men were sent to slave-labor camps or other concentration camps to do vital war work. Others were recruited into the regular German armed forces to clear away mines or perform other dangerous jobs, from which only a fraction returned.

Gypsy Treatment Throughout Europe

The total number of German and Austrian Gypsies who were deported and/or interned in camps was about 23,500. Most of them were eventually killed.

A group of Gypsy prisoners sit on the ground in an open field, awaiting instructions from their German captors in Bełżec.

Before the Germans invaded Czechoslovakia in 1939, 13,000 Gypsies lived in the territories that soon became the Protectorate of **BOHEMIA AND MORAVIA**. About half escaped to **SLOVAKIA** before the Nazis began to deport Gypsies. Some 4,000 were sent to Auschwitz between July 1943 and May 1944. Only a few hundred Czech Gypsies survived the war.

Information about the fate of the Gypsies in the rest of Europe is sketchy. According to one source, a total of more than 200,000 were killed in all of Europe. This may be a low estimate. In Yugoslavia, Gypsies were murdered together with Jews by the Ustaša regime; possibly as many as 90,000 Gypsies were killed in Yugoslavia alone.

In the occupied areas of Europe, the Nazis generally confined Gypsies and later transported them to Germany or Poland to work under forced labor conditions or to be killed. Apparently Bulgaria, **DENMARK**, Finland, and Greece were the only countries where the Gypsies escaped this treatment. In the **NETHERLANDS**, Gypsies, like the Jews, were interned in **WESTERBORK**, a transit camp, and from there sent to Auschwitz. Gypsies from **LUXEMBOURG** and **BELGIUM** were sent to Auschwitz as well.

Before the Nazi occupation of **FRANCE**, French authorities had already restricted the movement of Gypsies. After the defeat of France in June 1940, Gypsies from the regions of Alsace and Lorraine were interned in a camp at Schirmeck, where they were kept separate from "asocials" and "criminals." Shortly before Christmas 1941, they were deported. In unoccupied France, 30,000 Gypsies were interned under the supervision of Xavier **VALLAT** and the Ministry for Jewish Affairs. Later, most were sent to camps in Germany, including **BUCHENWALD**, Dachau, and **RAVENSBRÜCK**, where between 16,000 and 18,000 perished. Gypsies were interned in Algeria as well; 700 were restricted to the Maison Carrée area near Algiers.

Gypsies in **ITALY**, like the Jews, had a mixed experience. Often persecuted, many were also saved by the Italians. Before the war, the authorities rounded up Gypsies and put them on islands in the Venice region, off the mainland. Later, some were sent to Germany to work in forced labor or to extermination camps. Others,

Heinrich Himmler's November 1943 directions regarding the treatment of Gypsies included the following: "(1) Settled Gypsies and part Gypsies are to be treated as citizens of the country. (2) Nomadic Gypsies and part Gypsies are to be placed on the same level as Jews and placed in concentration camps. In cases of doubt, the police commanders will decide who is a Gypsy."

who managed to escape the Ustaša massacres in nearby Croatia, were sheltered there by the authorities. In the fall of 1943, when the Germans took over territories that the Italians had held in Yugoslavia and Albania, they interned the Gypsies and sent some to Buchenwald, **MAUTHAUSEN**, and other camps.

Although the Hungarians planned to intern Gypsies in labor camps as early as February 1941, the policy was never fully implemented. After the **ARROW CROSS PARTY** coup in October 1944, persecution of Gypsies began in earnest in **HUNGARY**. Germans and Hungarian collaborators rounded them up, deporting some together with Hungarian Jews. It is thought that about 31,000 Gypsies were deported within a few months, and only three thousand returned. The sources for these figures, however, have not been verified.

The large Romanian Gypsy population was not subjected to an extermination policy. According to a postwar Romanian People's Court, however, tens of thousands met their death as a result of expulsion. In 1941 and 1942, about 25,000 Gypsies from the Bucharest area were sent to Transnistria, and others were sent to the Ukraine.

Slovak Gypsies were treated somewhat better than those in the Protectorate of Bohemia and Moravia. On January 18, 1940, they were drafted, along with young Jewish men, into labor brigades. In 1941, orders were issued to expel them from their quarters in most towns and villages in Slovakia, but these orders were carried out inconsistently. Slovak fascists, however, massacred hundreds of Gypsies.

Most Gypsies in Poland faced deportation to concentration and extermination camps. Beginning in September 1944, the majority of those remaining in the ghettos were killed. About 25,000 persons, or two-thirds of the Polish Gypsies, died during the Nazi occupation.

In Estonia, **LITHUANIA**, and **LATVIA**, known as the Baltic States, and in the **SOVIET UNION**, Gypsies were murdered by the **OPERATIONAL SQUADS** (*Einsatzgruppen*). A report by the secret army field police dated August 25, 1942, stressed the need to "ruthlessly exterminate" bands of wandering Gypsies. Gypsies were murdered along with Jews at **BABI YAR**, in the Ukraine. In May 1943, Alfred **ROSENBERG**, the minister for the Eastern Occupied Territories, proposed that the Gypsies be concentrated in special camps and settlements. They were not, however, to be "treated as Jews." Himmler's instructions regarding treatment of Gypsies distinguished between "settled" Gypsies and "nomadic" ones; the latter were singled out for harsher treatment. The distinction between settled Gypsies and nomadic Gypsies was applied only in the Baltic states and the occupied areas of the Soviet Union. Some settled Gypsies in the Soviet Union were drafted into labor brigades or sent to concentration camps.

The Nazis' slaughter of wandering groups of Gypsies in the Baltics and Soviet Union seemed illogical, since the "pure" Gypsies they wished to spare were probably nomadic. On the other hand, there is no evidence that the Germans tried to find and spare settled Gypsies, or conduct special campaigns to find and register wandering Gypsies with the aim of murdering them.

A confused picture of Nazi conduct emerges. In Germany, the Nazis murdered those whom they saw as *Mischlinge*, while they mostly spared the "pure" Gypsies. In the rest of Europe, the Nazis did not have a very clear policy: Wherever they found wandering clans of Gypsies, they murdered them because they were "asocials," as Otto **OHLENDORF**, commander of SS-Einsatzgruppe D, said at his trial. The Nazis' treatment of the Gypsies was in keeping with their general way of thinking: Gypsies were not Jews, and therefore there was no need to kill all of them. Those Gypsies who were of "pure blood" or who were not considered dangerous on a racial level could continue to exist, but under strict supervision. The *Mischlinge* were doomed to death. The difference between the fate of the Gypsies and that of the Jews is clear. The Jews were slated for total annihilation, whereas the Gypsies were sentenced to selective mass murder on a vast scale. Even today the Gypsies are still a persecuted minority, and research about their history in the Nazi period is in an early stage.

SUGGESTED RESOURCES

Friedman, Ina R. *The Other Victims: First-person Stories of Non-Jews Persecuted by the Nazis.* Boston: Houghton Mifflin, 1990.

Ioanid, Radu. *The Holocaust in Romania: The Destruction of Jews and Gypsies Under the Antonescu Regime, 1940–1944.* Chicago: Ivan R. Dee, 2000.

Lewy, Gunther. *The Nazi Persecution of the Gypsies.* New York: Oxford University Press, 2000.

Ramati, Alexander. *And the Violins Stopped Playing: A Story of the Gypsy Holocaust.* New York: Franklin Watts, 1986.

HALUTS YOUTH MOVEMENTS. SEE YOUTH MOVEMENTS.

"HARVEST FESTIVAL." SEE ERNTEFEST ("HARVEST FESTIVAL").

HA-SHOMER HA-TSA'IR. SEE YOUTH MOVEMENTS.

HEBREW LITERATURE ON THE HOLOCAUST. SEE LITERATURE ON THE HOLOCAUST.

HE-HALUTS YOUTH MOVEMENTS. SEE YOUTH MOVEMENTS.

Heydrich, Reinhard

(1904–1942)

Reinhard Heydrich was the head of the Nazi Security Police; Sipo, the **SD** (*Sicherheitsdienst*; Security Service), and later, the Reich Security Main Office (*Reichssicherheitshauptamt*; RSHA). He was a key person in planning and implementation of the anti-Jewish policies of the Third Reich, including strategies for the **"FINAL SOLUTION"**.

Heydrich was born in Halle, a provincial Saxon town, to a family of musicians. His father was an opera singer and the director of a conservatory. In his youth Heydrich was exposed to his father's devotion to the music of Richard Wagner, his mother's stern discipline, and the worship of the authority of the state and its rulers. He was given the false notion that he was partly of Jewish origin.

Reinhard Heydrich.

Commissioned as an ensign and trained as a navy signal officer, Heydrich was discharged from the navy in April 1931. A naval court of honor found him guilty of misconduct toward a female friend, whom he had mistreated.

Frustrated by the rules of civil society, Heydrich, who initially had regarded the NAZI PARTY with contempt, was introduced by a family friend to Heinrich HIMMLER. Himmler made him an intelligence officer and charged him with the organization, in 1931, of the SS espionage and surveillance apparatus, the SD. Freed from the restraints of navy discipline and the civil code of behavior, Heydrich's ruthlessness, cynicism, and ambition were fully applied to this task. Inquiry into his alleged Jewish ancestry showed the rumor to be false, but his superiors blackmailed him with this suspicion, which guaranteed his loyalty. As SD chief, Heydrich was entrusted with the information-gathering, blackmail, and intrigue needed to establish Himmler's control over the secret state police, the GESTAPO. At the same time, Heydrich became executive director of the Bavarian political police, the nucleus of the Gestapo system under Himmler. The SD and the Gestapo, of which Heydrich later became executive director, were instrumental in establishing the Nazi system of terror. These groups executed the leaders of the Storm Troopers (*Sturmabteilung;* SA) on June 30, 1934.

Heydrich played a role in purging the German army high command in 1938, and also helped plant the false information that led to Joseph Stalin's purge of the Red Army's high command. Reflecting Himmler's fanatical race ideology, the SD developed into a political network of espionage and warfare, promoting ever more radical and deadly solutions to the "Jewish question," such as violent pogroms and forced emigration. In 1936 Heydrich was made chief of the Gestapo and the Kripo (*Kriminalpolizei*), retaining separate control over the SD.

pogroms
Organized and often officially sanctioned violent attacks on Jews and their property.

As Gestapo chief, Heydrich had unlimited power to send "enemies of the Reich," including Jews, to CONCENTRATION CAMPS. He encouraged competition between the SD and the Gestapo, which under his control vied with each other to carry out Adolf HITLER's Jewish policies. They also competed with other party elements. Under Joseph GOEBBELS' influence, they were encouraged to implement "solutions" to the "Jewish question," such as the assembly-line deportation organized primarily for Jews in AUSTRIA and Czechoslovakia.

In KRISTALLNACHT (Night of the Broken Glass), the pogrom of November 9 and 10, 1938, which was instigated by Goebbels, the SA Storm Troopers and the Nazi party took the lead. Heydrich, assisted by Heinrich MÜLLER and using prepared lists, saw to it that thousands of Jews were arrested by the Gestapo and SS. On January 24, 1939, Hermann Göring established the Reich's CENTRAL OFFICE FOR JEWISH EMIGRATION(Zentralstelle für Jüdisch Auswanderung). This transferred the implementation of the Reich's Jewish policy to the SS, and Heydrich was the chief administrator of this policy.

When war broke out in 1939, Heydrich was in charge of the OPERATIONAL SQUADS(Einsatzgruppen). In a special decree of September 21, 1939, he ordered them to isolate all Polish Jews into areas of cities called ghettos and to establish within each ghetto a Jewish administrative unit called the JUDENRAT (Jewish Council). Heydrich unified the Gestapo and SD within the framework of the newly established RSHA, giving ruthless SD functionaries, such as Eichmann, complete executive power in their anti-Jewish actions. Heydrich was instrumental in such schemes as the NISKO AND LUBLIN PLAN and the proposed mass deportations to Madagascar (*see* MADAGASCAR PLAN).

In 1941, prior to Hitler's assault on the SOVIET UNION, Heydrich arranged with the army high command to make military assistance for the Einsatzgruppen in

Russia. This was to facilitate the immediate annihilation of the Jews and Soviet officials in the Russian areas that were soon to be occupied.

On July 31 of that year, Göring, on Heydrich's urging, charged him with implementing the "final solution of the Jewish question" in all German-controlled territories throughout Europe. To carry out this task, Heydrich required the cooperation of the Reich's other departments. He convened a meeting of top officials at Wannsee, a Berlin suburb (*see* **WANNSEE CONFERENCE**), on January 20, 1942, to confirm the program for the planned extermination. Although Heydrich had direct access to Hitler and was given increasing power, it is not known to what extent he alone initiated the rationale and the methods adopted for the "final solution."

Late in 1941, Heydrich was rewarded for his anti-Jewish terror and extermination campaign by being appointed acting governor of the Protectorate of **BOHEMIA AND MORAVIA**. Attacked by Czech resistance fighters in an ambush near Prague, Heydrich died on June 4, 1942. Five days later the Germans retaliated by leveling the Czech village of Lidice; murdering all of its male inhabitants and shipping the remaining women and children to concentration camps.

SEE ALSO **AKTION (OPERATION) REINHARD.**

SUGGESTED RESOURCES

Calic, Edouard. *Reinhard Heydrich: The Chilling Story of the Man Who Masterminded the Nazi Death Camps.* New York: Morrow, 1985.

Cowdery, Ray R. *Reinhard Heydrich: Assassination.* USM, 1994.

MacDonald, C. A. *The Killing of Reinhard Heydrich: The SS "Butcher of Prague."* New York: Da Capo Press, 1998.

Himmler, Heinrich

(1900–1945)

Heinrich Himmler was Reich Leader (*Reichsführer*) of the **SS**, head of the **GESTAPO** and the Waffen-SS, minister of the interior from 1943 to 1945, and, next to Adolf **HITLER**, the most powerful man in Nazi Germany.

Himmler was born in Munich, Germany, into a middle-class Catholic family. His father was a schoolteacher with rigid views. Educated at a secondary school in Landshut, Himmler joined the army in 1917 as an officer cadet, but never served in active duty. After his discharge he studied agriculture and economics at the Munich School of Technology. He worked briefly as a salesman and as a chicken farmer in the 1920s. During this period he maintained close contact with the newly formed **NAZI PARTY**. Himmler took part in the Hitler Beer Hall Putsch of 1923 at the side of Ernst Röhm. Himmler joined Röhm's terrorist organization, the Reich War Flag (Reichskriegsflagge), and held various positions in the region of Bavaria.

Himmler became assistant propaganda leader of the Nazi party in 1926. He joined the SS in 1925, and became its head in 1929. The SS, which originally numbered 200 men who served as 's personal security force, became a key element in the power structure of the Nazi state under Himmler's leadership. Himmler was elected a Nazi Reichstag deputy in 1930, and immediately after the Nazi seizure of power in January 1933 was appointed police president in Munich and head of the political

Heinrich Himmler.

His role in strategizing the executions of the Holocaust years makes Himmler one of the most horrific mass murderers in history.

police throughout Bavaria. This gave him the power base to extend SS membership, organize the **SD** (Sicherheitsdienst; Security Service) under Reinhard **HEYDRICH**, and secure their independence from Röhm's Storm Troopers (Sturmabteilung; SA).

In September 1933 Himmler was appointed commander of all the political police units throughout the Reich (except Prussia). The following year, Himmler was appointed deputy head of the Gestapo in Prussia. He was instrumental in crushing the abortive SA putsch of June 1934, which eliminated Röhm and the SA as potential rivals for power and opened the way to the growth of the SS as an independent force. The next stage in Himmler's rise to power came in 1936, when he won control of the entire police force throughout the Third Reich, with the title of *Reichsführer-SS* and Head of the German Police. He created a state within a state, using his position to terrorize his personal enemies and all opponents of the regime. Himmler established the first **CONCENTRATION CAMP** at **DACHAU** in 1933. The organization and administration of the camps continued to be the work of the SS.

Himmler was inspired by a combination of fanatic racism and a belief in occult forces. His concern for "racial purity" led to the encouragement of special marriage laws that would further the systematic birth of children of perfect "Aryan" couples, and also to the establishment of the Fountain of Life (Lebensborn) institutions at which girls, serving as prostitutes for SS men, were selected for their perfect Nordic qualities. Himmler aimed to create an aristocracy of the "master race," based on his concepts of the virtues of honor, obedience, and courage. By recruiting "Aryans" of different nationalities into the Waffen-SS, he worked to establish a pan-European order of brotherhood, owing allegiance to Hitler alone. The war gave Himmler the opportunity to work toward his goal of the elimination of Jews and Slavs as "subhumans." Himmler was a master of efficiency, utterly lacking in scruples, and an extremely competent administrator.

He suffered, however, from psychosomatic illnesses that took the form of intestinal cramps and severe headaches. Himmler was squeamish, and on one occasion he almost fainted at the spectacle of a hundred Jews, including women, being shot to death on the Russian front. This physical weakness helped lead to the introduction of poison gas as "a more humane means" of execution.

In October 1939 Himmler was appointed Reich Commissar for the Strengthening of German Nationhood, and was given absolute authority in the newly annexed part of **POLAND**. This entailed responsibility for the replacement of Poles and Jews by **VOLKSDEUTSCHE** (Ethnic Germans) from the Baltic states. By the time of the invasion of the **SOVIET UNION** in 1941, Himmler controlled all the organs of police and intelligence power, and through the SS he dominated the concentration and **EXTERMINATION CAMPS** in Poland. His Waffen-SS (the military branch of the SS), with its 35 divisions, was practically a rival army to the Wehrmacht—the regular German combined armed forces. He also controlled the political administration in the occupied territories. As minister of the interior in 1943, Himmler gained jurisdiction over the courts and the civil service. He used these powers to exploit Jews and Slavs as slave laborers, to gas millions of Jews, and to institute pseudo-**MEDICAL EXPERIMENTS** on Jews, Gypsies, and other "asocial elements" to determine their resistance to extremes of cold and decompression.

The killing of the Jews represented for Himmler the fulfillment of a mission. The **"FINAL SOLUTION"** was the means to achieve the racial supremacy of the "Aryan" and purify the world of contamination by subhumans. His four **OPERATIONAL SQUADS** (Einsatzgruppen) in the east were the "agents of death" when the SS established the extermination camps of **BEŁŻEC**, **SOBIBÓR**, and **TREBLINKA** in the spring of 1942. After the July 1944 bomb plot on Hitler's life, Himmler received

even further advancement, as commander in chief of the Reserve Army and commander of Army Group Vistula.

Toward the end of the war, aware of the inevitable German defeat, Himmler made a number of gestures, apparently hoping to ingratiate himself with the Allies. He approved negotiations in Budapest that would have allowed the release of Hungarian Jews in return for trucks supplied by the Allies. In November 1944, he tried to conceal the evidence of mass murder in the extermination camps and permitted the transfer of several hundred camp prisoners to Sweden. He also tried to initiate peace negotiations with the Allies through the head of the Swedish Red Cross. Himmler ordered a stop to the mass murder of Jews at this time, and proposed that Germany surrender to U.S. general Dwight D. Eisenhower in western Europe while continuing the struggle in the east. This proposal infuriated Hitler, who stripped Himmler of all his offices. Even Admiral Karl Dönitz, who succeeded Hitler in the last days of the war as head of the German government, rejected Himmler's services. After the German surrender, Himmler assumed a false identity and tried to escape, but he was captured by British troops. He committed suicide on May 23, 1945, before he could be brought to trial as one of the major war criminals.

SUGGESTED RESOURCES

Breitman, Richard. *The Architect of Genocide: Himmler and the Final Solution.* New York: Knopf, 1991.

Hitler's Henchmen [videorecording]. Windsong/La Mancha, 1991.

Padfield, Peter. *Himmler: Reichsführer-SS.* New York: Henry Holt, 1991.

Russell, Stuart. *Heinrich Himmler's Camelot: Pictorial/Documentary.* Kressmann-Backmeyer, 1999.

Hirsch, Otto

(1885–1941)

Otto Hirsch was the chairman of the Reich Representation of German Jews, an organization formed in the early 1930s to help protect the interests of Jews living in **GERMANY** during the rise of Nazi **ANTISEMITISM**. Hirsch was born in Stuttgart, the capital of Württemberg, and studied law. He joined the civil service, first on the municipal and later on the provincial level.

In 1919 Hirsch represented Württemberg at the Weimar National Assembly and the Paris Peace Conference. Active in Jewish affairs, he became one of the leaders of the **CENTRAL UNION OF GERMAN CITIZENS OF JEWISH FAITH** (Centralverein Deutscher Staatsbürger Jüdischen Glaubens), and was among its members advocating that the Union promote Jewish settlement in Palestine. Hirsch was on the committee that helped establish the Jewish Agency, a Zionist organization; he also belonged to the Committee of Friends of the Hebrew University and the Provincial Council of Württemberg Jews, whose chairman he became in 1930. A meeting with Martin Buber aroused his interest in adult education, and on Hirsch's initiative a *Lehrhaus* (Bet-Midrash, or Jewish house of study) was established in Stuttgart, with Buber as one of its lecturers. Hirsch headed the *Lehrhaus* board along with Jews representing a variety of political and religious perspectives.

In 1933 Hirsch was among the founders of the Reich Representation of German Jews which, upon orders from the German authorities, became known in 1939 as the Reich Representation of Jews in Germany. As chairman, he played a major role in the organization's activities, which included providing economic aid to Jews, offering vocational training and retraining, expanding the Jewish network of schools, and enabling Jewish emigration. He also helped establish and operate the Center for Jewish Adult Education, which was headed by Buber.

Hirsch was a courageous leader of the Reich Representation of German Jews, deftly managing interaction with the German authorities. He guided the organization through internal problems, successfully mediating between opposing views and conflicting demands. Experienced in organization and budgeting, he was the liaison with Jewish aid organizations abroad, especially the British Council for German Jewry and the American **JOINT DISTRIBUTION COMMITTEE**, gaining their full confidence as a representative of German Jewry.

In the summer of 1935 Hirsch was arrested for the first time, in connection with a sermon that the Reich Representation of German Jews had written to be read in all the synagogues of Germany on the Day of Atonement. Refusing to go into hiding at the time of the **KRISTALLNACHT** ("Night of the Broken Glass") pogroms in November 1938, Hirsch was arrested for a second time and held for two weeks in the **SACHSENHAUSEN** concentration camp. On resuming his work, he focused most of his efforts on emigration and rescue. His plan was to establish transit camps for refugees in Britain and other countries. He hoped that this would facilitate and speed up the release of the many thousands of Jews who had been arrested in Germany and accelerate rescue efforts. He held numerous meetings in Britain and the United States in 1938 and 1939 with representatives of aid organizations and government officials, and was the Reich Representation of German Jews delegate to the **EVIAN CONFERENCE**.

On February 16, 1941, Hirsch was again arrested, and a few months later was taken to the **MAUTHAUSEN** concentration camp, despite the fact that his wife had obtained an entry visa for him to the United States. He was tortured to death in the camp, and his family was later informed by the camp administration that he had died on June 19, 1941. After the war, memorials to Otto Hirsch were established in his native city of Stuttgart and in Shavei Zion, a settlement in northern Israel founded by Jews from Württemberg.

SUGGESTED RESOURCES

"The Position of the German Jews, as Seen by Alfred Wiener, of the Leadership of the Centralverein." *Yad Vashem Online.* [Online] http://www.yad-vashem.org.il/holocaust/documents/16.html (accessed on August 23, 2000).

"Reichsvereinigung." *Simon Wiesenthal Center Museum of Tolerance Online.* [Online] http://motlc.wiesenthal.com/pages/t064/t06453.html (accessed on August 23, 2000).

Hitler, Adolf

(1889–1945)

Adolf Hitler was the leader of the Third German Reich (Nazi Germany). Born in Braunau, **AUSTRIA**, he was the son of a customs official. Hitler spent his youth in the country of his birth. He dropped out of high school in 1905. Two years later,

Adolf Hitler with a member of the Nazi Youth.

Hitler took the entrance test for the Vienna Academy of Art's School of Painting, and failed. His mother died that year of breast cancer. In 1908 Hitler made Vienna his home, living on the small sums of money he could earn selling his sketches and doing odd jobs. **ANTISEMITISM** was widespread in Vienna at the time. According to Hitler, this period of his life in Vienna shaped his views, and especially his concept of the Jews, though he may already have been an antisemite by then.

In 1913 Hitler moved to Munich, Germany. When World War I broke out in 1914, he volunteered for the Bavarian army. He served as a message runner in **BELGIUM** and **FRANCE** and was promoted to private first class. Hitler was awarded medals for bravery, including the Iron Cross, First Class, in 1918. In October of the same year, he was temporarily blinded in a British gas attack, and in the military hospital he learned of Germany's collapse. It was then and there, by his own admission, that Hitler decided to enter politics. He wanted to fight the Jews, whom he blamed for betraying Germany and ultimately bringing about its defeat.

After his return to Munich, Hitler served as a political spokesman and agent for the Bavarian army. In his first political document, he stated that the final goal of

When Hitler left school at the age of sixteen, he spent many untutored hours reading German history and mythology, dreaming of becoming an artist, and nurturing what would become a lifelong disdain for formal higher education and intellectualism. A fruitless and bitter struggle to succeed as an artist in Vienna followed. During these years, he began to publicly articulate his anger and hatred toward Jews, Marxists, democracy, and other social and political targets. Remarkably, despite his generally unkempt appearance, people listened.

chancellor:
Prime minister.

antisemitism must be "the total removal of the Jews." In 1919 he joined a small antisemitic political party that eventually took the name National Socialist Workers' Party (Nationalsozialistische Deutsche Arbeiterpartei, or NSDAP; *see* **NAZI PARTY**). The party's 1920 platform called for all the Jews of Germany to be deprived of their civil rights and for some of them to be expelled from the country. Hitler gained attention as a public speaker, and in 1921 became the party chairman. In November 1923 he led an attempt to bring down the government by force, for which he was sentenced in 1924 to five years' imprisonment in a fortress.

During his imprisonment in Landsberg, Hitler dictated the first volume of his book ***MEIN KAMPF*** (My Struggle). He was released after only nine months. In 1925 he reestablished the National Socialist party and created the **SS** (Schutzstaffel, or Protection Squad) to serve as the party's fighting force.

That same year, the first volume of *Mein Kampf* was published; the second one followed in 1926. Another book, written by Hitler in 1928, was published long after his death. Entitled *Hitler's Second Book*, it explains the grounds for Hitler's antisemitism, which was based on race theory (*see* **RACISM**). Antisemitism was, Hitler pointed out, at the center of his political thought.

Hitler's Rise to Power

Hitler aimed to use constitutional means to gain a majority in parliament. Then he intended to destroy the constitution. In 1928 the National Socialist party ran in the Reichstag (one of the houses of parliament) elections for the first time, receiving only 2.8 percent of the votes. In the Reichstag elections of July 1932, however, the National Socialist party received 37.3 percent, the highest it ever obtained in free elections. It became the largest political party represented in the Reichstag.

On January 30, 1933, Hitler was appointed **chancellor** which gave him sweeping powers. After a suspicious fire in the Reichstag on February 27, he suspended basic civil rights in Germany. On March 5, parliamentary rule was abolished. Antisemitic riots took place that month, culminating in the boycott of April 1, 1933 (*see* **BOYCOTT, ANTI-JEWISH**). A law was passed on April 7 eliminating Jews from public life in Germany. On July 14, all other political parties were dissolved, and the Nationalist Socialist Workers' Party became the only recognized party in the land.

A few weeks later, Hitler became commander in chief of the Wehrmacht (German army), and assumed the title of Leader and Reich Chancellor. He was now the dictator of Germany. Under his direction, the buildup of arms increased, as did the persecution of the Jews. The **NUREMBERG LAWS** were adopted on September 15, 1935, depriving Jews of their citizenship, barring them from some professions, and forbidding marriage between Jews and people with Germanic family backgrounds. Many other decrees issued by Hitler or in his name led to the exclusion of the Jews from German society. By the end of 1937 about 150,000 Jews had left Germany—approximately one-third of the country's Jewish population.

After the Germans took over Austria by force on March 13, 1938, nearly 200,000 Jews were added to the Reich; one quarter of them left the country within six months. In October, some 17,000 Jews of Polish nationality were expelled from Germany and sent to Poland. This was soon to be followed by the November **KRISTALLNACHT** ("Night of the Broken Glass") pogrom, several days of organized violence against Jews, their homes, and their businesses.

Hitler's Antisemitism

Hitler thought of Jews as a source of danger to Germany and to humanity in general. He believed Jews played a key role in democracy, liberalism, and socialism—political ways of thinking that Hitler abhorred. Hitler felt that the Jewish spirit was influencing western European civilization.

As early as the 1920s, in *Mein Kampf*, Hitler presented the Jews as the world's foremost enemy:

> [The National Socialist movement] must open the eyes of the people concerning foreign nations and must over and over again recall who is the real enemy of our present world. In place of the insane hatred for Aryans …; it must condemn to general wrath the evil enemy of humanity as the true creator of all suffering.… It must see to it that, at least in our country, the most deadly enemy is recognized and that the struggle against him, like an illuminating sign of a brighter epoch, also shows to the other nations the road of salvation of a struggling Aryan humanity.

On January 30, 1939, Hitler declared in the Reichstag that a new world war would lead to the destruction of the Jewish race in Europe. World War II officially began on September 1 of the same year, when the Germans invaded Poland. They immediately embarked upon the destruction of Jews in that country, although for a while this was done in a haphazard way. At about this time Hitler ordered the systematic killing of the mentally ill with toxic gas (*see* **EUTHANASIA PROGRAM**).

Eliminating the Jews

In September 1939, Hitler approved of a plan to expel the Jews from Germany into the Polish territories that had been taken over by the Reich. He informed Alfred **ROSENBERG** that he wished to concentrate all the Jews from the territories under German rule in an area between the Vistula and Bug rivers. This area in central Poland, known as the **GENERALGOUVERNEMENT**, would be a kind of Jewish transit camp, from which Jews would be sent to other destinations.

The systematic killing of Jews, which was known as the **"FINAL SOLUTION,"** began after the German invasion of the **SOVIET UNION** on June 22, 1941. Hitler's political strategy was to gain what he called "living space" (*lebensraum*) for the German people by acquiring new land and destroying the Jewish people. These two goals were the roots of his deadly legacy.

The first massacres of Jews in the Soviet Union were carried out by the **OPERATIONAL SQUADS** (Einsatzgruppen) in June 1941; the killing was then extended to include the rest of the Jews in Europe. On April 2, 1945, Hitler boasted that he had "exterminated the Jews of Germany and central Europe." His political testament of April 29, 1945, ended with a call for "merciless resistance to the universal poisoner of all nations—international Jewry." The following day he committed suicide in Berlin.

Decision Making and Jewish Policy Under Hitler

The Nazis believed in what they called the Leadership Principle; it involved the exercise of absolute authority from above and absolute obedience from below. The Nazis assumed that this sort of iron discipline and maximum efficiency would be an improvement over the more chaotic decision-making process that characterized the Weimar Republic. After 1933 many German institutions, including schools and universities, adopted the Leadership Principle to emphasize their allegiance to

the new regime. Hitler was glorified by the principle because it made him the source of all wisdom and the universal giver of orders.

Historians have discovered that the decision-making process of the Third Reich was considerably more chaotic than the Leadership Principle would suggest. Hitler's work habits alone were too unsystematic to allow him to run a smoothly functioning decision-making apparatus. In addition, his interests were not broad enough for him to perform the role of a universal giver of orders. He concentrated his attention most consistently and effectively in matters of foreign policy, rearmament, war, and the architectural reconstruction of Berlin.

Hitler's work habits were erratic. He was at times capable of working for weeks at a pace that left his aides exhausted, but these bouts of frenzied activity would be followed by weeks of lethargy. During these periods of lethargy, aides had difficulty getting him to perform even the most routine chores.

Hitler was not good at delegating responsibility. If he did not want to supervise a policy area himself, he usually did not assign the responsibility to a subordinate, either. The result was often a competitive struggle among ambitious subordinates who were eager to demonstrate their competence to Hitler and rise to the top ranks of the Nazi leadership. The most successful in this fight for survival, such as Hermann Göring and Heinrich **HIMMLER**, wound up in charge of vast empires. Those who were less able or less ambitious, like Alfred Rosenberg or Wilhelm Frick, had to be satisfied with a less prestigious rung on the Nazi ladder.

Hitler's strong, charismatic personality enabled him to maintain his authority over his subordinates. Although he rarely did so, Hitler could at any time intervene in any of the innumerable disputes between these ambitious underlings. He sometime did so with brutal swiftness. This was learned the hard way by Ernst Röhm and the Storm Troopers (Nazi military) leadership: on the night of June 30, 1934, Röhm and others were murdered on Hitler's orders.

Controversies about the Nazi decision-making process and Hitler's role in it have been widespread among scholars of the Holocaust. Some believe that the rivalries among Hitler's subordinates actually made the Nazis' policies against the Jews more extreme, propelling them from the **ANTI-JEWISH LEGISLATION** of 1933 to the **NUREMBERG LAWS** of 1935, the **ARYANIZATION** of Jewish-owned properties, the **DEPORTATIONS** of 1938 and 1939, and the "Final Solution." These scholars see Hitler primarily as the figure of authority who heartily approved of this process of persecution—a process in which he only occasionally played a directing role. According to this line of thinking, many of the Nazis' actions against the Jews were not part of a well-thought-out plan, but rather the result of rivals striving to out-do one another in currying favor from their leader.

Other scholars suggest that Nazi Jewish policy was from its beginning the product of long-term Nazi intentions. They point to statements made by Hitler from the 1920s about his intention to solve "the Jewish problem" by physical annihilation. In their view, Hitler and his underlings hid their murderous intentions until time and circumstances in 1941 were ripe for the "Final Solution" to be implemented.

It is clear to scholars on both sides of this debate that Hitler paid less attention to the details of Jewish policy than he did to foreign policy, rearmament, or war. It is interesting to study his role at several critical turning points in the making of Jewish policy: The notorious Nuremberg Laws of September 1935 and the infamous *Kristallnacht* pogrom of November 1938 came about by accident, rather than as a result of long-range planning. In the case of the Nuremberg Laws, the racist idea that people of Germanic background and Jews should no longer be allowed to marry was long part of Nazi ideology. Hitler made a sudden decision at the Nazi party rally in Nuremberg in 1935 to present a law forbidding such marriages. The officials called upon to draft the legislation were caught off guard, and had to improvise.

The circumstances leading to the *Kristallnacht* pogrom in November 1938 demonstrate a similar inclination on Hitler's part to act impulsively. On November 7 a Jewish youth, upset over the deportation of his parents from Germany, shot and killed a German diplomat in Paris. This inspired Propaganda Minister Joseph **GOEBBELS**, who was eager to gain additional influence in Jewish policy, to make a proposal to Hitler: He suggested that the Storm Troopers be set free all across Germany as an act of vengeance against the "Jewish crime in Paris." The result was a brutal night of murder, rioting, and looting. Decrees issued two days later confiscated one-fifth of the property of every German Jewish family. The Nazis announced those decrees as punishment, but in fact they had been ready for some time beforehand. Nevertheless, their sudden implementation was the result of Hitler's impulse. In this way, a significantly new stage in Nazi Jewish policy was inaugurated.

With this information in mind, it may be possible to understand more fully the implementation of the "Final Solution" in 1941. No one has found a document with Hitler's signature calling for the mass murder of Jews. Some scholars think this is simply the result of the chaotic way in which the Nazi system functioned. The order could have been delivered orally. And perhaps by 1941, the system no longer required an order from Hitler to set the machinery of murder in action. Another possibility is that Hitler and the Nazi leaders deliberately tried to keep the order secret, either by delivering it orally or marking it "Destroy after reading." Alternatively, such a document might have been destroyed by an act or accident of war. There is no debate among scholars, however, about Hitler's responsibility for the decision to implement the "Final Solution," even if its execution was carried out largely by the elaborate SS machinery under the command of Himmler.

SUGGESTED RESOURCES

Hitler [videorecording]. History Channel/A&E Home Video, 1996.

Hitler, Adolf. *Mein Kampf.* Reprint, Boston: Houghton Mifflin, 1998.

Rosenbaum, Ron. *Explaining Hitler: The Search for the Origins of His Evil.* New York: Random House, 1998.

Shirer, William L. *The Rise and Fall of the Third Reich.* New York: Simon and Schuster, 1960. Reprint, 1990.

Spielvogel, Jackson J. *Hitler and Nazi Germany: A History.* Englewood Cliffs, NJ: Prentice Hall, 1988. Reprint, 1996.

Thomsett, Michael C. *The German Opposition to Hitler: The Resistance, the Underground, and Assassination Plots, 1938–1945.* Jefferson, NC: McFarland, 1997.

Triumph des Willens [Triumph of the Will] [videorecording]. Connoisseur Video Collection, 1992.

Hitler Youth

Hitlerjugend, or The Hitler Youth (HJ), was the National Socialists' organization for children and young adults. The HJ had its origins in the *Jungsturm Adolf Hitler* (Adolf **HITLER** Boys' Storm Troop), an offshoot of the SA (*Sturmabteilung*; Storm Troopers) that was founded in 1922 and changed its name to Hitlerjugend in

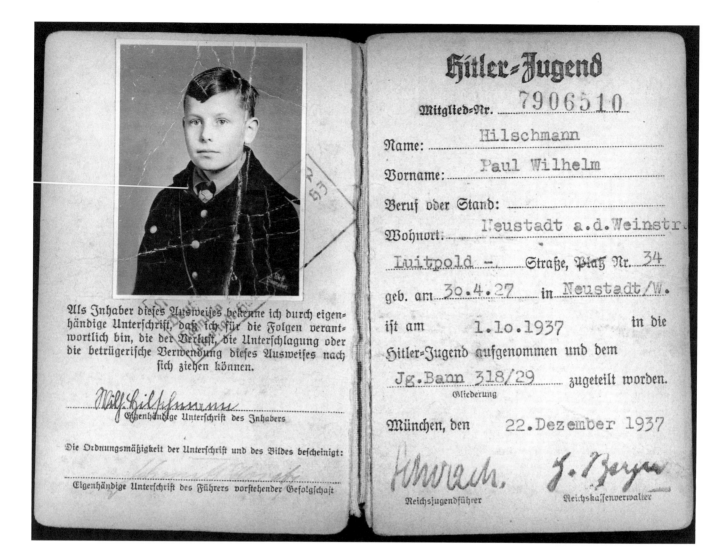

Hitler Youth identification card.

1926. Originally a movement for boys only, it began to admit girls in 1928 in a separate organization. In 1930, this organization became known as the *Bund Deutscher Mädel* (League of German Girls; BDM).

In 1931, Baldur von Schirach was appointed Reich Youth Leader (*Reichsjugendführer*) of the Nazi movement. Schirach's immediate goal was to bring the different youth organizations in the party under a single authority. In addition to the BDM, these organizations included the League of Nazi Students and the German Young Folk (Deutscher Jungvolk), which inducted youngsters at the age of ten. Schirach achieved his goal when he was appointed *Jugendführer des Deutschen Reiches* (Youth Leader of the German Reich) in June 1933. By 1935, the HJ was a huge organization, comprising 60 percent of the country's youth.

Like the Deutscher Jungvolk, the HJ admitted children at the age of ten. Its membership was organized into two age brackets, from ten to fourteen and from fourteen to eighteen. The organizational chart devised by Schirach followed the military pattern, involving squads, platoons, and companies. The companies were within territorial formations based on districts that corresponded with the **NAZI PARTY**'s geographic divisions. They were all subject to the authority of the Reich Youth Leadership.

The HJ and its organizational form were expressions of Hitler's ideology, in which children represented the reserve manpower that would ensure the continued existence of the "Thousand-Year Reich." Nazi educational doctrine was based on Hitler's anti-intellectualism and on a preference for body building at the expense of the mental and intellectual development of the individual. One of the guiding principles of Nazi education was to keep young people in constant action and to constantly spur them to activism. This was the system to which a boy was subjected from the moment he entered the HJ until he became a soldier or an **SS** man. He was equipped not only with a uniform, but with a bayonet as well. When boys reached 19, they were drafted into the Reichsarbeitsdienst (Reich Labor Service), which stressed physical work and iron discipline. Thousands of these youngsters were put to work on the land. As soon as they had completed the compulsory term in the Labor Service, the young men enlisted in the armed forces. This process enabled the Nazi party to control and supervise German youth from the ages of ten to twenty-one.

The objectives of the girls' organization, the BDM, were based on becoming the Nazi ideal woman. The values girls were to learn included obedience, performance of duty, self-sacrifice, discipline, and physical self-control. Two-thirds of the time that girls spent in the BDM was taken up with sports and one-third with ideology. German girls were taught that their primary role in life was to become mothers of genetically healthy Aryan children, whom they would educate, in turn, in the spirit of National Socialism. The BDM members were indoctrinated with "racial pride" and with the consciousness of being pure "German women" who would shun any contact with Jews.

During the war, the BDM became increasingly involved in the war effort, at the expense of ideological training. In the HJ, political and ideological indoctrination played a much larger role than in the BDM. The activities in which the HJ members were engaged overshadowed the formal education that they were receiving and estranged them from their families; quite often the youngsters became their family's Nazi propagandists—not to mention their ideological supervisors. The propaganda used for the implanting of Nazi ideas also drew on the mass media, and sophisticated methods were employed to gain the support of German youth for the HJ ideals. The film *Hitlerjunge Quex* (Hitler Youth Quex) is a typical example of the Nazi style of brainwashing. Produced in 1933, the film tells the life story of a boy who is strongly influenced by Nazi ideas.

Many of the young men who were converted to Nazi ideology during their membership in the HJ absorbed the poison of hatred through their training and activities. When they grew up, they became agents of the "Final Solution"—murderers by conviction.

SUGGESTED RESOURCES

Dvorson, Alexa. *The Hitler Youth: Marching Toward Madness.* New York: Rosen Pub. Group, 1999.

Heil Hitler! Confessions of a Hitler Youth [videorecording]. Ambrose Video Publishing, 1991.

Heyes, Eileen. *Children of the Swastika: The Hitler Youth.* Brookfield, CT: Millbrook Press, 1993.

Keeley, Jennifer. *Life in the Hitler Youth.* San Diego: Lucent Books, 2000.

Rempel, Gerhard. *Hitler's Children: The Hitler Youth and the SS.* Chapel Hill: University of North Carolina Press, 1989.

HITLERJUGEND. SEE HITLER YOUTH.

HOLLAND. SEE NETHERLANDS, THE.

Holocaust

The word "holocaust" is derived from the Greek *holokauston*, which originally meant a sacrifice, or offering to God, which was totally burned by fire. Over time, the word was used to describe the killing of masses of human beings in great numbers. By the 1950s, the term "holocaust" was used primarily to refer to the Nazis' destruction of the Jews of Europe and of other groups of people during World War II. The Hebrew term *sho'ah* and the word "holocaust" have become linked to the attempt by the Nazi German state to destroy European Jewry during World War II.

The use of the Hebrew word *sho'ah* to denote the destruction of Jews in Europe during the war first appeared in the booklet "The Holocaust of the Jews of Poland," published in Jerusalem in 1940 by the United Aid Committee for the Jews of **POLAND.** The booklet contains reports and articles on the persecution of Jews in Eastern Europe since the beginning of the war, as reported by eyewitnesses. Some of these witnesses were leaders of Polish Jewry.

Up to the spring of 1942 the term *sho'ah* was rarely used. The Hebrew term that was first used to describe the persecution and murder of Jews was *hurban*, which is similar in meaning to the word "catastrophe." It has a historical meaning for Jews because the word was used in reference to the destruction of the Temple. Leaders of the Zionist movement, who supported the establishment of a Jewish state in Israel, and intellectuals in Palestine began using the word *sho'ah* in reference to the destruction of European Jewry. One of the first to give the term a historical perspective was Jerusalem historian Ben Zion Dinur (Dinaburg). In the spring of 1942, he stated that the Holocaust was a "catastrophe" that symbolized the unique situation of the Jewish people among the nations of the world.

SUGGESTED RESOURCES

Adler, David A. *We Remember the Holocaust.* New York: Henry Holt, 1989.

Gilbert, Martin. *Never Again: A History of the Holocaust.* PresUniverse, 2000.

Gutman, Israel, ed. *Encyclopedia of the Holocaust.* New York: Macmillan, 1995.

The Last Days [videorecording]. PolyGram Video, 1998.

Shoah [videorecording]. New Yorker Video, 1999.

United States Holocaust Memorial Museum. [Online] http://www.ushmm.org/ (accessed on August 23, 2000).

Holocaust, Denial of the

The phrase "denial of the **HOLOCAUST**" refers to efforts to deny or misrepresent the events that came to be known as the Holocaust. Attempts to deny the Holocaust began even before World War II (1939–45) ended. Since then, denials have been spread systematically, and in various ways, in many countries.

The phenomenon includes:

1. denials of the fact that the extermination of the Jews by the Nazis ever took place;

2. statements that Jewish losses have been grossly exaggerated;

3. denials that the Holocaust was the result of deliberate policies of Adolf **HITLER** and his **NAZI PARTY**; and

4. the trivializing claim that the Holocaust was not unique and that there had been earlier such events, even precedents that had served as models for the Holocaust.

The phrase "denial of the Holocaust" also refers to the suppression of facts and the destruction of pieces of evidence documenting the mass murder.

Methods of Denial

People who deny the Holocaust use various methods to persuade others to their points of view. The most extreme among the deniers claim that the German authorities never planned to murder the Jews of Europe. They even say that no **EXTERMINATION CAMPS** were built and operated. They argue that there is no truth to the charges that a murder apparatus designed and run by the Nazis slaughtered up to six million Jews by deliberate, sophisticated methods. Other deniers do not totally deny the facts, but they deny that the murder was as thorough and as extensive as it actually was. Also included among those who seek to deny the whole truth of the Holocaust are those who may be called "revisionists." Revisionists—among them genuine scholars and historians—do not reject proven facts. But they do try to reduce the degree of responsibility held by the top Nazi levels and Hitler himself. They describe the Holocaust as an event that was essentially no different from earlier mass slaughters, such as those perpetrated by Joseph Stalin in the **SOVIET UNION**.

Another form of denial is the "partial denial." It is more sophisticated than extreme denial methods. As a result, partial denial can be viewed as more dangerous. Partial deniers try to weaken the power of historical facts by casting doubt on the numerical data, the credibility of documents and witnesses, and so forth. Those who adopt this approach also aim at total denial of the Holocaust. But they think that it is easier to reach this goal by questioning the reliability of various details in the total historical picture. This method poses as a revisionist approach that examines each event on its own merits. "Partial revisionists" include some people who regard the total denial as ineffective and damaging. Other partial revisionists believe that the propaganda material circulated by the most radical deniers addresses itself to the most uneducated audience, as well as members who hold extremely conservative political viewpoints. These partial revisionists also think, though, that articles posing as respectable theoretical discussions will reach an intelligent audience interested in studying the subject.

One of the most widespread tactics of revisionists is to question the legitimacy of the Nuremberg Trial (*see* **TRIALS OF THE WAR CRIMINALS**). That war-crimes trial is attacked from various legal angles, including by critics who do not question the facts of the Holocaust. One major approach relates to the Soviet participation in the trial and the ban on trying crimes committed by the Soviets. This argument was raised by many critics of the International Military Tribunal. Revisionists use it to cast doubt on the reliability of the many documents that served the prosecution as the basis for its case. In truth, however, the documents collected for the trial, along with the actual proceedings of the trial, are among the best-known, most widely circulated, and most reliable collection of primary source information.

Who are the deniers and revisionists? What kind of people are they, and why do they do this?

Revisionists also question the number of victims. Revisionists try to downplay the real number of victims and to sow doubt and confusion on this issue. They quote misleading pre-war population figures, or even invent statistics, to argue that the millions of Jews who were murdered did not even exist. Revisionists have also proposed a variety of theories concerning the present whereabouts of European Jews from the Nazi era.

Another target for revisionists is the enormous wealth of material examining and documenting the Holocaust years and the Nazi crimes. Nazi individual and party activities were recorded down to the last detail. Documents include official Nazi papers and thousands of diaries, testimonies, and memoirs. Very few events of historical dimensions have left behind such an enormous mass of documentation. The Nazis habitually put everything on paper, whatever the subject, even on the most confidential matters. And while part of the documentation was destroyed in the last stages of the war, large quantities fell into the hands of the victorious powers. Contrary to the usual practice with official records, this material was not subjected to a long freeze before its release to the general public, and it has been readily available for research and publication.

Among the most revealing documents are those from the war itself—the office diary kept by Hans **Frank**, the head of the **Generalgouvernement**; a book written by Hitler in 1928 and shelved (*Hitler's Second Book*); the diaries of Joseph **Goebbels**; the speeches of Heinrich **Himmler**, and his recently published desk calendar; and the minutes of the **Wannsee Conference** on the implementation of the **"Final Solution."** Among the important sources of information from after the war are the statements made by the many thousands of Nazi criminals in their interrogations and during their court trials. Also very revealing were the autobiography and other notes of Rudolf **Höss**, the commandant of **Auschwitz**.

Revisionists can not explain away or reject this huge accumulation of documents. They argue that diaries and testimonies of Jews are not believable, because Jews are an interested party. Thus, revisionists dismiss whatever Jews said or wrote down as one big lie. They also reject testimonies given by non-Jews, and documents forwarded from the German-occupied countries during the war (especially from **Poland**), that provide a record of events. These, they say, are biased and written under pressure from Jews. Revisionists take advantage of any contradiction or distortion in the documentation. Thus, when some witnesses let their imagination run free and incorrectly claim that the **Dachau** concentration camp had working gas chambers (*see* GAS CHAMBERS/VANS), revisionists pounce on this discrepancy to say that if some details in the evidence given by witnesses are incorrect, then the whole story of the Holocaust must be nothing but a pack of lies.

Generally, though, revisionists realize that such wholesale denials on their part weaken their case, and so they concentrate on seeking to discredit particular aspects. For example, one revisionist argued that it was impossible to use **Zyklon B** gas regularly in one place, as was the case in Auschwitz, and that therefore the story of the use of gas in Auschwitz is not true. Another revisionist tried to prove that it is impossible to cremate human bodies at the rate that this was done in the extermination camps. He based his conclusion on a comparison with the time it takes to cremate bodies in ordinary crematoria operating under normal conditions.

Motives of Deniers and "Revisionists"

Who are the deniers and revisionists? What kind of people are they, and why do they do this? Another question is, do they know the truth, yet deliberately fabri-

cate a web of lies? A careful analysis of their writings indicates that prominent revisionists know the truth. Their arguments carefully avoid the obvious weak points that could reveal them as liars. How they build their arguments shows that they are aware of the truth, but are trying to distort and suppress it.

Altogether, only a few dozen people are involved in preparing denial material. They write books and articles, hold conferences, and quote one another to create the impression that they represent a legitimate historical school. They have an international organization of sorts coordinating their activities. The organization distributes books and pamphlets from country to country and from continent to continent, and operates groups in different countries. The organization also establishes channels to reach various sectors of the population.

One of the revisionists' major problems is winning serious academic status for their arguments and their publications. They need this recognition in order to gain entry to universities and colleges and capture the attention of students and educators. A revisionist center in California specializes in these efforts. It conducts international conferences of revisionists and seeks to have them invited to prestigious universities. It publishes a journal using the style and format of authentic scholarly journals. Other major centers of revisionist activities are in Sweden, **GERMANY**, **FRANCE**, England, Argentina, and Australia.

Revisionists' motivations are varied. Some are Nazi activists who are using the denial of the Holocaust to repair the Nazi image. Some have joined because of their bitter hatred of communism and Communists—a hatred so extreme it forces them to adopt an apologetic position on Nazism. The **ANTISEMITISM** of some of the revisionists is so extreme that they will use any means to attack Jews. Most belong to neo-Nazi and neo-fascist movements. These movements have received little respect, largely because of the revelation of the horrors of the Holocaust. It is not surprising, then, that the present-day fascists and their sympathizers seek to hide or erase the truth about the Holocaust, which blocks their quest for power.

The arguments of revisionists have, however, received attention and acquired influence. In some quarters they may have an impact among young people who learn nothing about the Holocaust. It is natural that people who are hearing about the Holocaust for the first time refuse to believe that such horrible events could have occurred. Those who seek to deny that such events did take place, or to discredit them in one way or another, find a ready audience in these people. At some educational institutions, revisionist ideas have been given strength by holding them forth as counter-arguments to accepted historical facts concerning the Holocaust.

Revisionists also claim the right to be given access to the media. When no notice is taken of them, they complain that the principles of democracy and freedom of speech are being violated and that they are the victims of a conspiracy. In some cases, when revisionists used provocative means to promote their ideas, their attempts failed. In California, for example, they announced in 1980 and 1981 that they would give a prize to any person who could prove that murder by gassing was committed at Auschwitz. Revisionists were brought to court and sharply criticized for their action. Some countries have outlawed the revisionists' publications. Revisionists have also been put on trial in some places. In most cases, the judgment has gone against them. But there have also been instances when judicial authorities refused to take a clear stand on such issues as the murder methods used in the Holocaust or the dimensions of the Holocaust, on the grounds that these are historical matters that a court of law is not competent to judge.

Attempts to deny the Holocaust have also led to vigorous counter-action. The denial attempts have had the unintended effect of arousing interest in the subject and a

A**ttempts** to deny the Holocaust have had the unintended effect of arousing interest in the subject and a desire to learn more about the facts of the Holocaust.

103

desire to learn more about the Holocaust. They have spread awareness of the Holocaust and of the need to protect humanity from the scourge of RACISM and GENOCIDE.

SUGGESTED RESOURCES

Butz, Arthur R. *The Hoax of the Twentieth Century.* Torrance, CA: Institute for Historical Review, 1976. Reprint, 1992.

"The Leuchter Report: Holocaust Denial and The Big Lie." *The Nizkor Project.* [Online] http://www.nizkor.org/faqs/leuchter/ (accessed on August 23, 2000).

Lipstadt, Deborah E. *Denying the Holocaust: The Growing Assault on Truth and Memory.* New York: Macmillan, 1993.

Shermer, Michael. *Denying History: Who Says the Holocaust Never Happened and Why Do They Say It?* Los Angeles: Martyrs Memorial and Museum of the Holocaust, 1996. Reprint, Berkeley: University of California Press, 2000.

Stern, Kenneth S. *Holocaust Denial.* New York: American Jewish Committee, 1993.

HOLOCAUST LITERATURE. See LITERATURE ON THE HOLOCAUST.

HOLOCAUST MARTYRS' AND HEROES' REMEMBRANCE AUTHORITY. See YAD VASHEM.

HOLOCAUST SURVIVORS. See SURVIVORS, PSYCHOLOGY OF; UNITED STATES ARMY AND SURVIVORS IN GERMANY AND AUSTRIA.

Homosexuality in the Third Reich

In 1871, when the Prussian-dominated German Empire was established, there was a law that classified homosexuality as "an unnatural form of licentiousness," which could mean a prison term for persons caught in such an act. Under the democratic Weimar Republic in GERMANY (1919–33), the issue became a subject of free public discussion, and the Scientific-Humanitarian Committee was established for the defense of homosexuals. Even in that period the NAZI PARTY denounced homosexuality in no uncertain terms, declaring it a deviation from normal sexual behavior that placed the main emphasis on the sensual, pleasurable element of sex life to the detriment of the natural increase in population, the nation's strength, and a proper family life. Sexual relations, according to the Nazi view, "serve the reproductive process, their purpose being the preservation and continued existence of the *Volk* [the pure German race, society and culture], rather than the provision of pleasure to the individual." Homosexuality, in males and females, was not only an egotistic form of sex life; it also harmed the strength of the *Volk*, and was therefore incompatible with the ideal of racial purity.

In March 1933 the Nazi party launched a wave of "protective custody" (*Schutzhaft*) arrests of hostile political elements and opponents of the Party; this included persons who were known for their activities on behalf of homosexuals. In 1935, the penal code against homosexuality was made even more stringent than it had been under the previous government; now even the friendship between males that was based on homosexuality, and not just the homosexual act itself, was made an offense. In August 1936 arrests were made in several large cities, in places where homosexuals

were known to congregate. The attitude toward homosexuals was that they were asocial elements who should be put in prison. Persons who were found to be "recidivist" (repeat) and "chronic" homosexuals were incarcerated in CONCENTRATION CAMPS.

The Nazi position on homosexuality, however, was inconsistent. Officially, homosexuality was sharply denounced, but its practice in certain Nazi circles was tolerated or ignored. This was the case with Ernst RÖHM, chief of the SA (*Sturmabteilung*; Storm Troopers) and a Hitler confidant, who was a known homosexual, as were several of his aides in the SA command. Political opponents took the Nazis to task over Röhm's homosexuality, but Hitler chose to ignore his close aide's sexual preference. It was only after the "Night of the Long Knives" (June 30–July 1, 1934), when Röhm and a group of his SA cohorts were murdered by Nazi Party operatives following a political confrontation within the Nazi leadership, that Röhm's homosexuality was mentioned as one of the reasons for his murder.

The charge of homosexuality was also used to get rid of prominent figures who were no longer regarded as desirable. In 1938, the chief of the general staff, Gen. Werner Freiherr von Fritsch, was dismissed from his post because he disagreed with Hitler's political and military plans. The official reason given, however, was that he had been discovered to be a homosexual—a libel invented by the GESTAPO.

Under Nazi rule, tens of thousands of persons were punished on the charge of homosexuality. Thousands of them (some sources put the figure at 10,000 or more, but no precise figure is available) were imprisoned in concentration camps, where they were forced to wear pink triangular patches (*rosa Winkel*). Many of the homosexuals imprisoned in the camps perished there. Shortly before the end of the war, some of them were set free and drafted into frontline service with the Wehrmacht (combined German armed forces). This step, of course, violated the Nazi principle on the issue.

Persecution of homosexuals was restricted to the Reich and the areas annexed to it. There is no evidence of Nazi-instigated drives against homosexuality in the occupied countries.

SUGGESTED RESOURCES

Beck, Gad. *An Underground Life: The Memoirs of a Gay Jew in Nazi Berlin.* Madison: University of Wisconsin Press, 1999.

Friedman, Ina R. *The Other Victims: First-person Stories of Non-Jews Persecuted by the Nazis.* Boston: Houghton Mifflin, 1990.

Grau, Gunter, ed. *The Hidden Holocaust: Gay and Lesbian Persecution in Germany 1933–45.* Chicago: Fitzroy Dearborn, 1997.

Heger, H. *The Men with the Pink Triangle.* Boston: Alyson Publications, 1980. Reprint, 1994.

The Pink Triangles: The Persecution of Gays During World War II [videorecording]. Facing History and Ourselves, 1989.

Plant, Richard. *The Pink Triangle: The Nazi War against Homosexuals.* New York: Henry Holt, 1986.

Rector, F. *The Nazi Extermination of Homosexuals.* New York, 1981.

Horthy, Miklós

(1868–1957)

Miklós Horthy was regentregent: Head of state of HUNGARY from 1920 to 1944. In general, Horthy's rule was generally characterized by official and semiof-

Miklós Horthy.

ficial **ANTISEMITISM**. Between 1938 and 1941, Horthy authorized increasingly harsh and comprehensive anti-Jewish laws. Nevertheless, in 1942 and 1943, while facing Adolf **HITLER**'s challenge, he rejected German pressure to impose even harsher measures in Hungary, such as the excluding Jews from all economic activities, forcing Jews to wear the Jewish star (*see* **BADGE, JEWISH**), concentrating Jews in ghettos, and deporting all Jews to **CONCENTRATION CAMPS** and **EXTERMINATION CAMPS**.

After the German occupation of Hungary (March 19, 1944), Horthy nominated a government totally subservient to the Nazis, giving it unlimited authority for all anti-Jewish measures. Some 500,000 Jews never returned from the deportations that followed.

On July 7, however, Horthy ordered the deportations stopped, and one week later, on July 14, 1944, he proposed that several categories of Jews in Hungary be allowed to emigrate, primarily to Palestine. The public offer was made soon after Horthy halted the deportations of Jews from Hungary early that month under pressure from the Allies. The Swedes and the Americans in particular had appealed to Horthy to ameliorate the suffering of the remaining Hungarian Jews—in effect, the Jews of **BUDAPEST**. Three weeks later, the Germans allowed the Hungarians to inform the western Allies and neutral nations of the offer.

According to the plan, 1,000 children, as well as 8,243 holders of immigration certificates to Palestine and their families, would be allowed to leave Hungary for Palestine. Four days later Imre Tahy, the Hungarian official in Bern, informed Carl Burckhardt of the International Red Cross about the offer. He added two important clauses: Jews who had parents in Sweden or who maintained business relations with Sweden could go either to Palestine or to Sweden; and the Germans had agreed to the offer. In truth, however, the Germans were not at all willing to allow substantial emigration from Hungary.

The British, the Americans, and the Jewish Agency took the offer at face value, and the Jewish Agency urged the western Allies to accept it. Throughout the summer and fall, the United States sought to convince neutral governments in Europe and Latin America to provide a haven for any Jews who might succeed in leaving Hungary. As a result, *Schutzpasse* (safe-conduct passes issued by the neutral governments), some of which had already surfaced in Budapest, were issued by representatives of neutral governments to tens of thousands of Jews who were considered potential citizens of a number of neutral and Western countries, including Palestine. No Jews, however, were actually allowed to leave Hungary during the summer and early fall through the so-called Horthy Offer, because of German opposition.

On October 15, Horthy was deposed by the Germans and replaced as head of state by Ferenc Szálasi, the leader of the brutal fascist **ARROW CROSS PARTY**. With Horthy's ousting, his plan for saving Hungarian Jews had no chance of succeeding.

SUGGESTED RESOURCES

Fenyo, Mario D. *Hitler, Horthy, and Hungary; German-Hungarian Relations, 1941–1944.* New Haven, CT: Yale University Press, 1972.

Horthy, Miklós. *Memoirs.* New York: Robert Speller, 1957 Reprint, Westport, CT: Greenwood Press, 1978.

Sakmyster, Thomas L. *Hungary's Admiral on Horseback: Miklós Horthy, 1918–1944.* New York: Columbia University Press, 1994.

Höss, Rudolf

(1900–1947)

Rudolf Höss, born in Baden-Baden, **GERMANY**, was the camp commandant of **AUSCHWITZ**. When World War I broke out Höss volunteered for service, even though he was under age. On his return to Germany after the war he joined military organizations known as *Freikorps* in East Prussia and the Baltic states. He later participated in terrorist actions against the French occupation forces in the Ruhr (a region of Germany) and against the Poles in the 1921 struggle for Silesia.

In November 1922, Höss joined the **NAZI PARTY** while attending a reunion of members of the *Rossbach Freikorps* in Munich. In June 1923 he was arrested in the Ruhr district for participating, with a *Freikorps* underground group, in the murder of a German teacher who had collaborated with the French. Although he was sentenced to a ten-year prison term, Höss was pardoned by 1928. As soon as he was released he joined the Artamanen Society, a nationalist group that advocated work on the land and settlement of Polish territory in the east. Höss and his wife, Hedwig, were also members of Artamanen, and worked at recruiting members for militant Nazi organizations, mainly the **SS**.

In 1933, on instructions from the Nazi party and local estate owners, Höss formed an SS cavalry unit. In June 1934 he joined the SS for active service, at the suggestion of Heinrich **HIMMLER**, who was one of the leaders of the Artamanen Society. From December 1934 until May 1938 Höss held various positions in the administration of the **DACHAU** concentration camp. There he trained under Theodor **EICKE**, the first commandant of the camp. Then in May 1940 Höss was posted to Auschwitz, appointed *Obersturmbannführer* (lieutenant colonel), and became the actual founder of the camp and its first organizer and commandant. In the summer of 1941, Höss began preparing the camp for the extermination of masses of human beings. As of January 1942 he led the killing operations at Auschwitz-Birkenau.

A report about the Auschwitz exterminations, written by Höss while under investigation after the war in a **KRAKÓW** jail, opens with the following words:

> In the summer of 1941—I cannot state the precise date—I was summoned by the adjutant's office to Berlin, to report to *Reichsführer*-SS [Chief of the SS] Himmler. Without his aide-de-camp present—contrary to his usual practice—Himmler said to me: "The Führer has ordered the 'Final Solution of the Jewish Question.' We, the SS, are charged with the execution of this task. I have chosen the Auschwitz camp for this purpose, because of its convenient location as regards transportation and because in that area it is easy to isolate and camouflage the camp. I first thought to appoint one of the senior SS officers to this task, but then I changed my mind because of the problems of the division of authority that such an appointment would run into. I am herewith charging you with this task. This is a strenuous and difficult assignment that calls for total dedication, regardless of the difficulties that will arise. Further practical details will be conveyed to you by Sturmbannführer [Major] Adolf **EICHMANN** of the *Reichssicherheitshauptamt* [Reich Security Main Office], who will soon get in touch with you. The offices concerned will hear from him at the appropriate time. You must keep this order absolutely secret, even from your own superiors. After your talk with Eichmann let me know what arrangements you propose to be made."

Rudolph Höss after the conclusion of World War II.

On December 1, 1943, Höss was appointed chief of Section 1D of the SS **ECONOMIC-ADMINISTRATIVE MAIN OFFICE** (*WVHA—Wirtschaftsverwaltungshauptamt*). In late June of 1944 he was sent back to Auschwitz, on a temporary assignment, to preside over the murder of the Jews of **HUNGARY**. In what was called *Aktion* (Operation) Höss, 430,000 Jews were brought to Auschwitz in 56 days, to be annihilated there. In recognition of his "outstanding service" in the **CONCENTRATION CAMPS**, Höss was awarded war crosses classes I and II, with swords. After the fall of the Reich, Höss assumed the name Franz Lang. He was released from a prisoner-of-war collection point and put to work in agriculture.

In March 1946 Höss was recognized, arrested, and handed over to the Polish authorities, in keeping with the agreement on the Extradition of War Criminals. He was taken to **WARSAW** and from there to Kraków, where his case was investigated. In the Kraków jail where he was held in 1946 and 1947, Höss wrote an autobiography. He also wrote a series of notes about the SS commanders in the concentration camp and those who were in charge of putting the **"FINAL SOLUTION"** into effect, including a profile of Eichmann. The supreme court in Warsaw sentenced Höss to death, and he was hanged in Auschwitz on April 16, 1947.

SUGGESTED RESOURCES

Browning, Christopher R. *Nazi Policy, Jewish Workers, German Killers.* New York: Cambridge University Press, 2000.

Höss, Rudolf. *Commandant of Auschwitz: The Autobiography of Rudolf Höss.* Cleveland: World Publishing, 1960. Reprint, London: Phoenix Press, 2000.

Levi, Primo. *Survival in Auschwitz: The Nazi Assault on Humanity.* New York: Summit Books, 1986. Reprint, New York: Collier Books, 1993.

Hungarian Labor Service System

After the adoption of the major anti-Jewish laws in **HUNGARY** in 1938 and 1939, the Jews of military age (20 to 48) were classified as "unreliable" and therefore labeled unfit to bear arms. Instead, Hungarian Jews were drafted into special labor service units under the Hungarian Labor Service System (Munkaszolgálat). They were organized into military formations under the command of Hungarian army officers and, instead of guns, were supplied with shovels and pickaxes. These units were employed primarily in construction, mining, and fortification work for the military in Hungary proper as well as in Serbia, the Hungarian-occupied parts of Eastern Galicia, and the **UKRAINE**. Along the front lines, they were used for constructing trenches and tank traps, maintaining roads, and clearing minefields.

In addition to providing labor support for military operations, the drafted laborers worked in industries supporting the war effort. As of the summer of 1940, Hungarian Jewish labor servicemen worked at companies including the Manfred Weiss Ammunition Works in Csepel, the Polgari Brewery of Kobanya, the Air Defense Works in **BUDAPEST**, the Parquet and Furniture Plant in Budapest, and the Hungarian Car and Machine Works in Gyor. Beginning in June 1943, Hungarian Jewish forced laborers were sent to work in the copper mines at Bor in Serbia; 6,000 Jews, Seventh-Day Adventists, and Jehovah's Witnesses were forced to work there until September 1944. Some of the laborers were brought back to Mohács in October of that year. At Crevenka, during their journey back from the copper mines, the **SS** lined up more than 700 of the drafted laborers and shot them.

Jewish conscripts in Hungarian Labor Service System Brigade 108/56 (September 1941).

The legal basis for the labor service system was provided by Hungary's Law No. 2 of March 11, 1939, which dealt with general national defense and security issues. On the surface, the legal provisions were not necessarily discriminatory. Originally persons conscripted into labor service were to receive the same pay, clothing, and rations as those in the armed forces. However, after the outbreak of World War II, and especially after Hungary declared war on the **SOVIET UNION** on June 27, 1941, the condition of the Jewish labor servicemen deteriorated. Many of the non-Jewish officers and guards attached to the Jewish labor companies became increasingly antisemitic, and the treatment of the Jewish servicemen became more blatantly violent. Jewish laborers were gradually deprived of their uniforms and army boots, and were compelled to wear discriminatory badges—yellow armbands for Jews and white armbands for converts—that made them easy targets for abuse. The severity of the treatment varied from unit to unit and from place to place, depending on the attitude of the officers and guards in charge.

The situation was particularly tragic in many of the frontline units, especially in the Ukraine. There, far from the scrutiny of the central governmental and military authorities, many officers and guards (often joined by German military and SS elements) were abusive toward the labor servicemen under their authority. They mistreated them, withheld or stole their already meager rations, gave them inadequate housing, and forced them to remain for long periods without any kind of shelter.

Many of the labor servicemen had to perform their duties without adequate clothing or shoes. Some were subjected to brutal "sports" after a long workday, for the entertainment of the troops. Others were doused with water and commanded not to move until the cold of the Ukrainian winter caused the water to freeze on them.

By 1942, 100,000 men had been drafted into these units, with over 50,000 of them outside Hungary's borders, mostly in the Ukraine. During the winter of 1942–43, as the Soviet forces gained the upper hand, thousands of the laborers were killed and thousands more were taken captive by the Russians. During a chaotic retreat, the Hungarian soldiers killed many of the Jews and stole whatever they could from them. According to official Hungarian reports about 25,400 men fell or were captured at this time. It is estimated, however, that there were more than 40,000 casualties among the laborers in the Ukraine by the end of 1943, with about 20,000 prisoners falling to the Red Army and the rest dying during the fighting or perishing from maltreatment, hunger, cold, and disease.

Ironically, when the **"FINAL SOLUTION"** program was launched, soon after the German occupation of Hungary on March 19, 1944, the labor service system became a refuge for many thousands of Hungarian Jewish men threatened with deportation and almost certain death. This change came about primarily for two reasons: there was a need for labor in Hungary itself, and there was pressure from Hungarian government and military officials who supported Regent Miklós **HORTHY**'s desire to break out of the alliance with Nazi Germany and who were able to exploit the need for labor to help some labor servicemen.

After the **ARROW CROSS PARTY** came to power in October 1944, men from these work sites, as well as many others, were transferred into the hands of the Nazis. Many thousands were sent to Germany, supposedly on loan, for work on projects of interest to the Nazis. Many thousands more were marched to the Austrian border to build the "East Wall" for the defense of **VIENNA**. Relatively few of these "laborers" survived the Nazi captivity. Most of the Jewish labor servicemen who fell into Soviet hands were treated as prisoners of war, and were released as Hungarian or Romanian nationals only after the peace treaties with Hungary and Romania were signed in February 1947.

SUGGESTED RESOURCES

Handler, Andrew, and Susan Meschel, eds. *Young People Speak: Surviving the Holocaust in Hungary.* New York: Franklin Watts, 1993.

Hungary

After Adolf **HITLER**'s rise to power in **GERMANY** in 1933, the Hungarian government formed an alliance with him, for political and economic reasons. Germany soon became Hungary's main trading partner. Hitler offered German support for Hungary's desire to expand its territory. In return, Hungary offered Nazi Germany economic and political advantages.

Axis powers
Countries aligned with Nazi Germany, including Italy and Japan, and later Bulgaria, Croatia, Hungary, Romania, and Slovakia.

With the 1938 Munich Agreement, the relationship paid off, as Hungary received part of a former territory from Czechoslovakia. This convinced some Hungarian politicians that the Axis powers would play a leading role in Europe for the next several decades. Others, however, were afraid of a strong Germany, and they were concerned about the brutality of the Nazi system. Count Pál

Teleki, who became Hungary's prime minister in March 1939, tried to maintain some distance from Hitler and did not join the war effort later that year. And during the first months of the war, the Hungarian government allowed more than 100,000 Polish refugees to find shelter in Hungary, which also did not please Hitler.

1940–43

Since the end of World War I (1914–18), Hungary had wanted the return of Transylvania, which was 33 percent Hungarian and about 55 percent Romanian. In August 1940, the foreign ministers of Germany and **ITALY** signed an agreement that allowed the Hungarians to take possession of northern Transylvania and its 2.5 million inhabitants. Most Hungarians regarded this as a major foreign policy success. Several months later, Hungary joined the Tripartite Pact, which bound Germany, Italy, and Japan together. This sealed Hungary's formal military and political alliance with Nazi Germany as part of the Axis.

At home, the Hungarian government also made changes that were agreeable to the Germans. The fanatic leader of the **ARROW CROSS PARTY**, Ferenc Szálasi, was released from prison. A ban prohibiting government workers from joining extremist parties was lifted. And a new political party, which closely followed the **NAZI PARTY**'s platform, was formed.

In December 1940, in a show of independence, Hungary signed a pact of "eternal friendship" with Yugoslavia, which was not yet dominated by Hitler. But three months later, after a military takeover there by anti-Tripartite Pact forces, Hitler decided to invade Yugoslavia. He offered territorial rewards to the Hungary's head of state, regent Miklós **HORTHY**, if he would join the invasion. Horthy accepted. In the wake of these events, Prime Minister Teleki committed suicide. His successor, László Bárdossy, sent Hungarian troops to assist the Germans in Yugoslavia a few days after the German invasion. As a result, Hungary received territory with a population of more than 1 million (36 percent Hungarian).

Another major decision was to join the Germans in their war against the **SOVIET UNION**. The Hungarians joined the new offensive on June 26, 1941. And in December 1941, in another fateful move, the Hungarians declared war on the United States. This led to a British declaration of war on Hungary and the breaking of all major links with the West. The ill-fated Hungarian declaration came while Germany was suffering its first significant defeat in the Soviet Union. Hungary soon found itself isolated, committed to a long war, and at the mercy of increasing Nazi pressure. Instead of being a partner, the nation was becoming more and more a satellite of Germany. In January 1942, the Germans pressed Hungary to send most of its troops to the Soviet Union, and the Hungarians obeyed.

Some members of the Hungarian ruling elite began to view Bárdossy as being too subservient to Germany. Horthy appointed a new, more cautious prime minister, Miklós Kállay, in March 1942.

The Axis powers were defeated at Stalingrad. On January 13, 1943, the Red (Soviet) Army broke through the Hungarian lines, resulting in the loss of 150,000 of the 200,000 Hungarian soldiers. Prime Minister Kállay began to work on getting Hungary out of its alliance with Nazi Germany. No more troops were sent to the Soviet front in 1943, and preparations were made to allow more political freedom at home. Peace feelers were put out to the West. The Germans were aware of this change in attitude, but they did not interfere as long as Hungary maintained its eco-

The Hungrian Gendarmerie.

nomic agreements and as long as the British and U.S. armies were far from its borders. Still, as early as September 1943, the Germans prepared a contingency plan for the military occupation of Hungary.

German Occupation, 1944

Hitler decided to move against Hungary in March 1944, and he told Horthy of the plan. Horthy was afraid that if he did not obey, Romania would take part in the occupation. Thus, the Hungarians did not resist the Germans. On March 19, German soldiers entered Hungary, and a government that the Nazis considered reliable was set up under the former Hungarian ambassador in Berlin, Döme Sztójay. Horthy himself withdrew from public affairs, and various "experts" arrived from Germany to put Hungary back on a pro-German course.

Sztójay's government began carrying out Germany's orders. All anti-Nazi parties and politicians were eliminated. The government also mobilized 300,000 soldiers to try to resist the advance of the Red Army, which was less than 62 miles (100 km) from the Hungarian border.

In August, Horthy replaced Sztójay with General Géza Lakatos. Lakatos's government continued the earlier policy of seeking a way for Hungary to pull out of the war. A few attempts with the Western Allies failed, but Hungary did reach an agreement with the Soviet Union. Hungary agreed to give up territories gained through its alliance with Germany and to turn against the Nazis.

Rise of the Arrow Cross Party

On October 15, 1944, Horthy decided to carry out his planned change of course. The announcement was made, but the Germans had made contingency plans. They blocked Horthy's move, taking his son prisoner and threatening Horthy with his death if the reversal were carried out. The Germans replaced Horthy with Arrow Cross party leader Ferenc Szálasi, and Arrow Cross men took over strategic positions throughout the country.

As the Arrow Cross Party was turned loose, Hungary was in total chaos. The country was looted, and whatever could not be sent to Germany was destroyed.

The Arrow Cross began a reign of terror, plundering, pillaging, and murdering. Szálasi promised to send 1.5 million soldiers to the Russian front, intending to draft all males and females between the ages of 12 and 70 into the army or labor brigades. Factories were dismantled and sent to Germany, along with livestock. The population was ordered to retreat with the fascist troops in the direction of Germany. In November, political prisoners were turned over to the Nazis, who sent them to **CONCENTRATION CAMPS**, where most of them died.

As the Soviet forces overran Hungary, a handful of complete troop formations surrendered to them. Tens of thousands more Hungarians avoided being drafted and deserted from the army. To stop this, Szálasi ordered summary trials and executions. Signs of active opposition also increased by November, when the Soviets had taken two-thirds of the country. But on the whole, there was little organized Hungarian armed resistance.

In January 1945, a Hungarian armistice agreement was signed with the Soviet Union. On January 17, the Pest section of Budapest fell to the Red Army. Buda succumbed less than a month later. By April 4, 1945, no more Germans were fighting in Hungary.

Jews during the Holocaust

According to the census of 1941, Hungary had a Jewish population of 725,007, representing 4.94 percent of its total population of 14,683,323. There were approximately 100,000 converts and Christians of Jewish origin.

Jewish settlement in the area of what is now Hungary goes back to Roman times. In the modern period, the Jewish community of Hungary became highly integrated into the economic and cultural life of the country. For the most part, this Hungarian national identification remained quite firm, despite the increased **ANTI-SEMITISM** that marked the years between the world wars. It continued to influence the response of Hungarian Jews to their situation during World War II.

The "Jewish question," which had emerged earlier in Hungary, became prominent during the 1930s. Demands for its "solution" came from a variety of pro-Nazi political groups and from the heads of the **CHRISTIAN CHURCHES**. The anti-Jewish climate was encouraged by the mass media, especially the largely German-financed press. In addition, the Hungarian armed forces were among the most radical and aggressive hotbeds of antisemitism in Hungary. In the late 1930s, Hungary adopted a number of anti-Jewish laws that restricted Jews' roles in the economy and society of the country. One major anti-Jewish law (May 1939) identified the Jews in racial terms—a process that culminated in the racial law of 1941, which resembled Germany's **NUREMBERG LAWS**. Hungary also introduced (1939–40) a system designed for Jewish men of military age: the **HUNGARIAN LABOR SERVICE SYSTEM** (*Munkaszolgálat*). Close to 42,000 Hungarian Jews perished in these mobile forced-labor units before the German occupation of Hungary on March 19, 1944.

Before the occupation, Hungarian Jewry also suffered as many as 18,000 other losses. Of these, around 17,000 were "alien" Jews seized by the Hungarian authorities in July and August 1941 and deported to a site near **KAMENETS-PODOLSKI**. Most them were massacred there by **SS** troops under the command of Friedrich **JECKELN**. More than 1,000 Jews were murdered in Novi Sad (Ujvidék) and other areas of the Délvidék region in early 1942 by Hungarian military and gendarmerie units "in pursuit of partisans." (*See* **PARTISANS**.)

Most Hungarian Jews lived in safety until the German occupation. The government consistently rejected German demands that Hungary follow the other

Most Hungarian Jews lived in relative safety until the German occupation of Hungary, which brought with it all the violence, destruction, and anti-Jewish legislation that characterized Nazi control over the Jews elsewhere in Europe.

Nazi-dominated countries in Europe by implementing the "**FINAL SOLUTION**" program. It was for this reason, among others, that the Jewish leadership was convinced that Hungary would retain its independence to the end.

These illusions were shattered when Germany intervened militarily. The occupation forces included a **SPECIAL COMMANDO** (*Sonderkommando*) headed by Adolf **EICHMANN**. It provided guidance and technical assistance for the speedy implementation of the "Final Solution" program.

More anti-Jewish decrees were put into place. They provided, among other things, for the isolation, marking, plundering, ghettoization, and deportation of the Jews. The isolation of the Jews began with travel restrictions and the confiscation of telephones and radios. It was completed with forcing them to wear the yellow badge (*see* **BADGE, JEWISH**), which made them easy targets for antisemites. Next, Jewish-owned businesses and offices were taken over. Jews' personal property, including their valuables, bank accounts, and jewelry, were also taken. On April 16, the Jews of Carpathian Ruthenia and northeastern Hungary were ordered into ghettos. At the crack of dawn, they were ordered to pack and leave their homes within a half-hour. Their dwellings were looted soon afterward.

In the rural areas, the Jews were normally first ordered into the local synagogues or community centers, and a few days later transferred to ghettos in the county seats. In some cities, the ghettos were established in the Jewish sections. In others, they were set up in brickyards or idle factories. In still others, the Jews were forced to "set up camp" in neighboring forests under the open sky. The ghettos were closed off and were guarded by both local policemen and gendarmes brought in from other parts of the country. The ghettos lasted only two to six weeks. The conditions there were horrible, including a lack of food and adequate sanitary facilities. The Jews, especially those perceived as well-to-do, were treated cruelly by police and gendarmes searching for "hidden wealth."

The 434,351 Jews who were deported mostly from the countryside ended up in **AUSCHWITZ**-Birkenau. They were deported between May 15 and July 9, 1944, from 55 major ghettos and concentration centers, in 147 trains composed of sealed freight cars. Most of the Hungarian Jews were gassed in Birkenau soon after their arrival. Miklós Horthy halted the deportations on July 7, but the "de-Judaizers" continued their operations for two days, liquidating the Jewish communities in western Hungary and around the capital. Jews remained only in the capital, Budapest. A few transports, with about 21,000 Jews from the southern part of Hungary, were directed to Strasshof near Vienna, to be "put on ice" pending the outcome of Zionist-SS negotiations. Most of these Jews survived the war.

Budapest's Jews had been confined since June 1944 to living in special buildings designated with a yellow star. That anxiety-filled but relatively safe period ended on October 15 of that year, when the Arrow Cross Party came to power. Thousands of Jews, mostly women, were forced to march to a region near Nazi Germany to build fortifications for the defense of Vienna. Terror was rampant, with armed Arrow Cross gangs roaming the streets, robbing and killing Jews. Many of the victims were taken to the banks of the Danube, where they were shot and thrown into the river. Early in December, during the Soviet siege of Budapest, close to 70,000 Jews were ordered into a ghetto that was established in the Jewish section, near the Dohány Street synagogue. Although this period was relatively short-lived (Budapest was liberated on January 17–18, 1945), the people in the ghetto suffered horribly. Thousands died as a result of disease, starvation, and the cold. In total, the Hungarian Jewish community lost 564,500 lives during the war, including 63,000 before the German occupation.

The plight of the Jews during the Arrow Cross era was eased by the heroism of many. Resisters saved many lives by forging and distributing various types of documents, and by supplying the ghetto with food. Similar rescue activities were undertaken by the representatives of the neutral states, above all Raoul **WALLENBERG** of Sweden and Carl **LUTZ** of Switzerland. Many Jews, especially children, owed their lives to the activities of those associated with various Christian orders and agencies of the International Red Cross.

SEE ALSO **YOUTH MOVEMENTS.**

SUGGESTED RESOURCES

Anger, Per. *With Raoul Wallenberg in Budapest: Memories of the War Years in Hungary.* New York: Holocaust Library, 1981. Reprint, 1995.

Handler, Andrew, and Susan Meschel, eds. *Young People Speak: Surviving the Holocaust in Hungary.* New York: Franklin Watts, 1993.

Jackson, Livia Bitton. *I Have Lived a Thousand Years: Growing Up in the Holocaust.* New York: Simon & Schuster, 1997.

Schimmel, Betty. *To See You Again: A True Story of Love in a Time of War.* New York: Dutton, 1999.

Wallenberg, Raoul. *Letters and Dispatches, 1924–1944.* New York: Arcade, 1995.

I. G. Farben

I. G. Farben (IGF) was a German corporation, a conglomerate of eight leading German chemical manufacturers, including Bayer, Hoechst, and BASF (BadischeAnilinund Sodafabrik), the largest such firms in existence at the time. As early as World War I these firms had established a "community of interests" (*Interessengemeinschaft*; thus the initials I. G.). They merged into a single company on December 25, 1925, creating the largest chemical enterprise in Europe and, in fact, the whole world. Its share capital in 1926 was 1.1 million reichsmarks. Its turnover increased from 1.2 million reichsmarks in 1926 to 3.1 billion in 1943. On the German market IGF had a monopoly, and it was the country's largest single exporter. The first chairman of its board was Dr. Karl Bosch, who had previously been the chief executive officer of BASF.

Costly innovations, such as the production of synthetic fuel from coal and of synthetic rubber (Buna) from coal or gasoline, convinced IGF, at the time the economic crisis came to an end, that the company should establish close ties with Adolf **HITLER**. Early on, Hitler had become aware of the opportunity for **GERMANY** to become independent of imports of raw materials, thanks to the production processes in IGF's possession. To be profitable, the new IGF products needed a guaranteed market, and Hitler indicated that he would be ready to guarantee state purchase of these products, in appropriate quantities. Because the products of the great chemical conglomerate were an indispensable element in the Nazi re-armament program, the contacts between IGF's management and the government became increasingly close. This relationship occurred despite the presence on the IGF board of several Jewish members, and despite the fact that Nazi propaganda continued to attack IGF as an example of an international Jewish firm that was exploiting its workers. At a meeting of leading German industrialists with Hjalmar Schacht, Hermann Göring, and Heinrich **HIMMLER**, held on February 20, 1933, IGF contributed 400,000 reichs-

In 1933, the directorial board of I. G. Farben included several Jewish members, and Dr. Karl Bosch, chief executive officer of the company, objected to the firing of Jewish scientists from the company. Within four years, no Jews held executive positions or seats on the board of directors, and most of the board members had joined the Nazi Party. I. G. Farben would, before long, become an important partner with the Nazi regime in the destruction of the Jews of east Europe.

marks to the **NAZI PARTY**. It was the largest single contribution in a total sum of 3 million reichsmarks raised at this meeting for the Nazi party's election campaign.

The Four-Year Plan proposed by Hitler in 1936 was designed to prepare all of German industry for war. The plan further enhanced IGF's influence. A member of IGF's board, Carl Krauch, was given a leading position in the organization headed by Göring that had the task of implementing the Four-Year Plan. By that time the company was also adapting itself to the regime's ideological requirements. In 1933 Bosch had still objected—although in vain—to the removal of Jewish scientists from the company and from various other scientific institutions. Nevertheless, by 1937 no Jews were left in executive positions in the IGF or on its board of directors. The majority of the remaining board members joined the Nazi party. Using economic and political blackmail, IGF took over important chemical factories in the areas annexed to the Reich or occupied by it. Bosch resigned his post as chief executive officer in 1935 and was instead elected chairman of the board. His successor as chief executive officer was Hermann Schmitz, a member of the BASF board. After Bosch's death in April 1940, Krauch took his place as board chairman, adding this position to the different posts he held in the Four-Year Plan administration. More than anyone else, Krauch personified the link between private industry and growing government involvement in economic life during the Nazi period.

In connection with the economic preparations for the forthcoming war against the **SOVIET UNION**, the IGF board, with government support, decided to establish additional facilities for the production of synthetic fuels. The board decided on **AUSCHWITZ**, in Upper Silesia, as the place where the new installations were to be located. Auschwitz was chosen not only because of its convenient proximity to the railway and to coal mines but, more importantly, because the **CONCENTRATION CAMP** offered IGF up to 10,000 prisoners for work on the construction of the new plant. Board members Otto Ambros and Heinrich Bütefisch were responsible for the Auschwitz plant in their capacity as the officers in charge of Buna and gasoline, respectively. Dr. Walter Dürrfeld became general manager. At first, the plant management protested against the maltreatment of the prisoners working in the plant and their poor physical condition, but Dürrfeld eventually went along with the **SS**. In the middle of 1942 a new section of the concentration camp (Auschwitz-Monowitz) was established, close to the site of the IGF factory, to house the prisoners working there and thereby save the time-consuming daily march from and to the main camp. The prisoners' performance, however, never came close to IGF expectations and was always considerably inferior to that of free workers. Only small quantities of synthetic fuel were actually produced.

The location of this factory at Auschwitz was not IGF's only Auschwitz connection, however. **ZYKLON B** gas, used in Auschwitz for the killing of Jews, was a product of DEGESCH, a firm in which IGF had a decisive share.

In the Subsequent Nuremberg Proceedings, the United States, as the occupying power, conducted trials against the top officers of three major industrial concerns—Krupp, Flick, and I. G. Farben. In the IGF trial the accused were the chairman of the board, Carl Krauch, and several of his associates, including Dürrfeld. The major charges were: (1) preparing and waging aggressive war; (2) crimes against humanity, by looting the occupied territories; and (3) enslaving and murdering civil populations, prisoners of war, and prisoners from the occupied territories. All the defendants were acquitted of the first count; nine were found guilty of the second; and Krauch, Fritz ter Meer, Ambros, Bütefisch, and Dürrfeld were found guilty of the third. The decisive factor against the last four defendants was their role in the construction of the Auschwitz installations. The tribunal did not find the IGF board criminally involved

Panel of judges (l to r) James Morris, Curtis Grover Shake, Paul M. Hebert, Clarence F. Merrell (and a lower tier of unidentified men) presiding at the I. G. Farben trial, Nuremberg Trials, August 27, 1947.

in the poison-gas deliveries made by the DEGESCH company. The sentences of eight years each, imposed on Ambros and Dürrfeld, were the most severe. By 1951, however, all the IGF officers convicted had been released from prison.

Under Allied Control Council Law No. 9, of November 30, 1945, IGF assets were seized by the Control Council, which in turn handed them over to the four occupying powers. They were instructed that installations for the manufacture of war material were to be destroyed, certain plants were to be appropriated as war reparations, and the entire conglomerate was to be broken up. The IGF plants existing in the Soviet zone of occupation were nationalized. In the Western zones, however, no change of ownership ever took place. Basically, the conglomerate was broken up into its original three major component parts—Bayer, BASF, and Hoechst—whose balance sheet, by the end of the 1950s, already exceeded that of the original IGF. The final IGF Liquidation Act, of January 21, 1955, removed all the remaining restrictions imposed by the Allies. Many of the former top officers of IGF, including Ter Meer and Ambros, were soon again in leading positions in the German chemical industry.

In a 1953 decision, a court of the Federal Republic of Germany established the principle that a Jewish prisoner who had been forced to work for IGF in Monowitz had a right to sue the company for compensation. Following this decision and after lengthy negotiations, the residual company—I. G. Farben in Liquidation—agreed to put 27 million deutsche marks at the disposal of the Jewish Material Claims Conference to cover the claims of all Jewish forced laborers and prisoners who had been compelled to work at Monowitz. The payment was described as having been made on a purely voluntary basis and was not to be interpreted as an admission of guilt. IGF did not pay any compensation to non-Jewish forced laborers and prisoners.

The issue was raised again in the late 1990s when U.S. attorneys representing former slave laborers threatened class action lawsuits against many German businesses that had used slave labor. On July 6, 2000, after protracted negotiations, the German Parliament passed a bill setting up a $5 billion compensation fund to be paid for equally by industry and the German government.

See also **FORCED LABOR**.

SUGGESTED RESOURCES

Borkin, Joseph. *The Crime and Punishment of I. G. Farben.* New York: Free Press, 1978.

Hayes, Peter. *Industry and Ideology: I. G. Farben in the Nazi Era.* New York: Cambridge University Press, 1987. Reprint, 2000.

United Nations War Crimes Commission. "The Zyklon B Case; Trial of Bruno Tesch and Two Others." *Law-Reports of Trials of War Criminals.* [Online] http://www.ess.uwe.ac.uk/WCC/zyklonb.htm (accessed on August 22, 2000).

IMMIGRATION TO PALESTINE. See Aliya Bet; St. Louis.

IMT. See Trials of the War Criminals.

INTERNATIONAL MILITARY TRIBUNAL. See Trials of the War Criminals.

Italy

Benito Mussolini.

The Jewish community in Italy is the oldest continuous settlement of the Jews in Europe, dating back well over 2,000 years. Italian Jews in Sardinia gained rights as citizens in 1848; by 1870, that emancipation extended to the whole peninsula. Italian Jews had more security, opportunities, and acceptance than in many other countries. They were fully integrated into Italian society and politics and had access to careers in the diplomatic corps, the civil service, and the army—careers generally closed to them elsewhere in the West.

Until 1936, fourteen years after Benito Mussolini seized power, antisemitism was not part of the mainstream of Italian life and Jews were generally assimilated into Italian society. Jews made up only about one tenth of one percent of the total population, and without Jewish immigration from eastern Europe, there was little interest in or need for a separate Jewish "community" identity. Italy itself contributed to this level of assimilation through the "universalistic" nature of Italian nationalism (which, until 1938, was defined in cultural and not in "racial" terms) and a blend of respect for individual Jews and disregard for Judaism as a religion and as an ethical system. This subtly encouraged Italian Jews to identify themselves more as Italian than as Jewish.

Countercurrents of Jewish cultural revival surfaced in Italy early in the twentieth century. Zionism emerged, Jewish periodicals proliferated, and a Jewish youth movement was founded. These signs of Jewish "separatism" sparked criticism, which increased with the advent of FASCISM. Some Fascists believed that Jewish internationalism threatened the "monolithic unity" of the future Fascist state. Mussolini denounced "Jewish" Bolshevism and "English" Zionism in his newspaper *Il Popolo d'Italia* and he warned Italian Jews not to stir up antisemitism in the only country where it had never existed.

The Fascists Seize Power

Italian Jewish leaders expressed some alarm when the Fascists seized power on October 30, 1922. The international Jewish press and some world Zionist leaders

Map of Italy showing the locations of concentration camps during World War II.

charged the new regime with antisemitism. Members of the Italian government assured Jewish leaders that Fascism was free from antisemitic tendencies; this was consistent with established Fascist principles.

Fascist policy toward the Jews can be divided into four periods: (1) a phase of outwardly cordial relations (1922–32); (2) a transitional phase of ambivalent posturing (1933–36); (3) a six–year span of increasingly violent antisemitism (1937–43); and (4) the final period of German domination (1943–45).

CORDIAL RELATIONS In the decade after Mussolini seized power, the civil and religious rights of the Jewish minority were respected. Mussolini condemned racism and antisemitism. The government issued a series of decrees that gave a coherent and unified legal status to Italian Jewry and provided a stable financial base for Jewish religious, cultural, and charitable activities.

TRANSITIONAL PHASE Hitler's rise to power in 1933 ushered in a period of change. For the next three years, Mussolini alternated declarations and acts in favor of the Jews with unofficial antisemitic moves and expressions of sympathy for the German position. No anti-Jewish measures were enacted during these three years.

ANTISEMITISM INCREASES In 1936, as **GERMANY** and Italy intervened in the Spanish Civil War and strengthened their alliance, the Italian government's policies toward Jews began to reflect Hitler's policy, even though these partners disagreed about Hitler's doctrine of Nordic superiority, which had anti-Italian as well as anti-Jewish implications. Racial laws were finally issued in 1938, making it clear that

In 1923 Mussolini emphatically declared: "The Italian government and Italian Fascism have never had any intention of following, nor are following, an antisemitic policy...."

In response to rising Zionist activity in Italy during the 1920s and 1930s, Mussolini warned Italian Jews not to stir up antisemitism where it had never before existed, implying that by drawing attention to their political, religious, and cultural differences, the Zionists would be responsible for whatever anti-Jewish response might occur.

Mussolini had committed to adopt antisemitism in the interest of unity with Hitler and Nazism. The Fascist race laws turned out to be an unsuccessful attempt to adapt German racial theories to Italian conditions. The result was a weakened version of Hitler's **NUREMBERG LAWS** that antagonized Italian and Western opinion, alienated the Catholic church, and still displeased the Germans.

When Italy entered into World War II on June 10, 1940, anti-Jewish legislation and propaganda intensified. However, Germany and Italy still disagreed about certain matters, including Fascist Jewish policy. Mussolini needed German economic and military aid too much to back away from his anti-Jewish legislation, but he retained some independence in carrying out Italy's anti-Jewish policy. This explains why Italian-occupied territories in **FRANCE**, Yugoslavia, and Greece became havens of refuge for persecuted Jews. Mussolini approved of security measures against hostile Jewish elements but he refused to deport Italian citizens to the east. And Hitler, though determined to impose his anti-Jewish obsession throughout Europe, including Italy, chose not to jeopardize relations with Rome on this question until after the Italian armistice with the Allies on September 8, 1943.

"FINAL SOLUTION" APPLIED TO ITALY Three important facts help to explain how the Holocaust unfolded in Italy. First, most Italian Jews lived in the north part of the country—the part of Italy that came under German control in 1943. Second, Hitler decided, against the advice of his experts, to restore Mussolini to power in 1943. The creation of a Fascist puppet republic made it possible to implement the "Final Solution" in Italy. Third, Hitler backed away from his intent to forcibly occupy the Vatican. This was the only decision Hitler took after the Italian "betrayal" that helped the Jews, for it enabled the Catholic church to save thousands of Jewish lives.

Concentration Camps in Italy

Before World War II began, **CONCENTRATION CAMPS** did not exist in Italy. Persons suspected of acting against the Fascist regime were exiled to remote villages; political prisoners served their terms in regular prisons or special wings of such prisons. This changed when Italy entered the war on June 10, 1940. Non-Italian Jews who had not complied with the expulsion order issued in 1938 were arrested in large numbers. Men, women, and children were thrown into jail with no charges brought against them. On September 4, the Ministry of the Interior ordered 43 concentration camps to be established, for the imprisonment of enemy aliens and Italians suspected of subversive activities. The prisoners in these camps included thousands of Jews who were foreign nationals or stateless persons, and 200 Italian Jews who openly opposed the Fascist regime.

Prisoners in the Italian camps fared better than those in Nazi camps elsewhere in Europe. Families lived together, there were schools for the children, and a broad program of social welfare and cultural activities was in place. For the most part, the prisoners were assigned only to jobs that were related to the camp itself.

The fall of the Fascist regime on July 25, 1943, and Italy's surrender to the Allies on September 8, 1943, were dramatic turning points. The country was split into two; the Allies controlled the south and the Germans held the central and northern parts. Many Jewish prisoners in Fascist concentration camps were liberated, since most of the camps, including the largest one, were situated in the Allied-controlled southern districts. On the other hand, most of Italy's Jews, who were concentrated in Rome and the north, were caught in the German-occupied part of Italy.

The Germans began to seize Jews in all the major northern cities, where they had been living peacefully. In a single day—October 16, 1943—the Germans arrested more than 1,000 persons in Rome. Throughout October and November, similar actions took place in Trieste, Genoa, Florence, Milan, Venice, Ferrara, and other cities. Jews were held first in local jails, then confined to concentration camps, usually in Fossoli di Carpi and Bolzano. When a certain number of prisoners had been collected, they were deported to EXTERMINATION CAMPS, mainly to AUSCHWITZ; a few went to BERGEN-BELSEN while political prisoners were sent to MAUTHAUSEN.

The Fascist satellite state took increasingly harsher actions against the Jews, whom they now called aliens "belonging to an enemy nation." On November 30, 1943, the state called for all Jews to be put in concentration camps and their property confiscated. By then most Jews had either fled for their lives or had been imprisoned or deported. In Italy, the Germans avoided issuing special anti-Jewish decrees, such as the wearing of the yellow badge (*see* BADGE, JEWISH) or the establishment of ghettos and Judenräte (Jewish councils). They focused on arresting and deporting Jews.

Between September 8, 1943, and April 1945, the Germans conducted massive manhunts for Jews. More than 20 percent of Italy's Jews were imprisoned in Italy for weeks or months prior to being deported to the extermination camps. Conditions in transit and concentration camps varied. Some were labor camps; others were transit camps where the Jews were held pending deportation.

The Fossoli camp, established in 1940 to house prisoners of war, was located near Carpi, north of Modena. After Italy surrendered, Fossoli was handed over to the Germans, who soon filled it with Jews—individuals and families—who were destined for deportation. Political prisoners and Italian army personnel who refused to serve under the Fascist satellite state were also confined here, in separate barracks. Before it was enlarged, Fossoli had room for only 800 prisoners. Between November 1943 and the end of 1944, at least 3,198 Jews—more than a third of the number deported from Italy—passed through Fossoli. German officers ran this camp, with the help of SS men and Fascist militia. Although the camp's conditions were generally tolerable, it was not completely without the violence and starvation that characterized Nazi concentration camps, however.

The Germans established the Bolzano camp in late 1943 or early 1944. It had the largest capacity of all the concentration camps in Italy, housing as many as three thousand prisoners at a time. In 1944, most of the prisoners and the administrative staff of the Fossoli camp were moved to Bolzano. Several transports left Bolzano for Auschwitz and then for concentration camps in Germany (RAVENSBRÜCK and Flossenbürg). The last transport apparently left on January 25, 1945; thereafter, no more than eight hundred prisoners remained, including several dozen Jews. Bolzano was liberated at the end of April 1945, before the Germans could remove the prisoners.

In its layout and established procedures, Bolzano was more like a typical German labor camp than any other camp in Italy. On arrival, the prisoners had to go through the usual routine: their hair was shaved, their possessions were seized, and their clothes were exchanged for prison uniforms. Every prisoner had to sew a triangular patch on his or her clothing displaying a registration number. The prisoners were put on hard forced labor inside and outside the camp, working in the fields, making railway repairs, digging tunnels near the camp, and so on. Only the political prisoners classified as "dangerous" were not put to work, for security reasons.

The La Risiera di San Sabba camp near Trieste was not an extermination camp in the standard meaning of the term, but this camp did have a crematorium. It was

In contrast to conditions in other Nazi camps, life at Fossoli was relatively civilized. Jewish prisoners lived in several barracks, men and women separately; they were allowed to care for their children, even the infants and those who were without parents. Prisoners could keep the few possessions they had brought and did not have to wear prison garb.

A unit of Italian Blackshirts (SS men) stands at attention holding spades during a fascist demonstration.

used for burning the corpses of prisoners who had been executed or had died under torture. The camp was housed in an abandoned rice processing plant that had occasionally been occupied by the Italian soldiers. After Italy surrendered to the Allies, Trieste was put under the direct and exclusive German control. Two notorious SS officers, Odilo **GLOBOCNIK** (a native of Trieste) and Franz **STANGL**, operated in this zone at different times. SS officer Christian **WIRTH** served as camp commander from the fall of 1943 to May 1944; he was followed by Dietrich Allers, who had been director of the German euthanasia campaign in 1939. All the camp staff was German, except perhaps for a few Ukrainian auxiliaries. More than 20,000 prisoners passed through La Risiera. Several thousand persons were murdered, generally by having their skulls cracked with heavy clubs. Their bodies were burned in the crematorium. Several dozen Jews were killed at La Risiera; some 650 were deported to Auschwitz or, as of the end of 1944, to camps in Germany. The last transport left the camp on January 11, 1945.

Between September 15, 1943, and January 30, 1944, at least 3,110 persons of Jewish "race" were shipped from Italy to Auschwitz; 2,224 are known to have died in the Holocaust. Between February and December 1944, at least another 4,056 were deported to the east; 2,425 of them lost their lives. About 2,700 Italian Jews were deported from various other areas. Others were murdered in Italian prisons and internment camps for individual infractions, in retaliation for the acts of other Jews, or as group punishment by the authorities.

Collaboration and Aid Given

At the trial of Eichmann in 1961, it was stated that "every Italian Jew who survived owed his life to the Italians." But while it is true that Italian "Aryans" of all classes saved most of the Jewish survivors, it is also true that Italians contributed to the persecution and death of many Italian Jews. Italian collaborators with the Germans included the men of the Fascist Black Brigades and the volunteers of the Italian SS. They helped the Germans round up thousands of Jews, question them, and

deport them. Some Italian civilians betrayed Jews in hiding in exchange for monetary rewards. Even some Jews betrayed their own peers.

Nonetheless, during World War II the Italians, more than most other Europeans, extended aid to the Jews. From the onset of the war to mid-1942, the Italian authorities protected Jews of Italian nationality living in German-occupied territories or in countries in the German sphere of influence. Italians in occupied France took particularly forceful actions, saving thousands.

From mid-1942 to September 1943, Italians witnessed the arrest, roundup, and deportation to the east of entire Jewish populations in France, Belgium, and Greece, and saw with their own eyes the unspeakable atrocities committed against Jews in CROATIA. Moreover, they had heard rumors of what was happening in eastern Europe. Many of the Italian military personnel and Italian diplomats serving in these places were outraged, and persuaded their superiors in Rome to help Jews, whatever their nationality, who were seeking asylum in the Italian zones of occupation. Thus, genuine rescue operations were launched in areas under the supervision or control of the Italian army: in Dalmatia-Croatia, where 5,000 Jews found refuge; in southern France, where at least 25,000 had gathered; and in Athens and the Greek islands, where 13,000 Jews had congregated. At least 40,000 Jews who were not Italian nationals found refuge. The Italians treated them humanely and did not hand them over to the Croats, the Vichy police, or the Germans, despite unceasing demands and protests.

The Germans repeatedly pressured Italian military officials and diplomats to hand over the Jews to them. On at least two occasions, Mussolini was ready to yield; he even agreed to surrender the Jewish refugees from Croatia. But the high-ranking diplomats and officers who would have had to implement this order refused.

After the Italian government surrendered to the Allies on September 8, 1943, Jews in Italy feared for their lives. Until the day of liberation, the German occupation forces hunted them down mercilessly. In this period of endless terror, Jews desperately needed help. Many Italians, including a substantial numbers of Italian clergy, responded, helping them cross the borders to neutral territory or hiding them in homes, remote villages, and monasteries.

At the time of the armistice in 1943, there were some 44,500 Jews in Italy and the Greek island of Rhodes, about 12,500 of them foreigners. By the war's end, at least 7,682 of these had died in the Holocaust. Of the 8,369 deportees who have so far been identified, only 979 returned to Italy after the war, including a baby born at Bergen-Belsen. In addition, at least 415 Jews survived imprisonment or detention in Italy itself. A few escaped while on their way to the extermination camps.

But although about four-fifths of the Jews of Italy survived the war, Italian Jewry suffered a grievous blow. Thousands emigrated; many of those who remained were physically and spiritually broken. The habit of Jewish life had been interrupted, and in many places its very setting had disappeared, leaving Italian Jewry a shadow of its former self.

Italian diplomats, Army officers and Italian police officers stood firm on protecting Italian "nationals," whether Jewish or not.

SUGGESTED RESOURCES

Caracciolo, Nicola. *Uncertain Refuge: Italy and the Jews During the Holocaust.* Urbana: University of Illinois Press, 1995.

Herzer, Ivo, ed. *The Italian Refuge: Rescue of Jews During the Holocaust.* Washington, DC: Catholic University of America Press, 1989.

Levi, Primo. *The Reawakening.* Boston: Little, Brown, 1965. Reprint, New York: Macmillan, 1993.

Stille, Alexander. *Benevolence and Betrayal: Five Italian Jewish Families Under Fascism.* New York: Summit Books, 1991.

Zuccotti, Susan. *The Italians and the Holocaust: Persecution, Rescue, and Survival.* New York: Basic Books, 1987. Reprint, Lincoln: University of Nebraska Press, 1996.

Jäger, Karl

(1888–1959)

An **SS** officer, Karl Jäger was born in Schaffhausen, Switzerland. Following an early career in business, he joined the **NAZI PARTY** in 1923 and the SS in 1932. From 1935 he served in Ludwigsburg, Ravensburg, and Münster, successively. In Münster, where he was assigned in 1938, he was appointed chief of the **SD** (Sicherheitsdienst; Security Service). After serving in the occupied Netherlands for a time, Jäger was appointed commanding officer of Einsatzkommando 3 in Einsatzgruppe (Operational Squad) A, which was attached to an army corps in northern Soviet Russia (*see* **OPERATIONAL SQUADS**). He later became commander of the Security Police and SD for the General Commissariat of **LITHUANIA** in **KOVNO**.

In this capacity, Jäger was in charge of the extermination of the Lithuanian Jews, as witnessed by the reports that he submitted. In a report dated December 1, 1941, Jäger stated: "There are no more Jews in Lithuania, except for those in three small ghettos, Šiauliai, Kovno, and **VILNA**." In another report, of February 9, 1942, Jäger summed up the killings accomplished by the unit under his command: 136,421 Jews, 1,064 Communists, 653 mentally ill persons, and 134 others. Among the 138,272 victims there were 55,556 women and 34,464 children.

In the fall of 1943 Jäger was reassigned to Germany and was appointed chief of police in Reichenberg, in the Sudetenland. When the war ended he succeeded in assuming a false identity and became a farmer. In April 1959 he was arrested, and on June 22 of that year he committed suicide in his cell.

SUGGESTED RESOURCES

Gitelman, Zvi, ed. *Bitter Legacy: Confronting the Holocaust in the USSR.* Bloomington: Indiana University Press, 1997.

A Teacher's Guide to the Holocaust: Perpetrators. [Online] http://fcit.coedu.usf.edu/holocaust/people/perps.htm (accessed on August 22, 2000).

Janówska

Janówska was a labor and **EXTERMINATION CAMP** located in the suburbs of **LVOV**, in German-occupied **UKRAINE**. In September 1941, the Germans set up a factory on Lvov's Janówska Street, to meet the needs of the German army. Soon after, they expanded it into a network of factories as part of the German Armament Works, a division of the **SS**.

These factories used the Jews of Lvov as forced labor. In September 1941, some 350 Jews worked there; by the end of October, they numbered 600. At that point, the factories' status underwent a change: The area became a restricted camp, enclosed by barbed wire, which the Jews were not permitted to leave. In November

The Janówska camp orchestra played while the inmates set out to work and when they returned. It was established by the Germans, who amused themselves by mocking and humiliating the inmates.

1941, the Germans asked the Lvov **JUDENRAT** (Jewish Council) to supply more workers for the camp, but the Judenrat chairman, Dr. Joseph Parnes, refused. As a result, he was executed.

In 1942, the labor in the camp was intensified, and its inmates were used in metalwork and carpentry. The prisoners were also given jobs with no practical purpose, such as digging trenches and moving loads from one place to another. In this way, the Nazis hoped to break them in body and spirit before sending them to their death. In the wake of Nazi violence against the Jews of Lvov in March 1942, several hundred more Jews were put into the camp.

When the mass deportation of Jews from Eastern Galicia (a part of Ukraine) to the **BEŁŻEC** extermination camp began in March 1942, the role of the Janówska camp changed. From time to time, groups of Jews from towns and villages in the area were held there before being sent on to the death camp. Inside Janówska, periodic "selections"—*selektionen*—classified some as fit for work. These inmates stayed behind, while the other prisoners were sent to die at Bełżec. Later that spring, the camp was enlarged and it became more like a **CONCENTRATION CAMP**, with beatings and killings, starvation and disease. The Lvov Judenrat, working with the prisoners' families, organized a committee that sent food to the camp. Only a fraction of the food reached the prisoners, however; most was taken by the camp staff.

Following more brutal SS campaigns against the Jews in Lvov in the summer of 1942, thousands more prisoners were added to the camp population. By mid-1943, Janówska, while still functioning as a labor camp, was being turned into an extermination camp. Fewer prisoners were working in the factories. In addition, the length of stay of newcomers was shortened, with most being taken directly to places of execution on the city outskirts. In the middle of May 1943, more than 6,000 Jews from Janówska camp were murdered. The harassment and killing of Jews continued unabated.

Despite the reign of terror in the camp, there were cases of mutual help and even efforts at organizing resistance. The prisoners especially tried to help the ill, so that they could recover and not be put to death immediately. In the middle of 1943,

underground activists smuggled in arms with the help of inmates who worked outside the camp, hoping to offer armed resistance when the camp was about to be liquidated.

The liquidation did begin in November 1943, and it has been suggested that the Germans moved up the date in order to avoid a general uprising in the camp. While the Jewish underground did not have the time to organize a full-scale revolt, some prisoners attempted armed resistance while being taken to the execution sites. On November 19, a revolt broke out among the group of prisoners known as *Sonderkommando* (Special Commando) 1005 (*see* **AKTION [OPERATION] 1005**), whose task it was to collect and cremate the bodies of the victims. Several of the guards were killed. Some among the *Sonderkommando* escaped, but most were caught and executed.

While no precise figures are available on the number of Jews who perished in the Janówska camp, estimates suggest that tens of thousands of Jews died there.

SUGGESTED RESOURCES

Kaplan, Helene C. *I Never Left Janówska.* New York: Holocaust Library, 1989.

Wells, Leon Weliczker. *The Janówska Road.* London: Cape, 1966. Reprint, Washington, DC: United States Holocaust Memorial Museum, 1999.

JDC. SEE JOINT DISTRIBUTION COMMITTEE.

Jeckeln, Friedrich

(1895–1946)

Born in Hornberg, Germany, Friedrich Jeckeln joined the **NAZI PARTY** in the 1920s; by 1930 he was an **SS** officer with the rank of SS-*Obergruppenführer* (general). Following the German invasion of the **SOVIET UNION** in June 1941, Jeckeln was appointed Higher SS and Police Leader on the southern front, which included the occupied areas of the **UKRAINE**. On September 1, 1941, the units under his command slaughtered at least 14,000 Hungarian Jews who had been deported to the **KAMENETS-PODOLSKI** area. From July to October of that year they participated in the massacre of the Jews of Kiev at **BABI YAR** and in the mass killings at **ROVNO** and Dnepropetrovsk. On October 11, Jeckeln was appointed Higher SS and Police Leader on the northern front and in Ostland, which encompassed the Baltic countries—**LITHUANIA**, **LATVIA**, and Estonia—and parts of **BELORUSSIA**. Jeckeln was in charge of the annihilation of the Jews of **RIGA** in November and December 1941, including the Jews from Germany and **AUSTRIA** who were sent to that city in the last months of 1941. In Operation Malaria, carried out in early 1942, the anti-partisan units under his command in Belorussia liquidated many ghettos and slaughtered tens of thousands of Jews.

After the war, Jeckeln was arrested by the Allies and handed over to the Soviet Union. He was tried in Riga before a Soviet military court, which sentenced him to death by hanging on February 3, 1946. The sentence was carried out immediately.

Friedrich Jeckeln.

SUGGESTED RESOURCES

Press, Bernhard. *The Murder of the Jews in Latvia, 1941–1945.* Evanston, IL: Northwestern University Press, 1999.

Schneider, Gertrude. *Journey into Terror: Story of the Riga Ghetto.* New York: Ark House, 1979. Reprint, Westport, CT: Praeger, 2000.

A Teacher's Guide to the Holocaust: Perpetrators. [Online] http://fcit.coedu.usf.edu/holocaust/people/perps.htm (accessed on August 22, 2000).

JEWISH BADGE. SEE BADGE, JEWISH.

Jewish Brigade Group

The Jewish Brigade Group was a group of the British army, composed of Jewish volunteers from Palestine. Formed in September 1944, the Jewish Brigade Group fought on behalf of the Allied forces in ITALY from March to May 1945.

The origins of the brigade can be traced back to the earlier stages of World War II. When the war began, Chaim Weizmann, as president of the World Zionist Organization, offered the British government the full cooperation of the Jewish people in the war effort, and began negotiations to create a Jewish fighting force within the British army. The British were at first reluctant. But in the summer of 1940 they changed their minds, hoping that by forming a Jewish force, they could achieve greater support in American public opinion for a policy of assistance to Britain, which was then alone in its efforts to fight GERMANY. In October 1940 the War Cabinet decided to establish such a force, amounting initially to one division. Most of the recruits were to come from the neutral United States and from refugees. Palestine would provide this division with a nucleus of commanding staff to safeguard its national-Zionist character.

The talks with Weizmann on the establishment of the division dragged on inconclusively until March 1941. In the meantime the war situation changed considerably. The threat of invasion to the British Isles faded, while the Middle East and the Balkans became Britain's principal theater of war. The British generals in the Middle East were apprehensive of the likely Arab reaction to the establishment of a Jewish division. Britain's prime minister, Winston Churchill, was persuaded first to postpone implementation for a few months, and then to cancel it altogether in October 1941.

With the occupation of Europe by the Nazis and the imminent entry of the United States into the war, the whole idea of a Jewish formation within the British army had to be modified. It was to be completely based on volunteering in Palestine. In July 1940 the British renounced their earlier idea of mixed Jewish-Arab units, and accepted the principle of Jewish companies in most supporting units of the ground forces. At the same time, the Jewish Agency agreed to help recruit 2,500 individuals for ground crews of the Royal Air Force and to form Jewish Auxiliary Military Pioneer Corps companies. In September 1940, the British responded to another Jewish request and created the Jewish infantry companies known as the "Buffs" and several Jewish anti-aircraft and coastal artillery batteries as a part of the garrison in Palestine.

About 3,000 of the volunteers who had enlisted at the beginning of the war were dispatched to Greece in early 1941. About 100 were killed in action and 1,700 were captured by the Germans in the campaigns of Greece and Crete. The remainder were evacuated to Egypt. Under the growing threat to Britain's position in the Middle East, enlistment increased in the spring of 1941.

> Was it fair to deny the Jews the right to fight their oppressors, when the Allies were doing practically nothing to stop the mass murder?

Although the Jewish Brigade Group was not the first Jewish unit to take part in combat, it was the first and only Jewish formation to fight in World War II under the Jewish flag, recognized as representing the Jewish people.

The recruitment campaign reached its peak in July 1942. Under pressure from American and local public opinion, on August 6, 1942, the British declared the establishment of the Palestine Regiment, consisting of three Jewish battalions and one of Arabs. The low status of the Palestine Regiment disappointed the *Yishuv*—the Jewish population in Palestine—and recruitment began to dwindle. Many soldiers asked for transfer into supporting units, which at least served nearer the front lines in Egypt and the Western Desert, and sometimes participated in the fighting.

The news of the extermination of the Jews in Europe, which reached Palestine in November 1942, had little influence on enlistment in the army. Eighty percent of the 30,000 recruits joined the army in the first half of the war, and only one-fifth enlisted in the following years. The Holocaust had more impact within the ranks, particularly among the soldiers of the infantry battalions and artillery batteries stationed in Palestine. Against the official stance of the Jewish Agency, they then demanded to be dispatched out of the country and sent to the front, where they would be able to take their revenge on the Nazis and assist the surviving remnant of European Jews upon its liberation. The demand persisted throughout 1943.

New Zionist proposals in the summer of 1943 for the creation of a fighting force were not connected with the Middle East and its sensitive equilibrium between Arabs and Jews. This time the British were more responsive. Although the generals still had several misgivings, moral considerations carried more weight than before. It did not seem fair to deny the Jews the right to fight their oppressors, when the Allies were doing practically nothing to stop the mass murder. Churchill exercised all his personal authority in favor of accepting the Zionist proposal and urged his colleagues to approve it. On July 3, 1944, the British War Cabinet decided that although the formation of a Jewish division was not logical on practical grounds, the creation of a brigade should be immediately and positively considered.

The cabinet decision opened the way to intensive talks, resulting in an official communiqué by the War Office on September 20, 1944, announcing the formation of the Jewish Brigade Group. Brigadier Ernst Benjamin was appointed its commanding officer, and the Zionist flag was officially approved as its standard.

The three infantry battalions of the brigade assembled near Alexandria, Egypt. In early November they sailed for Italy. The brigade took part in the early stages of the final Allied offensive in Italy in April 1945 and then was withdrawn for reorganization. Its casualties at the front totaled 57 killed and about 200 wounded, including non-Jewish personnel.

After the termination of hostilities, the brigade was stationed in Tarvisio, near the border triangle of Italy, Yugoslavia, and **AUSTRIA**. Several missions set out from Tarvisio to eastern Europe and to the **DISPLACED PERSONS'** camps in Austria and Germany. Soon the brigade became a source of attraction for the surviving Jewish youth from all over the continent. During the two-month sojourn in the region, about 150,000 Jews were smuggled to Tarvisio, where they were hospitalized and fed by the soldiers until their eventual transfer by the Jewish transport units to the refugee centers farther south.

In July 1945, the brigade moved to **BELGIUM** and the **NETHERLANDS**. About 150 soldiers were secretly dispatched to conduct organizational and educational work in the displaced persons' camps, and to assist in the preparations for "illegal" immigration to Palestine (*see* **ALIYA BET**). Other soldiers concentrated on illegal arms purchase for the Hagana (the Jewish underground military organization in Palestine). Despite last-moment attempts by the Jewish Agency to prolong the brigade's existence, the British were determined to disband it according to their demobilization plan, and this was accomplished in June and July of 1946.

Thirty thousand Jews volunteered in Palestine for service in the British army between 1939 and 1946. They sustained 700 fatalities; 1,769 were taken prisoner; several thousand were wounded; and 323 were decorated or mentioned in dispatches. Five thousand served in the Jewish Brigade.

SEE ALSO **RESISTANCE, JEWISH.**

SUGGESTED RESOURCES

Beckman, Morris. *The Jewish Brigade: An Army with Two Masters, 1944–1945.* Sarpedon, 1998.

In Our Own Hands: The Hidden Story of the Jewish Brigade in World War II [videorecording]. Chuck Olin Associates, 1998.

Morris, Henry. *We Will Remember Them: A Record of the Jews Who Died in the Armed Forces of the Crown, 1939–1945.* Washington, DC: Brassey's, 1989. Reprint, London: AJEX, 1994.

JEWISH COUNCIL. SEE JUDENRAT.

Jewish Fighting Organization

The Jewish Fighting Organization (*Żydowska Organizacja Bojowa*; ŻOB) was a Jewish armed group. It was established in **WARSAW** on July 28, 1942, when mass **DEPORTATIONS** from the ghetto were in full swing. The group allowed the Jews to defend themselves and offer armed resistance to the Nazi enemy. First to join the ŻOB were the pioneering **YOUTH MOVEMENTS**—*Ha-Shomer ha-Tsa'ir, Dror,* and *Akiva.* The first command of the ŻOB consisted of Yitzhak **ZUCKERMAN**, Josef **KAPLAN**, Zivia Lubetkin, Shmuel Braslav, and Mordechai **TENENBAUM**. Arie Wilner was deputized to be the organization's representative with the Polish underground, to establish contacts with the underground's fighting organizations and obtain assistance from them.

The Early Struggle for Unity

The political groups in the Warsaw ghetto began discussing the formation of a military defense organization in March 1942. The talks were in reaction to a number of circumstances, including reports of massacres being carried out by **OPERATIONAL SQUADS** (*Einsatzgruppen*) in Soviet territories occupied by the Germans in the second half of 1941. There were also reports on the emergence of the **UNITED PARTISAN ORGANIZATION** (*Fareynegte Partizaner Organizatsye*) in **VILNA**, and eyewitness accounts of the mass murders taking place in the **CHEŁMNO** camp. The Warsaw ghetto factions and their leaders had been unable to reach agreement because some believed that Warsaw Jews were not in danger of being deported. They felt that even if that danger did materialize, the greater part of the ghetto population might escape, whereas military organization and resistance in the ghetto might lead to its immediate and total **liquidation**. Until the deportations, the Bund (Jewish Socialist Party) representatives opposed any separate Jewish organization, believing that the Jews should join the general Polish underground. For a long time the Bund members also opposed forming part of a general Jewish organization together with Zionist and bourgeois groups, their political antagonists. For these

liquidation
The emptying of a Jewish ghetto through deportations and violence.

reasons, and because the Polish underground elements refused to recruit Jews to their ranks or to establish their own branches in the ghetto, a broadly based fighting organization could not be created prior to the deportations.

The first such fighting organization to be set up in the Warsaw ghetto was the Antifascist Bloc. Formed at the end of March and in early April 1942 by the Communists, it also attracted factions from the Zionist left. The **Zionists** in the bloc assumed that the Communists had the support of the **SOVIET UNION** along with access to military power and equipment that could arm and strengthen the defense organization in the ghetto. It turned out, however, that the Communists in the **GENERALGOUVERNEMENT** territory had no direct link with the Soviet Union, they possessed few resources of their own, and they had little status among the Polish population. The Communists wanted to use the ghetto as a manpower reserve for partisan operations, and did not support resistance in the ghetto itself. The Zionists, and especially the Zionist youth movements, disagreed, believing that the struggle in the ghetto was the main purpose of any defense organization. Soon it became obvious that the Communists' promises to transfer groups of fighters from the ghetto to partisan units in the forests were groundless. The Communist organization had no territory established there and all their attempts to transfer people to the forests ended in disaster. Then on May 30, 1942, several Communist activists in the ghetto were arrested, one of whom had come from the Soviet Union and taken charge of the military arm of the Antifascist Bloc in the ghetto. The arrests were the result of their political activities as Communists and had nothing to do with the bloc. However, the arrests caused shock and fear among the movements that had joined the bloc, and ultimately led to its dissolution.

Warsaw Ghetto Deportations

The great wave of deportations from the Warsaw ghetto took place from July 22 to September 12, 1942. Nearly 300,000 Jews were uprooted from the ghetto and 265,000 of them were taken to the **TREBLINKA** extermination camp. The ŻOB came into being on July 28, and called on the Jews in the ghetto to stand up for themselves and resist deportation. But the fear-ridden population was concerned only with survival. Because of the lack of weapons and the atmosphere of terror in which the deportations took place, the ŻOB was unable to carry out any large-scale attacks or revenge actions. However, several small-scale actions took place. On August 20 a member of ŻOB shot and severely wounded Joseph Szerynski, the commandant of the **JEWISH GHETTO POLICE**, which had taken an active part in the deportations. ŻOB members set fire to several warehouses belonging to German factories in the ghetto, and in various places they interfered with the hunt for the Jews. On September 3 the ŻOB suffered losses when two of its leaders, Josef Kaplan and Shmuel Braslav, were captured and killed. That same day, the ŻOB's pitiful collection of arms—five pistols and eight hand grenades—fell into German hands. In the eyes of many of the ŻOB members this setback was a decisive blow. Only the encouragement of senior members Yitzhak Zuckerman and Arie Wilner prevented the others from giving up. The two leaders argued that after the mass deportation there would be a lull, which could be used for re-arming and planning a revolt.

When the wave of deportations came to an end, the ŻOB's methods and its standing among the remaining population underwent a change. Some 55,000 Jews were left in the ghetto, 35,000 of whom were recognized as workers in factories that belonged to the Germans and were under German supervision. The other 20,000

Zionists
Members of a social and political movement promoting the creation of a homeland for Jews in Palestine.

had succeeded in eluding deportation and gone into hiding. The tension of the preceding months was gone and was replaced by a sense of anticlimax. The survivors missed their family and friends, and now that they knew what was happening in Treblinka, they realized they, too, were living on borrowed time and their end was near. Many regretted not having offered resistance to the deportations, and insisted that they would fight if an opportunity arose again.

New Life for the Jewish Fighting Organization

With new interest from the remaining Jews, the ŻOB entered a new stage of growth and entrenchment. In October 1942 negotiations with the underground political groups were concluded. A broader ŻOB emerged, now composed also of Po'alei Zion Zionist Socialists, Po'alei Zion Left, the Bund, Gordonia, *Ha-No'ar ha-Tsiyyoni* (The Zionist Youth), and Communists, in addition to the founding pioneering Zionist youth movements. For a while, Betar and the Revisionist Zionists also belonged to the ŻOB, but internal disagreements led to the Revisionist camp's secession and the establishment of their own military formation, the Jewish Military Union (*Żydowski Związek Wojskowy*; ŻZW). Individuals from other political groups also joined the ŻZW, as did some who had not previously belonged to any underground organization. In this period of intensive operations there was great tension and frequent confrontation between the ŻOB and the ŻZW, and they were on the verge of armed clashes. In the end, however, representatives of the two bodies held talks and reached a settlement in which the ŻZW agreed to coordinate any action it was planning with the ŻOB.

A strategic plan was also agreed upon regarding armaments, arms procurement, and the division of sectors and positions in the ghetto between the two organizations. All was in preparation for the struggle that would be waged when, as expected, the Germans renewed the deportations. Mordecai **ANIELEWICZ** (of *Ha-Shomer ha-Tsa'ir*) was appointed the commander of ŻOB. The other members of the command were Yitzhak Zuckerman (*Dror*), Berk Schajndemil (Bund; later replaced by Marek Edelman), Yohanan Morgenstern (Po'alei Zion Zionist Socialists), Hersh Berlinski (Po'alei Zion Left), and Michael Rosenfeld (Communists). The Zionist factions that had joined and supported ŻOB decided to set up a civilian body as well, made up of well-known leaders. This was established as the Jewish National Committee (*Żydowski Komitet Narodowy*). It played an important role in legitimizing the ŻOB in the final stages of the ghetto's existence, collected funds for the procurement of arms, and gave ŻOB the authority of a general Jewish organization representing the Jews before the Polish underground leaders. *Oneg Shabbat*, the underground archive established by Emanuel **RINGELBLUM**, became affiliated with the National Committee.

Beyond the Ghetto's Borders

The ŻOB was created in Warsaw, which was the center of its operations. From the very beginning, however, the ŻOB made efforts to spread the concept of resistance and preparation for a revolt to the provinces, especially to cities with a strong underground core. In pursuit of this objective, Mordechai Tenenbaum was dispatched to **BIAŁYSTOK**, where he brought about the unification of the Jewish forces and led the uprising there. Zvi Brandes and Fruma **PLOTNICKA** were sent to Zagłębie (Będzin), and Avraham Leibovich ("Laban") to **KRAKÓW**.

The ŻOB's principal emissary on the "Aryan" side of Warsaw was Arie Wilner, who was assisted by Adolf Abraham Berman of Po'alei Zion Left and Leon **FEINER**

of the Bund. Wilner was able to establish ties with both the Home Army (*Armia Krajowa*; AK), the military arm in **POLAND** of the Polish government-in-exile in London, and the People's Army (*Armia Ludowa*), the Communists' fighting force among the Poles. The AK recognized ŻOB officially, but did not provide much in the way of weapons to the group. The AK did train ŻOB members to make their own hand grenades out of explosives.

One of the first operations undertaken by the ŻOB, even before its base was broadened, was to purge the ghetto of elements that had assisted the Germans in the deportations: the **JEWISH GHETTO POLICE** commanders and spies who reported to the Germans on developments in the ghetto. Before the first uprising, which took place in January 1943, Jacob Lejkin (the acting chief of the Jewish police at the time of the deportations) was executed. Later, in the wake of the uprising, such activity was intensified. Dr. Alfred Nossig, once an active Zionist who had become a Nazi informer, was also killed. The ŻOB's original aim had been simply to take revenge, but their punitive actions also struck fear into the hearts of other collaborators and neutralized them. In the last weeks of the ghetto's existence, the ŻOB was firmly in control of ghetto life, having subdued both the **JUDENRAT** (Jewish Council) and the Jewish police.

SEE ALSO **RESISTANCE, JEWISH.**

SUGGESTED RESOURCES

Gutman, Israel. *Resistance: The Warsaw Ghetto Uprising.* Boston: Houghton Mifflin, 1994.

Landau, Elaine. *The Warsaw Ghetto Uprising.* New York: New Discovery Books, 1992.

A Teacher's Guide to the Holocaust: Resisters. [Online] http://fcit.coedu.usf.edu/holocaust/people/resister.htm (accessed on August 22, 2000).

"Zydowski Zwiazek Wojskowy." *Simon Wiesenthal Center Museum of Tolerance Online.* [Online] http://motlc.wiesenthal.org/pages/t088/t08818.html (accessed on August 22, 2000).

Jewish Ghetto Police

The Jewish Ghetto Police (*Jüdischer Ordnungsdienst*) were referred to by the Jews as the "Jewish police." These police units were organized in Jewish communities on orders of the Nazi occupying forces throughout eastern Europe.

In every occupied city or region, the Jews were ordered to form an administrative committee called the **JUDENRAT** (Jewish Council). This was usually in anticipation of concentrating all the Jews into areas known as ghettos. The leaders of the Judenrat were then forced to organize the Jewish ghetto police force, according to guidelines from the Germans.

Whereas the Judenrat itself, although also created on German orders, often contained elements of voluntary association, the Jewish police force was strictly a German-initiated phenomenon. There was no precedent in the life of the Jewish community for the existence of a separate Jewish police force.

According to the German guidelines Jewish ghetto police personnel should have a high degree of physical fitness, some military experience, and secondary or higher education. In practice, however, these guidelines were not always observed. From the very beginning many Judenräte (Jewish Councils) were apprehensive

Jewish police in Lublin.

about the way these police units would function. They suspected that the Germans would eventually have direct supervision of the police and use them to implement their own anti-Jewish policies. Aware of this danger, many Judenräte tried to attract to the police young Jews who would be loyal to the Jewish community. At first, some recruits did tend to join the police force because it gave them an opportunity to serve their community. But there were other reasons for joining. As members of a protected organization, recruits were immune to being seized for forced labor. Police service also offered greater freedom of movement and more possibilities of obtaining food. There was a certain degree of power that came with their role as police agents.

A study of the records of more than 100 Jewish police officers in the **GENERAL-GOUVERNEMENT** reveals that the Judenräte did not succeed in their efforts to ensure that the police had public credibility. Seventy percent of the men who served in the police force had taken no part in Jewish community life before the war, and some 20 percent were refugees and strangers to the ghetto population. Only 10 percent had participated in community affairs in the prewar period. The Germans themselves often made sure, when a police unit was set up, that it would be headed by men who

would blindly follow orders. The Jewish police force was perceived by many Jews as a potential danger to the community. Some of the Jewish **YOUTH MOVEMENTS** and Jewish political parties did not permit their members to enlist in the police, recognizing that the priorities of the German-controlled Jewish police were in conflict with the pro-Jewish priorities of their underground organizations.

The size of a Jewish police force depended on the size of the Jewish community it served. Thus, in **WARSAW** the Jewish police at first numbered 2,000, in **LVOV** 500, in **ŁÓDŹ** 800, in **KRAKÓW** 150, and in **KOVNO** 200. There was no uniform structure for the police units. In the large ghettos, the commanders held officer rank and the units were made up of subdivisions and district stations. The policemen were identified by the different caps they wore and by the unit's designation inscribed on their armband, the yellow badge that they, like all other Jews, had to wear (*see* **BADGE, JEWISH**). In the small ghettos where a police unit consisted of a few men only, no such organizational differentiations were made.

Police Duties

The duties carried out by the Jewish police can be divided into three categories:

1. Duties in response to specific German demands as conveyed via the Judenrat
2. Duties related to the Judenrat's activities among the Jews that were not directly related to German demands
3. Duties related to the Jewish population's needs

The first two categories included collecting ransom payments, personal belongings and valuables, and taxes; searching out people for forced labor; guarding the ghetto wall or fence and the ghetto gates; escorting labor gangs who worked outside the ghetto; and, as time went on, conducting random seizures of persons to be sent to labor camps and participating in the roundup of Jews for mass **DEPORTATIONS**. The Judenrat was often ordered by the Germans to supply ghetto inhabitants or their financial "contributions" for specific purposes; the Jewish ghetto police were enlisted to ensure that the quotas were met. Meeting the peace-keeping or regular police needs of the ghetto or community was of secondary priority to the first two classifications of duty.

The isolation of the Jewish population in ghettos and their exclusion from standard public services created serious health and welfare problems. Early on, it was the role of the Jewish police to attend to the sanitary conditions of the community and assist in the distribution of food rations and general assistance to the needy. They also helped in the control of epidemics, and in the settling of disputes—all this, of course, in addition to complying with German demands. The ghetto population appreciated the Jewish police for these public-welfare activities. However, even at an early stage, there were signs of corruption and misconduct among the Jewish police.

Dilemmas

As time passed, the ability of the Jewish police to spend time on community living conditions was reduced. As their roles demanded that they take harmful actions against their peers, as in rounding up Jews for deportation, many Jewish police chose to quit the force. Some quit in an overt manner, as a way to express their identification with their families and with the Jewish population as a whole. Most of those who did so lost their immunity to deportation, and were subsequently sent to the extermination camps.

There were a few benefits for members of the Jewish ghetto police: the possibility of increased freedom, larger food rations, and protection of family members from deportations persuaded some men to volunteer for these jobs.

But not all Jewish police felt that kind of pressure from the Jewish community. They stayed on their jobs up to the final phases of the ghettos' existence, submitting to German authority and obediently following orders. When this happened in a ghetto, the Jewish police took on an entirely different character. As Jews resigned, the Germans recruited new men into the force, as both officers and rank and file. Generally, these men had no commitment at all to the Jewish population. Among the new Jewish police personnel were criminals, opportunists, and refugees with no ties or loyalties to the surviving remnants of the local Jewish community. In ghettos where the Judenrat was not willing to submit blindly to German orders, the Jewish police gained in strength, often taking over the Judenrat or usurping its administrative role.

The Underground

The attitude of the Jewish police toward ghetto **underground activists** took on three different forms:

1. The most common relationship was one of tension. In several ghettos—such as those of Będzin, Sosnowiec, Kraków, and Warsaw—the Jewish police tried to do away with the underground, although not all members of the police in these places took part in such efforts. The underground rarely trusted the Jewish police. In Warsaw, in August 1942, during the mass deportations, the Jewish police commander, Joseph Szerynski, was attacked by the underground and seriously wounded. His successor, Jacob Lejkin, was assassinated in October of that year, on orders of the **JEWISH FIGHTING ORGANIZATION**.

2. Sometimes the Jewish police followed a policy of nonintervention in the activities of the underground that took on the form of "benign neglect."

3. In some ghettos, such as Kovno, the Jewish police gave active help to the underground, and some policemen were also members of clandestine organizations.

underground activists
Those who joined or formed illegal organizations designed to undermine the Nazi authorities; some, but not all, were Zionists or Communists.

Conclusion

When the war ended, the conduct of the Jewish police in the ghettos came under investigation by groups of survivors. In Munich, 40 Jewish policemen were found guilty of improper conduct and were ostracized by the Jewish public. In Israel, several policemen were charged under the Nazis and Nazi Collaborators (Punishment) Law. A few were convicted but most were acquitted, as the courts took into account the extraordinary circumstances under which the Jewish policemen in the ghettos had been forced to function.

SUGGESTED RESOURCES

Trunk, Isaiah. *Judenrat: The Jewish Councils in Eastern Europe Under Nazi Occupation.* New York: Macmillan, 1972. Reprint, Lincoln: University of Nebraska Press, 1996.

Jewish Law (Statut des Juifs)

The *Statut des Juifs,* translated as "Jewish Law," was a set of anti-Jewish legislation passed by the Vichy government of **FRANCE** in October 1940 and June 1941. The laws applied to all of France despite the fact that at the time the Germans occupied only the northern three-fifths of the country—not the southern portion where the Vichy government was headquartered. Vichy's first comprehensive anti-Jewish statute, of October 3, 1940, defined a Jew as a person with three grandparents "of the Jewish race," or with two Jewish grandparents if the spouse was also Jewish.

In its explicit reference to race, the Vichy definition of Jewishness was both harsher and more inclusive than the policy set by the Germans in the occupied zone of France and elsewhere. The law went on to provide the basis for drastically reducing the role of Jews in French society. It excluded Jews from top positions in the French civil service, the officer corps of the army, the ranks of noncommissioned officers, and all professions that influence public opinion—teaching, the press, radio, film, and theater. Jews were permitted to hold menial public-service positions, provided they had served in the armed forces between 1914 and 1918 or had distinguished themselves in the military campaign of 1939 and 1940. The statute also called for a quota system to limit the presence of Jews in the liberal professions, including law and medicine. Formulated purely on French initiative, the law was prepared by the Justice Ministry of Raphaël Alibert, a militant anti-Semite, friend of the monarchist Action Française movement, and the formulator of the Vichy motto "Travail, Famille, Patrie" (Work, Family, Fatherland).

The Vichy regime's efforts to broaden the principles of this statute and to tighten some of its provisions led to a second *Statut des Juifs*, on June 2, 1941. It emerged from Xavier **VALLAT**'s General Office for Jewish Affairs, and was carefully drafted in a series of cabinet meetings and consultations with Justice Minister Joseph Barthélemy. After more clearly defining who was a Jew, and tinkering with the provisions for the removal of Jews from public posts, the law opened the way for a massive purging of Jews from the liberal professions, commerce, and industry. Only a handful of well-established French Jews could benefit from the exemptions provided by the statute. Even Jewish men who had served in France's military and survived captivity as prisoners of war were not exempt from this decree.

Keenly attentive to detail, Vallat was careful to close every loophole, to ensure that no Jew escaped the jurisdiction of the anti-Jewish program. Never fully satisfied with the handiwork of the General Office for Jewish Affairs, the coordinator of the anti-Semitic legislation worked on a new *Statut des Juifs* during the fall and winter of 1941, but this law was never enacted. Mean-spirited and filled with contradictions on the matter of race and religion, the statutes at the heart of the Vichy regime's policy toward the Jews reflected the legalistic approach of the government and its hatred toward all Jews, whether or not they were French citizens.

SUGGESTED RESOURCES:

Josephs, Jeremy. *Swastika Over Paris.* New York: Arcade, 1989.

Weisberg, Richard H. *Vichy Law and the Holocaust in France.* New York: New York University Press, 1996.

JEWISH YOUTH MOVEMENTS. SEE YOUTH MOVEMENTS.

Joint Distribution Committee

The American Jewish Joint Distribution Committee (JDC; also known as the Joint) was established in 1919 by American Jewry's overseas relief and rehabilitation agency to aid European Jews economically and in their emigration efforts. As early

Similar Name, Separate Organization

There were many relief agencies worldwide that sought to aid the Jews of Europe during the Nazi reign of terror. The Joint Rescue Committee—not to be confused with the Joint Distribution Committee—was established by leaders of various organizations in the Jewish community in Palestine (*Yishuv*), to contribute to this effort. This committee's early work focused on providing emergency food supplies and immigration certificates to Jews in the Polish ghettos. The committee was expanded from four members to twelve in 1943, in recognition of the need to centralize all European rescue and assistance efforts undertaken by the Yishuv. Despite internal divisions, the committee remained active because the participating organizations knew that the situation of European Jews was too complex for any one of them to act effectively alone. By 1945, the Joint Rescue Committee's efforts focused on helping war refugees. The committee disbanded shortly before the establishment of the state of Israel.

as 1930, it became clear to some Joint leaders in Europe that mass emigrations would be forthcoming as the National Socialists, with a vehemently antisemitic agenda, began to gain favor in **GERMANY**. However, no one was, at that point, able to imagine the scope of the horror that would overtake European Jewry in just a few years' time. Additionally, American Jews were feeling the effects of the economic crisis of 1929, so funds for early intervention and assistance programs were not available, anyway.

The central figure in the committee during the World War II years was Joseph J. Schwartz, who became head of the Joint's European operation. When the war broke out, the Joint became a major factor in an overall effort to help European Jews find new means for economic survival in Europe. At the same time, it aided in the emigration of those who could not stay there in what it hoped would be an organized exodus. Some of its funds went to support the eastern European communities, which were in a far worse economic situation than even German Jewry during the first years of Adolf **HITLER**'s regime.

Activities of the Joint Distribution Committee

The Joint's activities centered on raising money to fund rescue and rehabilitation programs and to assist self-help and underground resistance activity in Europe. Until the United States entered the war, in December 1941, the Joint sent food and money by various means to **POLAND**; after the American entry into the war, the committee was forbidden to help "enemy" countries. Several thousand Jews were evacuated from **LITHUANIA** to East Asia, largely with Joint support. In **WARSAW**, a very active Joint committee under the leadership of Yitzhak Gitterman raised funds by promising repayment in dollars after the war (these promises were later honored). Children's centers, hospitals, and house committees providing social, cultural, economic, and moral support were established under the Joint's supervision in the Warsaw ghetto. Educational services were funded by the Joint. The Joint office in Warsaw also provided funds for armed resistance, both in Warsaw and in **BIAŁYSTOK**.

The Joint funds were used to provide aid to French Jews and to support orphanages, hospitals, and public kitchens. Schools, theaters, and study groups received aid, as did efforts to help Jews obtain false identity papers and cross international borders. Small groups of surviving Jews were supported in **BERLIN** in 1944, and the remnants of the community in Zagreb were helped. Parcels were sent to a number of **CONCENTRATION CAMPS** and to the ghetto of **THERESIENSTADT**. Other aid efforts took place as circumstances allowed.

The Joint became a very active participant in the attempts to rescue Slovak Jewry. Some Polish Jews were smuggled into **SLOVAKIA**, where the Joint supported work camps that were to provide relative safety for their inmates. The Joint also supplied large sums of money, channeled through Switzerland, to aid Romanian Jewry. Joint funds went to save what was left of the Bessarabian and Bukovina Jews who had been expelled to the southern **UKRAINE** (Transnistria) in 1941. In **HUNGARY**, after the March 1944 occupation of that country by the Germans, funds were made available to establish children's shelters and were given to neutral diplomats to provide aid to Jews. Raoul **WALLENBERG** received the money he needed from the Joint, as did Carl **LUTZ**, the Swiss vice-consul in Budapest, both of whom used the funds to help rescue Jews through diplomatic channels. In Hungary, particularly in late 1944, the Joint's help became crucial in saving the remnants of Hungarian Jewry until Budapest was liberated.

Expenditures of the Joint

The Joint Distribution Committee sent funds totaling $12.29 million in 1938–39, and $11.9 million in 1940–41. The decrease resulted from the American Jews' disinterest in what was happening in Europe, despite tireless fund-raising efforts on the part of the committee. In 1942, the crucial year of the Holocaust, the committee had $6 million at its disposal for European relief, but funds could no longer be transferred to Europe except under crippling conditions. Switzerland was slated to be the main center for distribution of funds, with Saly **MAYER** as its representative. However, in 1942–43, owing to disagreements between the American and Swiss governments, no funds could be transmitted to that country. Global expenditures increased in 1943 to $8.9 million, to $14.8 million in 1944, and to $26.8 million in 1945. Tragically, by that time most of European Jewry had been murdered. Nevertheless, the funds did help some of those who had a chance of survival.

American Jewry and the Work of the Joint

The Joint's operations, on the whole, were the main way in which American Jews aided their European brotherhood during the Holocaust.

After the war, the conscience of American Jews was finally stirred up, and self-accusations were made regarding what had not been done during the Holocaust. Perhaps as a result of this, the Joint, working together with the United HIAS Service and other organizations, became the central Jewish agency supporting survivors in the **DISPLACED PERSONS'** camps in Germany, Austria, and **ITALY**, and in Poland, Hungary, Romania, and elsewhere. Between 1946 and 1950, the sum of $280 million was spent (compared to $169 million between 1914 and 1945), and quantities of food were sent to supplement the official rations. Also provided were clothing, books, and school supplies for children, cultural amenities, religious supplies, and much more. In addition, vocational training centers were supported. After the establishment of Israel in May 1948 the Joint became responsible for bringing immigrants there. Until 1949, it also funded the social activities in the detention camps that the British

Jewish displaced persons in Athens try on new shoes supplied by the American Jewish Joint Distribution Committee.

had set up in Cyprus. The Joint's work with survivors terminated with the closing of the last displaced persons' camp (Föhrenwald) in 1957, and with the committee's participation in the Claims Conference, which received and administered German reparation funds to Holocaust survivors after 1953. Without the Joint, the survivors' fate would have been much bleaker than it was.

SUGGESTED RESOURCES

Bauer, Yehuda. *American Jewry and the Holocaust: The American Jewish Joint Distribution Committee, 1939–1945.* Detroit: Wayne State University Press, 1981.

Milton, Sybil, ed. *American Jewish Joint Distribution Committee, New York.* New York: Garland, 1995.

Judenrat

A Judenrat (plural, Judenräte) was a "Jewish Council" established by the Nazis in many of the communities of occupied Europe. Judenräte were first set up in the Jewish communities of **POLAND**, under the orders of Reinhard **HEYDRICH**. Heydrich issued the instructions on September 21, 1939—just weeks after **GERMANY**'s invasion of Poland. Hans **FRANK**, the head of the **GENERALGOUVERNEMENT**, saw that the orders were fulfilled.

According to Heydrich's guidelines, the members of the Judenräte would be fully responsible for carrying out German policies regarding the Jews. The Jewish Councils would be made up, "as far as possible, of influential people and rabbis." Including leading community members in the Judenräte had two purposes: to make

"It is the duty of the Judenrat ... to receive the orders of the German Administration. It is responsible for the conscientious carrying out of orders to their full extent. The directives it issues to carry out these German decrees must be obeyed by all Jews and Jewesses."

Hans Frank, "Regulation for the Establishment of the Judenräte," November 28, 1939.

sure that German orders were put into place to the fullest possible extent, and to discredit Jewish leadership in the eyes of the Jewish population.

Under Frank's order, the Judenrat was to have 12 members in places where the Jewish population was 10,000 or less. In larger towns or cities, there would be 24 members. The councils were to be elected by the members of the community, but the council members themselves were to choose their chairman and vice-chairman. The results were subject to the approval of German district or city officials—thus, the elections were actually meaningless. On some occasions, though, members of the Jewish communities did have a say in determining the composition of the councils.

In some cases, Jewish activists refused to join the Judenräte, because they were suspicious—with good reason—of how the Germans would use them. But generally, local Jewish leaders did become members of the councils, either under Nazi pressure or because they thought they were best able to represent their communities in dealing with the German authorities. This reasoning met with approval from the Jewish population.

Decisions on Implementation

Once the Judenräte were established, the Germans lost no time in presenting them with daunting tasks. The councils were ordered to draft people for forced labor, take a census of the Jewish population, evacuate apartments and hand them over to Germans, pay fines or ransoms, confiscate valuables owned by Jews, and so on. In most cases, the Judenrat members tried to delay or negotiate the administrative and economic measures imposed by the Germans. However, traditional methods used for dealing with the authorities, such as lobbying officials and utilizing personal contacts, were not of help under the totalitarian Nazi regime.

The Judenräte believed that by complying with the Germans' early demands, they would impress upon the Nazis the vital importance to the Germans of the Jewish community. In this way, they hoped to avoid or moderate some of the blows, to gain time, to ward off or delay punishments, and perhaps even to persuade the Germans to reconsider their Jewish policy, to view the Jews as a reservoir for the manpower the Germans sorely needed. In the meantime, the Jews hoped, the war would end in a German defeat. It took a while before these theories and assessments were put to the test—until the mass deportations of 1942, when the true nature of German policy became increasingly obvious.

Providing Basic Needs

Judenrat members were also involved in providing the community with its basic needs. The war destroyed the Jewish economic structure, which had already been shaky. There had always been Jews requiring public assistance, but the hardships created by the German occupation were unprecedented. Tens of thousands of Jews were displaced from their homes and became refugees, without a place to live or a source of food. Jews were no longer covered by the general public services and required their own health services and public institutions, such as homes for the aged, orphanages, and, in part, educational institutions. The Judenrat's efforts to ease the plight of the Jewish population were among the ways in which it sought to counter the Nazi policy of starving communities and breaking their resistance. However, some Judenrat activities displayed instances of protectionism, favoritism, misuse of public trust for personal advantage, and so on. Such practices caused bitter resentment and were harshly criticized.

An unidentified Judenrat official, sitting at the desk in his office, gathered with other employees of the area.

More functions were imposed upon the Judenräte by the Germans with the ghettoization of the Jews. The Judenräte were expected to oversee the transfer Jews from their homes into the areas allotted for the ghettos, provide living quarters for the new inhabitants, maintain public order, and prevent smuggling. Some of these duties were carried out by the **JEWISH GHETTO POLICE** (*Jüdischer Ordnungsdienst*), an internal police force mandated by the Germans.

Under ghetto conditions, which separated the Jews from the general population, the hardships became much worse. Large sections of the Jewish community faced starvation. It was the Judenrat's responsibility to distribute the meager food rations permitted by the Germans. In a number of ghettos, the Judenräte tried to obtain more food by buying provisions on the black market or on the "Aryan" side, or by trading products manufactured in the ghetto.

SELF-HELP As a result of starvation, overcrowding, and the lack of basic sanitary facilities, diseases spread in the ghetto. The Germans welcomed the resulting rise in the Jews' death rate, but held the Judenrat responsible for making sure that contagious diseases did not cross the ghetto borders. The Judenrat set up hospitals and clinics and organized other forms of medical aid. In some cases, the Judenrat worked with voluntary organizations to contain and treat disease, with varying success.

COMPLIANCE OR REFUSAL? Beginning in 1940, the Judenräte were given the task of providing forced labor for the camps that were being set up by the Nazis. This was a fundamental change from previous assignments. It did not mean sending people on forced labor in or near their place of residence, where they could return in the evening to their community and family. It meant total separation and transfer to remote locations where a much harsher regime was in force—a regime that many prisoners could not endure for long.

The Judenräte had to decide how to meet these German demands. They usually did supply the required quota of able-bodied young men as workers for the labor camps, causing friction with the community when people had to be seized on the streets for deportation to the camps. In the initial stages of forced-labor deportations, the Judenräte tried to maintain contact with the members of their community imprisoned in the camps, sending them food, clothing, and medicines. But when German policy became even harsher, the contact was broken off. In some cases councils

> 66 ... the Council has become the sole *representative and mediator* between the Jewish population and the authorities.... The Council has become the central place where all the various Jewish affairs are organized."

—From a Jewish newspaper published with the approval of the German authorities.

Gazeta Zydowska, No. 46, December 23, 1940.

refused to supply quotas for the labor camps. When Joseph Parnes, chairman of the Judenrat in **LVOV**, refused to send men to the **JANÓWSKA** camp, he was killed.

As time went on and Nazi policy approached the next phase, that of mass extermination of Jews, the Judenräte had very little room left for maneuvering between the needs of the Jewish population and the demands made by the Germans. Judenrat members had to decide where to draw the line—Would following German orders help the overall community's struggle for survival? There were bitter discussions on this issue both within and outside the Judenräte. The decisions taken by the Jewish Council members and the answers they gave to this crucial question differed from one council to the next in substance. They also depended on the specific moment when they had to be made.

The pattern of behavior of Judenrat members fell into four categories:

1. Refusal to cooperate with the Germans, even with regard to economic measures or other relatively mundane issues;

2. Compliance with extreme measures of a material nature, such as the seizure of property, but absolute refusal to hand over human beings;

3. Resignation to the destruction of some Jews, on the assumption that this would enable other members of the community to be saved;

4. Compliance in full with all German orders, without any consideration for their effect on the Jewish public, and with concern only for one's own personal interests.

Most Judenrat members died either before the mass **SS** "operations" (*Aktionen*) took place, or during the deportations to **EXTERMINATION CAMPS**. In very many cases, they were murdered for refusing to comply with German orders.

In the first phase of the existence of Judenräte, the chairmen (or, at least, some of them) were responsible leaders who looked after the interests of the Jewish community and did not give in to German pressure. Those who followed them—that is, those who assumed their posts after the original chairmen had been dismissed or killed—were, for the most part, German appointees. They were less sensitive to the needs of the people. In the final stages of mass extermination and relentless terror, these Judenrat chairmen almost always carried out Nazi orders.

In their search for ways to prevent, slow down, or reduce the onslaught upon their communities, many Judenräte adopted a policy of "rescue by labor." They tried to convince the Nazis of the importance, for Germany, of the continued existence of the Jewish community, as a source of labor. As the war went on and the economy required additional manpower, authorities in charge of the production of military equipment and supplies wanted to use Jewish labor. This was not a rejection of the Nazis' **"FINAL SOLUTION"** policy to exterminate the Jews of Europe. It was simply a practical decision based on the prevailing conditions. But there were Judenräte that saw opportunities in such circumstances that could be exploited to save Jews. They were resigned to the hopelessness of trying to save the entire Jewish community, but they felt they might salvage a part of it by providing laborers who would be kept alive as long as they could work.

Resistance

Relations between the Judenrat and the resistance movements—the Jewish underground and fighters' organizations in the ghettos—were highly complex. They varied from place to place. Many Judenräte were opposed to the idea of armed resistance (*see* **RESISTANCE, JEWISH**) or of fleeing to the forests to join the

---

"The Community Council—the Judenrat, in the language of the Occupying Power—is an abomination in the eyes of the Warsaw Community.... It was not elected by the Community, but reached its position of power through appointment and with the support of the Nazi Authorities...."

From the diary of Chaim A. Kaplan, April 23, 1941

MORESHET ARCHIVES, D.2.138.

PARTISANS. Some members believed that resistance activities in the ghetto would endanger the entire community, in view of the rule of "collective responsibility" that the Nazis had introduced. This created tension in many ghettos where the Judenrat and the underground competed for influence. In some places, feelings ran high enough for violent clashes to erupt.

Some Judenräte supported the concept of resistance, but felt it should be used only when it was clear that the community was about to be liquidated. Others helped the resistance without reservations of any kind, and some even took a leading part in uprisings.

National and Local Function

As the war progressed, the Germans and their allies continued to establish Judenräte. In the areas of Eastern Europe where the Germans exercised direct control, the Judenräte were local institutions and, for the most part, had no contact with one another. Some of the Judenräte held authority in one location only, while others administered Jewish communities throughout a district or even an entire country. In some parts of Europe, the councils were set up as country-wide institutions, or were gradually given that responsibility. This affected the way they functioned, their relations with the Germans and the local governments, and their ties with the Jewish population.

Historical View

The role played by the Judenräte in Jewish public life during the Holocaust is one of the most controversial issues relating to the period. Some historians believe that the institution of the Judenrat weakened the inner strength of the Jewish communities. Others think that the Judenräte reinforced the Jews' power of endurance in their struggle for survival. Scholarship has been divided. At one time there was strong, indiscriminate condemnation of the Judenräte. Closer analysis of the various elements that made up the councils' activities has resulted in more examination of the different phases of Nazi policy on the "Final Solution," changes that took place in the composition of the Judenräte, and the effect of these changes on the conduct of Judenrat members. New efforts have been made to understand how the Judenrat used its limited authority—given to it by the Germans with the sole aim of enabling it to carry out German orders—for the good of the Jewish population; how it acted during the mass deportations; how Judenrat members viewed resistance and rescue efforts; and other issues. An objective assessment of all these elements permits a more realistic and accurate historical evaluation of the Judenrat.

SUGGESTED RESOURCES

"Judenrat." *The Jewish Student Online Research Center.* [Online] http://us-israel.org/jsource/Holocaust/judenrat.html (accessed on August 22, 2000).

Trunk, Isaiah. *Judenrat: The Jewish Councils in Eastern Europe Under Nazi Occupation.* New York: Macmillan, 1972. Reprint, Lincoln: University of Nebraska Press, 1996.

JÜDISCHER CENTRALVEREIN. SEE CENTRAL UNION OF GERMAN CITIZENS OF JEWISH FAITH (CENTRALVEREIN DEUTSCHER STAATSBÜRGER JÜDISCHEN GLAUBENS).

Kaltenbrunner, Ernst

(1903–1946)

Ernst Kaltenbrunner was a Nazi politician who was born in Ried im Innkreis (Upper Austria) and attended school in Linz. After studying chemistry and law in Prague and elsewhere, he practiced as a lawyer. He joined the National Socialist party and the **SS** in 1932. In 1934 and 1935, Kaltenbrunner was imprisoned in **AUSTRIA** on a charge of high treason. Upon his release, he headed the SS in that country from 1935 until 1938.

After the *Anschluss* (the forcible annexation of Austria to **GERMANY**), Kaltenbrunner, now a major general, was promoted to the post of under-secretary of state for public security in the Ostmark, as Austria was renamed by the Nazis, and he remained there until 1941. During the same period, Kaltenbrunner was a member of the ReichstagGerman parliament of elected representatives. Together with District Leader Josef Bürckel, Kaltenbrunner was responsible for the **CENTRAL OFFICE FOR JEWISH EMIGRATION** (*Zentralstelle Für Jüdische Auswanderung*) in Vienna, headed by Adolf **EICHMANN**. By the time Eichmann was transferred to Prague in April 1939, 150,000 Jews had emigrated from Austria. After Reinhard **HEYDRICH'S** was mortally wounded in an assassination attempt on May 27, 1942, Kaltenbrunner was appointed head of the **REICH SECURITY MAIN OFFICE** (RSHA). Heydrich died on June 4. Kaltenbrunner was formally named his successor as chief of the Security Police (*Sicherheitspolizei*) and the **SD** (*Sicherheitsdienst*; Security Service) on January 30, 1943.

With Heinrich **HIMMLER**, Kaltenbrunner was one of the main initiators of **AKTION (OPERATION) REINHARD** and assumed much of the responsibility for the implementation of the **"FINAL SOLUTION"** from 1942 to 1945, although few documents from that time period record his activities in this connection. The same is true for his participation in the **EUTHANASIA PROGRAM**. This may be partly attributed to Himmler's growing tendency to reserve the credit for himself. Evidence exists, however, of Kaltenbrunner's role as instigator of the deportation from **THERESIENSTADT** in 1943 of Jews unfit for work, and of Bulgarian Jews.

Kaltenbrunner ensured that many of his department heads appeared to be more important than they actually were in the power structure of the RSHA. His personal assistant was an SS officer who in 1941 had been responsible for the murder of at least 60,000 Jewish men, women, and children in Lithuania. Kaltenbrunner allowed others to assume credit for actions that he could later disavow knowledge of, apparently because he believed that, in contrast to many of his subordinates, he had a very real chance to survive after the end of the war. Even at his trial, Kaltenbrunner attempted to play the part of someone who simply followed orders and "had absolutely no idea." Nevertheless, on October 9, 1946, the International Military Tribunal sentenced him to death by hanging. The sentence was carried out on October 16.

The so-called Kaltenbrunner reports are a collection of reports on the interrogations conducted by the **GESTAPO** after the attempt on Hitler's life of July 20, 1944. They were drawn up for Martin **BORMANN**, on Kaltenbrunner's orders, by an improvised RSHA unit headed by SS-*Obersturmbannführer* lieutenant colonel Walter von Kielpinski. According to historians, the reports were the result of "thousands of investigations" carried out by some 400 RSHA officials operating in eleven groups that took part in suppressing the attempted coup.

Bodies of Jews massacred at Kamenets-Podolski.

SUGGESTED RESOURCES

Conot, Robert E. *Justice at Nuremberg.* New York: Harper & Row, 1983.

Sprecher, Drexel A. *Inside the Nuremberg Trial: A Prosecutor's Comprehensive Account.* Lanham, MD: University Press of America, 1999.

Taylor, Telford. *The Anatomy of the Nuremberg Trials: A Personal Memoir.* New York: Knopf, 1992.

Kamenets-Podolski

Kamenets-Podolski is a city in Ukraine where mass killings of Jews, mostly from **HUNGARY**, took place in August 1941. Shortly after Hungary declared war on the **SOVIET UNION**, on June 27, 1941, a plan was devised by Ödön Martinides and Árkád Kiss. They were two leading officers of the National Central Alien Control Office (*Külföldieket Ellenőrző Országos Kozponti Hatosag*; KEOKH), the agency with jurisdiction over foreign nationals living in Hungary, to "resettle" the Polish and Russian Jews in the Hungarian-administered part of "liberated" Galicia. Under Decree No. 192-1941, adopted on July 12, and a subsequent secret directive of the KEOKH, a drive was begun to deport "the recently infiltrated Polish and Russian Jews in the largest possible number and as quickly as possible." Among the "alien" Jews rounded up that month were also a considerable number of Hungarian Jews who could not prove their citizenship simply because their papers were not immediately available. Other Hungarian Jews were caught up in the turmoil. In the Transcarpathian Ukraine, an area inhabited by Orthodox and Hasidic Jews, many Jewish communities were uprooted in their entirety. Since the Jews were rounded up hastily, usually in the dark of night, very few of them could take along adequate provisions.

The "alien" Jews were packed into freight cars and taken to Kőrösmező, near the Polish border. From there, they were transferred across the border at the rate of about 1,000 a day. By August 10, approximately 14,000 Jews had been handed over to the **SS**. An additional 4,000 were transferred by the end of the month, when the operation was completed. From Körösmezö the Jews were first taken to Kolomyia, and then marched in columns of 300 to 400 to Kamenets-Podolski. Their fate was decided on August 25 at a conference held at the Vinnitsa headquarters of the *General-quartiermeister-OKH*, where SS-*Obergruppenführer* (lieutenant general) Friedrich **Jeckeln** assured the conference attendees that he would complete the liquidation of the Jews by September 1, 1941. The *Aktion* (Operation) took place on August 27 and 28 near the city and claimed (according to Jeckeln's Operational Report USSR No. 80) 23,600 Jewish lives. This was the first five-figure massacre in the Nazis' **"Final Solution"** program. Of these, 14,000 to 18,000 Jews were from Hungary. The remainder were local.

SUGGESTED RESOURCES

Gitelman, Zvi, ed. *Bitter Legacy: Confronting the Holocaust in the USSR.* Bloomington: Indiana University Press, 1997.

"Jews in the Soviet Union." *The Jewish Student Online Research Center.* [Online] http://us-israel.org/jsource/Holocaust/sutoc.html (accessed on August 21, 2000).

Kaplan, Josef

(1913–1942)

Josef Kaplan was a leader of the **Warsaw** Jewish underground and a founder of **Jewish Fighting Organization** (the Żydowska Organizacja Bojowa; ŻOB). He was born in Kalisz, a city in western Poland, into a poor family and a strict religious atmosphere. Early in his youth he was drawn to secular education and culture. He joined the Ha-Shomer ha-Tsa'ir Zionist youth movement in the town, attracted by the political zeal of its members and their vision of a homeland for Jews in Palestine. As an adult, in the late 1930s, he was one of the leaders of the Zionist movement in Poland. During the first few days of World War II, in September 1939, Kaplan joined the flood of refugees to the east, and took charge of the illegal border-crossing point at Lida on the Polish-Lithuanian border. Early in 1940 Kaplan returned to Nazi-occupied Poland to take charge of the underground movement, Ha-Shomer ha-Tsa'ir. From then on, Kaplan devoted all his time to the underground. He consolidated the movement's structure in the various ghettos and ensured the continuation of agricultural training even on a clandestine basis; he published and distributed underground newspapers, and was his movement's representative in the overall Jewish underground organizations and institutions.

In the spring of 1942, Kaplan organized a group of Jews to fight against the Nazis. He took part in the activities of the Antifascist Bloc in Warsaw and, in July of that year, in establishing the ŻOB in Warsaw. On September 3, 1942, during the mass deportation of Jews from Warsaw, the Nazis caught Kaplan in the act of preparing forged documents for a group of fighters who were about to join the partisans, and he was killed.

Kaplan kept a diary, but it was not preserved. **Irena Adamowicz**, who knew him well, described him in the following terms: "The activist who had been likable but quite average turned into a great man, very strong … and very calm. He was an excellent organizer and an ideal underground operator, painstaking and resourceful in all humdrum day-to-day affairs, and with a clear and inspiring approach to matters of principle, of life and death."

Josef Kaplan.

Irena Adamowicz
A Polish woman who served as a liaison officer coordinating efforts among various ghetto underground movements.

SUGGESTED RESOURCES

Roland, Charles G. *Courage Under Siege: Starvation, Disease, and Death in the Warsaw Ghetto.* New York: Oxford University Press, 1992.

Stewart, Gail. *Life in the Warsaw Ghetto.* San Diego: Lucent Books, 1995.

A Teacher's Guide to the Holocaust: Resisters. [Online] http://fcit.coedu.usf.edu/holocaust/people/resister.htm (accessed on August 21, 2000).

Kapo

Kapo, from the Italian word *capo*, meaning "chief" or "boss," was the term used in the Nazi **CONCENTRATION CAMPS** for an inmate appointed to head a work gang *(Kommando)* made up of other prisoners. The term "Kapo" is sometimes also used to refer to any prisoner who was given an assignment and collaborated with the Nazis, and, beyond that, for any Nazi **collaborator**. In the German-occupied countries and in the camps, however, only the bosses of prisoner work gangs were referred to as Kapos. At the workplaces, the work gangs were split up into smaller groups, each headed by a foreman *(Vorarbeiter)* responsible to the Kapo.

Generally, Kapos were not skilled workers. Their job was to escort the prisoners to their place of work and make sure that they did their tasks properly. But work as such was generally not the major objective in the camps. The real purpose was to break the prisoners in mind and spirit. Kapos, therefore, were an instrument by which a regime of humiliation and sheer physical cruelty was imposed upon the prison population.

collaborator
A person who assisted the enemy authorities, i.e., the Nazis.

Striped prisoner's jacket that originally belonged to a German Kapo (trustee).

Many Kapos mistreated prisoners in a criminal fashion and were put on trial after the war. In numerous other instances, however, the Kapos just pretended to be strict with the prisoners and tried to handle them as humanely as possible, under the circumstances. But at all times a deep gulf divided the ordinary camp inmates from the Kapos and other supervisors. The Kapos' clothing was relatively warm, they had enough to eat, and they had their own reserved section in the prison barracks (the "block"). These privileges were unthinkable for the regular prisoners, and the differences in living conditions naturally affected the relationship between the groups.

SUGGESTED RESOURCES

Kapo [videorecording]. Jerusalem: Set Productions, 1999.

Tisma, Aleksandar. *Kapo.* New York: Harcourt Brace, 1993.

The Trial of Adolf Eichmann [videorecording]. PBS Home Video, 1997.

Kasztner, Rezső

(1906–1957)

Hungarian journalist and lawyer Rezső (Rudolf or Israel) Kasztner was a Labor Zionist activist, first in his hometown of Cluj and then, after the annexation of Transylvania by **HUNGARY** in 1940, in Budapest. In early 1943 he became the vice chairman of the Relief and Rescue Committee of Budapest of the Zionist movement.

The committee tried to warn others about what was happening to Jews in Poland and elsewhere. Jews in Hungary did not feel threatened, however, in spite of the accounts of Polish Jewish refugees arriving in Hungary after 1942. Despite internal dissension, the committee tried to prepare for the inevitable German occupation, even attempting to organize armed resistance. There was little interest in resistance on the part of the Hungarian Jewish community. Perhaps this was due to growing anti-Jewish hostility on the part of the general population, or it may have been related to the fact that most young Jewish men were compelled to serve in the labor service system under Hungarian army control (*see* **HUNGARIAN LABOR SERVICE SYSTEM**). Whatever their reasons, many in the Jewish community felt that resistance was not in the best interests of Jews as a whole, and they generally ignored Kasztner's warnings.

The Germans occupied Hungary in March 1944. Kasztner believed that the only way to save Hungarian Jews was to negotiate with the Germans. Consequently, money was paid to the **SS** for the release of large numbers of Jews in return for trucks and other materials (the operation was called "Blood for Goods"). At the end of June 1944, a train with 1,684 Jews left Hungary, ostensibly for Spain or Switzerland; it was, however, directed to the **BERGEN-BELSEN** camp, where these Jews were interned. On the train were Kasztner's family and friends from Cluj, along with representatives from all political and religious factions, and wealthy people who had paid to be included. Kasztner's idea was that this exodus would serve as a precedent for undoing the murder program, and that more trains would follow. However, none did.

In July 1944 SS officer Kurt Becher received Heinrich **HIMMLER**'s permission to negotiate with Kasztner. The first meeting, on August 21, 1944, led to Himmler's order to refrain from deporting the Jews of Budapest, and 318 Jews in Bergen-Belsen from the "Kasztner train" were released to Switzerland. In December of that year the remainder of the Bergen-Belsen internees were also sent to safety. Himm-

ler's willingness to make these lifesaving gestures was likely related to the impending German defeat. Perhaps Himmler and the German negotiators hoped that these gestures of decency might place them in a more favorable position with the Allied victors. After the war, Kasztner was called to Nuremberg (*see* TRIALS OF THE WAR CRIMINALS) to help prosecute Nazi criminals. His written testimony in favor of Becher undoubtedly helped to save the latter from a closer investigation.

In 1954, Kasztner filed a lawsuit against one Malkiel Grünwald, who had accused him of being a traitor and causing the deaths of many Jews. The trial, in Israel, became instead a trial of Kasztner himself. The judge accused Kasztner of having "sold his soul to the devil." This referred to the negotiations with the Nazis, and to the trainload of Jews he arranged to have sent to safety, which was seen as an avenue of rescue for Kasztner's relatives and friends. He was also accused of not warning Hungarian Jews of impending disaster and of covering up for the Nazis after the war. The Israeli Supreme Court was debating Kasztner's appeal when he was murdered by nationalist extremists. In a final verdict, the court posthumously exonerated Kasztner from all accusations except the charge that he had helped Nazis to escape from justice.

In retrospect, it seems evident that Kasztner's attempt to save Jews through negotiation was the only avenue of action available to him, and that by putting his own family members on that train in 1944 he likely persuaded many others to board it. In any case, he saw this as a breakthrough for future rescues.

Perhaps the most unfounded charge against him was that Kasztner did not warn Hungarian Jewry. Kasztner was not a well-known Jewish leader, and he had no authoritative position through which to warn anyone. In Cluj, where he was known, even important local citizens failed to convince most of the Jews that danger was near.

SUGGESTED RESOURCES

Hecht, Ben. *Perfidy.* New York: Messner, 1961. Reprint, New London, NH: Milah Press, 1997.

Rezső Kasztner Memorial. [Online] http://www.kastnermemorial.com/ (accessed on August 21, 2000).

KAUNAS. SEE KOVNO.

Kharkov

Kharkov was the second-largest city in the Ukrainian SSR (now the independent state of UKRAINE) at the beginning of World War II. According to the 1939 census, the city had a Jewish population of 130,200, one-sixth of the total number of Kharkov citzens. In the summer of 1941, when the Germans were approaching the city, many of its inhabitants fled, including the majority of the Jewish population. After Kharkov was captured by the Germans on October 23, 1941, it became the headquarters of the German Sixth Army. It remained under a military government throughout the German occupation and did not become part of *Reichskommissariat* Ukraine.

The military government issued all decrees concerning the city, including those affecting the Jews. On November 3, 1941, the military government announced that, of the meager food rations that would be available, Jews would receive only 40 percent. The daily bread ration was set at 150 grams (5.25 oz), but

Jews received only 60 grams (2 oz). Hostages were taken daily, and most were Jews. They were either shot or hanged. On November 26, **SPECIAL COMMANDO** (*Sonderkommando*) 4a arrived in Kharkov, headed by Paul **BLOBEL**. This meant the murder of more Jews. They were seized in groups from streets and houses and taken to the Hotel International. There they were tortured, and then murdered, mostly in gas vans. (*See* GAS CHAMBERS/VANS.)

On December 14, 1941, the military governor of Kharkov ordered the city's Jews to assemble on the site of a nearby tractor plant by December 16. The plant was situated 7.5 miles (12 km) from Kharkov, and the Soviets had removed all its equipment before their retreat. In order to terrorize the Jews, Special Commando 4a murdered 305 Jews, on the pretext that they had been spreading false rumors. The sheds in which the prisoners were housed had no doors, windows, or heating facilities, and the winter of 1941–42 was severe. Many died from cold, disease, and hunger.

Only three weeks after the establishment of this ghetto, the liquidation of the Jews of Kharkov was set in motion. On the first day, "volunteers" were called for work in Poltava and Lubny, located west of Kharkov. The 800 men who reported for the trip were taken by truck to a nearby site, the Drobitski Ravine, where they were murdered in pits that had been prepared in advance. In the following days more Jews were taken to the same site, by truck or on foot, and murdered. Gas vans were also used for killings. The mass slaughter was carried out by men of Special Commando 4a, assisted by members of German Police Battalion 314 and *Waffen*-SS soldiers, who were probably from **SS DEATH'S-HEAD UNITS** (*Totenkopfverbände*).

Following the war, a special committee investigated Nazi crimes in Kharkov and opened the burial pits in the Drobitski Ravine. The committee issued a report that stated that 15,000 people had been murdered there. However, according to evidence given at the trial of the officers and men of Special Commando 4a by the intelligence officer of the German Sixth Army (to which the Special Commando had been attached), the actual number of victims, as he had heard it from Blobel himself, was 21,685. This figure includes all the Jews killed from the beginning of the German occupation until early January 1942, when the liquidation of the Jews of Kharkov was completed.

The city was liberated on February 16, 1943, reconquered by the Germans, and liberated again on August 23. A few Jews survived, because they had gone into hiding with the help of local inhabitants.

SUGGESTED RESOURCES

Glantz, David M. *Kharkov 1942: Anatomy of a Military Disaster.* Rockville Centre, NY: Sarpedon, 1998.

Restayn, Jean. *The Battle for Kharkov, Winter 1942/1943.* Manitoba: J. J. Fedorowicz, 2000.

Kherson

Kherson is the capital of the district by the same name in **UKRAINE**, which was formerly a republic of the **SOVIET UNION**. Jews lived in Kherson from its founding in the eighteenth century. On the eve of World War II there were more than 15,000 Jews in a city population of 167,108.

Prisoners were not permitted to have water or food. They had to bribe the guards for these things. They were forbidden to leave the sheds at night, though there were no sanitary facilities inside.

By the time Kherson was captured by the Germans on August 19, 1941, two-thirds of its Jewish population had been evacuated or had fled the city on their own. In the first few days of the occupation, the Jews were ordered to form a "Jewish committee," a **JUDENRAT**, which was to register all the Jews between August 24 to 27. On August 25, the Jews were ordered to wear a Jewish star (*see* **BADGE, JEWISH**) on their chests; they were also forced to hand over to the German administration all of their money and valuables. When the registration was completed, the Jews were all concentrated in a ghetto, the only region of the city where Jews were permitted to live. Between September 16 and 30, 1941, the 5,000 Jews left in the city of Kherson were taken to a ditch outside the city and murdered.

The Kherson district contained the self-governing Jewish subdistricts of Kalinindorf, Stalindorf, and Nay Zlatopol. There were Jewish collective farms in these subdistricts. The farms were what remained of the Jewish agricultural settlements that had been established there in the second half of the nineteenth century. On the eve of World War II, these three subdistricts had a Jewish population of 35,000, most of whom were farmers.

The fate of the Jews living in the collective farms can be deduced from the course of events in the Stalindorf subdistrict. In the second half of September 1941, groups of Jewish men were murdered by Nazis on several collective farms. Heavy fines were imposed on the Jews. They were robbed of their belongings, and the community property of the collective farms was confiscated. Early in the spring of 1942 the Jewish farmers were told to sow potatoes and grow vegetables for the German administration. In April, many Jewish men were drafted and put into eight labor camps, to work on the construction of the Dnepropetrovsk-Zaporozhye highway. The old men, women, and children left behind in the collective farms were rounded up and killed on May 29. On December 5, 1942, all the men were put into the Lyubimovka camp, where they were murdered or died as a result of hard labor and disease.

The Kherson region was liberated in mid-March 1944. Surviving Jewish farmers who returned, expecting to rehabilitate their farms, found them occupied by Russians and Ukrainians. Jews appealed unsuccessfully to the authorities in Kiev to restore the Jewish subdistricts. When the war ended they were officially abolished.

SUGGESTED RESOURCES

Gitelman, Zvi, ed. *Bitter Legacy: Confronting the Holocaust in the USSR.* Bloomington: Indiana University Press, 1997.

Kielce

Kielce is the district capital in southeast **POLAND**, situated north of **KRAKÓW** and south of Radom. The Jewish community of Kielce was established in 1868, but only at the turn of the century did many Jews begin moving there from the neighboring townships. By 1921 the Jews in the city numbered 15,550, about one-third of the total population. According to the 1931 census, the number of Jews in Kielce was 18,083. By 1939 the Jewish population was estimated at 24,000.

The city was captured by the Germans on September 4, 1939, a few days after the outbreak of World War II, and anti-Jewish atrocities began immediately: seizure of property and possessions, heavy fines, forced labor, the taking of

Jüdische Soziale Selbsthilfe
K I E L C E
Żydowska Samopomoc Społeczna

Dział dożyw. dzieci.

Leg. Nr

upoważnia do korzystania
z kuchni Ż. S. S.

Ś N I A D A N I A

Nazwisko i imię
*1600 śniadań
dziennie*

Adres

Miesiąc maj 1941 r.

| 31 | 30 | 29 |

Child's identification card for breakfast rations from a soup kitchen in the Kielce ghetto, run by the Judenrat (Jewish Council); May, 1941, Kielce, Poland.

hostages, beatings, and killings. The first head of the **JUDENRAT** (Jewish Council) in Kielce, Dr. Moses Pelc, was soon sent to **AUSCHWITZ**. He was replaced by the industrialist Hermann Levy, who served the Germans until the liquidation of the ghetto. Levy was murdered by the **SS** in September 1942.

The Kielce ghetto was established early in April 1941 in accordance with an official order issued by Hans Drechsel, the German civilian administrator of the city. By the end of 1941 there were 27,000 Jews in the Kielce ghetto, including 1,000 deportees from Vienna who were brought to Kielce, and several thousand who were brought from neighboring small towns and more distant areas around Poznań and **ŁÓDŹ**. The able-bodied males were used by the Germans as laborers in the local stone quarries. Others worked in the ghetto as tailors, shoe-makers, and carpenters, and at other trades. Between April 1941 and August 1942, when the ghetto was liquidated some 6,000 Jews died of hunger, cold, and typhus within the ghetto confines.

In January 1942 seven Jews were shot for trying to leave the ghetto. Several other executions had taken place in the preceding summer, especially of activists and community leaders. Under the command of two SS officers, Ernst Karl Thomas and Hans Geier, the liquidation of the ghetto began on August 20. The violent removal of Jews lasted until August 24, when all the Jews, with the exception of 2,000 who were young and healthy, were loaded on freight trains and sent to **TRE-**

BLINKA. The sick Jews and the children of the Jewish orphanage had been killed by the Germans before the deportation. Some 500 Jews managed to escape.

The remaining 2,000 Jews of Kielce were placed in three labor camps in Kielce: Hasag-Granat (quarries, workshops, and munitions), Henryków (carpentry), and Ludwików (foundry). A projected revolt was aborted by an informer. In August 1944 the surviving inmates were sent to **BUCHENWALD** or Auschwitz. The last surviving group, consisting of 45 Jewish children, was taken to the Jewish cemetery and killed there by the Germans.

When the Soviet army captured Kielce on January 16, 1945, only two Jews remained of what had once been a 20,000-strong community. However, during the 18 months that followed, about 150 Jews—former residents who had survived the camps or were hiding in the forests, along with Jews who had never lived in Kielce—gradually gathered in the former Jewish community building at No. 7 Planty Avenue. Most of them lived on funds sent by the **JOINT DISTRIBUTION COMMITTEE**, forming a **kibbutz** and waiting for an opportunity to go to Palestine.

The hatred of the Poles toward the Jews was so intense that whenever a former Jewish resident appeared in town he was greeted with the words: "What? You are still alive? We thought that Hitler killed all of you." Rumors spread that masses of Jews would soon return to reclaim their former houses and belongings. The incitement culminated at the end of June 1946 when a woman ran through the streets shouting that the Jews on Planty Avenue were killing Polish children and drinking their blood. Another rumor was spread that a Polish boy had been killed in the basement of the community building and his blood used to make matzoth.

On July 1, 1946, mobs began gathering around the building. When the police were called in, all they did was confiscate the few licensed weapons that the Jews had. Appeals to the church dignitaries were dismissed with the excuse that they could not intercede for the Jews because the latter had brought communism into Poland. On July 4 the mob attacked and massacred 42 Jews and wounded about 50 more. The central Polish authorities in Warsaw sent in a military detachment and an investigation committee. Order was quickly restored, and seven of the main instigators and killers were executed. The missing Polish boy was soon found in a nearby village.

Thus, the thousand-year history of the Jews of Poland came to a disgraceful end with a medieval-style pogrom—a planned, violent, and organized attack. This event touched off a mass migration of hundreds of thousands of Jews from Poland and other countries of eastern and central Europe who had somehow survived World War II and the Holocaust.

In 1946 the tomb with the names of the 42 victims that had been erected in the Kielce Jewish cemetery was destroyed by the local Poles. It was rebuilt in 1987, and an iron fence placed the cemetery. The monument for the 45 children killed in 1944 was rebuilt as well.

kibbutz
Communal farm or settlement, often organized by Zionists seeking the creation of a Jewish homeland in Palestine.

SUGGESTED RESOURCES

Blumenfeld, Laura. "50 Years After the Lie; In Poland, a Ceremony of Peacemaking Finds Feelings Are Still Raw." *Washington Post,* July 15, 1996.

Perlez, Jane. "50 Years After Pogrom, City Shrinks at Memory." *New York Times,* July 6, 1996.

Jews being rounded up by the SS and taken to the Kistarcsa camp (after 1944).

KIEV. SEE BABI YAR.

Kistarcsa

Kistarcsa was a camp located 9 miles (5.6 km) northeast of **BUDAPEST, HUN-GARY**. Before the Germans occupied Hungary in 1944, Kistarcsa was an internment camp for political prisoners and other detainees. With the start of **DEPORTATIONS** from Hungary in the spring of 1944, Kistarcsa became a transit camp from which Jews in the Budapest area were sent elsewhere for extermination, primarily to **AUSCHWITZ**.

During the 1930s, the head of state of Hungary, Miklós **HORTHY**, had imprisoned political opponents (among them Jews) in Kistarcsa and several other camps. After World War II broke out in 1939, Jewish refugees who managed to obtain legitimate papers were also held there. The five buildings of the Kistarcsa camp, which were originally meant to house 200 prisoners, soon became overcrowded with 2,000 Jews.

When **GERMANY** occupied Hungary on March 19, 1944, the **SS** began rounding up Jews. They were first held in railway stations in various Budapest suburbs. From there, they were transferred to Kistarcsa. During the German occupation, the

SS took over the camp, but it was administered directly by the Hungarian police. By all accounts, the camp commandant, István Vasdenyei, was humane and did whatever he could to ease the plight of the Jews under his control. He cooperated with various Jewish relief organizations that cared for the inmates.

The first transport of 1,800 Jews left the camp for Auschwitz on April 29, 1944. Adolf **EICHMANN** sent eighteen more trainloads from Kistarcsa to Auschwitz before Horthy stopped the deportations on July 7 of that year. Furious at Horthy's intervention, Eichmann tried to send another train on July 15. Acting on information from Vasdenyei, Horthy turned back the transport before it reached the Hungarian border. On July 19, Eichmann sent Franz **NOWAK** and a special team of deportation experts to the camp. They sent 1,200 Jews to Auschwitz on what was the last deportation train from Kistarcsa. About 1,000 Jews stayed in the Kistarcsa camp until it was dismantled on September 27, 1944. Its remaining inmates were sent to various labor camps in Hungary.

SUGGESTED RESOURCES

Handler, Andrew, and Susan V. Meschel, eds. *Young People Speak: Surviving the Holocaust in Hungary.* New York: Franklin Watts, 1993.

KOCH, ILSE. SEE KOCH, KARL OTTO.

Koch, Karl Otto

(1897–1945)

Karl Otto Koch participated in the German military administration as a commandant of numerous concentration camps. Koch was born in Darmstadt, where he attended a commercial secondary school and became a bank clerk. Toward the end of World War I he was wounded and captured by the British, and was a prisoner of war until October 1919. In 1930 he became a member of the Nazi party and a year later joined the **SS**. He held senior command posts in the Sachsenburg, Esterwegen, and Lichtenburg (Prettin) concentration camps in 1934, and the following year was appointed commandant of the notorious Columbia Haus, a prison in **BERLIN**. In 1936 Koch was commandant of the Esterwegen and **SACHSENHAUSEN** concentration camps. In May 1937 he married Dresden-born Ilse Köhler (1906–1967). On August 1 of that year Koch was appointed commandant of the newly established **BUCHENWALD** camp. His wife was made an overseer in the same camp. Before long she became notorious for her extreme cruelty to the prisoners and for her nymphomania, which she vented on the SS guards in the camp.

In September 1941 Karl Otto Koch was appointed commandant of **MAJDANEK**, which was then a Soviet prisoner-of-war camp run by the Waffen-SS in **LUBLIN**. Under his tenure the camp was greatly enlarged, and civilian prisoners, including Jews, were brought in. Crematoria were constructed, and many more prisoners were killed. In July 1942, after a mass outbreak from the camp, Koch was suspended and put on trial before an SS and police court in Berlin, but was acquitted in February 1943. He then held administrative posts in postal-service security units, only to be arrested again in August of that year on charges of embezzlement, forgery, making threats to officials, and "other charges." The last apparently referred to murders for which he was responsible that went beyond existing orders, and to his hobby of

Karl Otto Koch, commandant of the Buchenwald concentration camp, with his wife Ilse and their son and dog.

collecting patches of tattooed human skin and shrunken human skulls. His wife was also arrested as an accomplice to her husband. It was she who selected the living prisoners whose skin she wanted, after they were killed, for her own collection and for use in making lampshades. In early 1945 Karl Otto Koch was sentenced by the Supreme Court of the SS in Munich, and in April of that year he was executed.

Ilse Koch was acquitted and went to Ludwigsburg to live with her two children and her husband's stepsister. She was arrested by the Americans on June 30, 1945, tried in 1947, and sentenced to life imprisonment. In 1949 she was released under a pardon granted by Gen. Lucius D. Clay, the military governor of the American zone in GERMANY. Under pressure arising out of hearings held by a U.S. Senate committee, she was immediately re-arrested upon her release, and in January 1951 was again sentenced to life imprisonment, by the State Court in Augsburg. In September 1967 she committed suicide in her prison cell.

SUGGESTED RESOURCES

Hackett, David A., ed. *The Buchenwald Report.* Boulder, CO: Westview Press, 1995.

Memory of the Camps [videorecording]. PBS Video, 1989.

A Teacher's Guide to the Holocaust: Perpetrators. [Online] http://fcit.coedu.usf.edu/holocaust/people/perps.htm (accessed on August 21, 2000).

Kolbe, Maximilian

(1894–1941)

Maximilian Kolbe was a Polish monk, philosopher, and priest, who, because of his work during the German occupation, was canonized a Catholic saint. Kolbe was born in Zduńska Wola, in the ŁÓDŹ district. His Christian name at birth was

Raymond and at the age of seventeen he entered the Franciscan order and became Friar Maximilian. In 1912 he went to Rome to study theology and philosophy. Kolbe founded the Order of the Knights of the Immaculata in 1917, and was ordained a priest the following year. He returned home to **POLAND** in 1919. In Poland, which by then had gained independence, Kolbe served as a priest. In 1927 he founded the City of the Immaculata (in Polish, Niepokalanow), a center near **WARSAW** that was to disseminate the Catholic faith in the spirit of the Virgin Mary; membership at the center grew to more than seven hundred followers.

In 1930, in spite of being afflicted with tuberculosis, Kolbe went to the Far East, along with several assistants, to establish a Catholic mission in Nagasaki, Japan. The new mission was modeled on the Niepokalanow Center in Poland. Kolbe named it Garden of the Immaculata. In 1936 Kolbe was summoned back to Poland, where he was appointed head of the Niepokalanow Center and its operations. His special interest was the center's publications network, which included a monthly, a youth magazine, and a popular daily newspaper. Kolbe was very active in spreading his religious views and his social ideas. Consequently, he gained a reputation for piety and devotion.

Early in the German occupation, Father Kolbe was arrested and removed from Niepokalanow, but by December 1939 he was allowed back to his "city," where he set up an institution for the care of refugees from Poznań and its environs and, it was reported, also extended help to Jewish refugees. In February 1941 Father Kolbe was again arrested and imprisoned. Three months later he was deported to **AUSCHWITZ**. According to eyewitness accounts by other prisoners, Father Kolbe remained true to his faith and sought to bring comfort to other victims. In July 1941, a prisoner from Kolbe's block succeeded in escaping from the camp. As punishment the **SS** decided to execute every tenth prisoner in the block. Standing in line next to Kolbe was a Polish man by the name of Gajowniczek, who was slated to be one of the victims. When the man cried out, "What will happen to my wife, to my children?" Kolbe stepped out of the line and declared that he wanted to take Gajowniczek's place. The Germans agreed, and Kolbe was moved to a starvation cell, where he was later put to death with a phenol injection.

In 1971 the Vatican proclaimed the beatification of Father Kolbe (a step below sainthood), and in October 1982 he was canonized as a saint of the Catholic church. Since 1971, and with even greater intensity after his canonization, a debate has raged in Poland, **AUSTRIA**, the United States, and Britain concerning Kolbe's true personality and work. Some claimed that while Kolbe was to be admired for what he did in his life and for his act of self-sacrifice, he had also been contaminated with antisemitic views, and the newspapers he published had an anti-Jewish slant.

An examination of these claims showed that the newspapers published under Kolbe's supervision, and especially the daily, which had had a wide circulation, did have a strong antisemitic flavor. While Kolbe had made attempts to restrain the daily's extreme antisemitism, his own letters and writings had an antisemitic tone. In addition, Kolbe had justified the exclusion of the Jews from the Polish economy. Kolbe's brand of antisemitism was not racist, and he preached that the Jews should convert. Some of his expressions against Jews, however, were quite extreme, and his writings contain references to the anti-Jewish **PROTOCOLS OF THE ELDERS OF ZION**.

Maximilian Kolbe in 1982.

SUGGESTED RESOURCES

Mohan, Claire Jordan. *St. Maximilian Kolbe: The Story of the Two Crowns.* Worcester, PA: Young Sparrow, 1999.

Stone, Elaine Murray. *Maximilian Kolbe: Saint of Auschwitz.* New York: Paulist Press, 1997.

Treece, Patricia. *A Man for Others: Maximilian Kolbe, Saint of Auschwitz, in the Words of Those Who Knew Him.* San Francisco: Harper and Row, 1982.

Kommissarbefehl (Commissar Order)

The *Kommissarbefehl* (Commissar Order) was the order issued by the German army that instructed all personnel involved in the attack on the **SOVIET UNION** to immediately kill all political commissars in the Red Army who fell into German hands. The guidelines that Adolf **HITLER** gave the *Wehrmacht* (Armed Forces) for the attack on the Soviet Union (Operation "Barbarossa") ordered leaders to plan the attack not only from its military aspects but from the ideological aspect as well. Thus, the attack was to include the physical destruction of political activists and those who promoted Communist ideals.

commissars
Communist officials assigned to military units; their function was to reinforce Communist Party principles and ensure loyalty.

On June 6, 1941, two weeks prior to the invasion of the Soviet Union, the *Oberkommando der Wehrmacht* (Armed Forces High Command) issued the *Kommissarbefehl.*

> It must be expected that the treatment of our prisoners by the political commissars of all types, who are the true pillars of resistance, will be cruel, inhuman, and dictated by hate.... Therefore, if captured during combat or while offering resistance they must on principle be shot immediately. This applies to commissars of every type and position, even if they are only suspected of resistance, sabotage, or instigation thereto.

> According to the Directive for the Conduct of the Troops in Russia, ... in their capacity as officials attached to enemy troops, political commissars ... will not be recognized as soldiers; the protection granted to prisoners of war ... will not apply to them. After having been segregated they are to be liquidated....

> Commissars seized in the rear area of the army group ... are to be handed over to the Einsatzgruppen [*see* **OPERATIONAL SQUADS** (Einsatzgruppen)] or Einsatzkommandos of the Sicherheitspolizei [Security Police].

The order was signed by Gen. Walter Warlimont and its issue was authorized by Gen. Wilhelm Keitel, the Armed Forces High Command chief of staff. It was based on the Order on Jurisdiction in the Operation "Barbarossa" Area of May 13, 1941, which gave the army and the **SS** wide powers and opened the door to the establishment of a regime of terror and tyranny in the Soviet territories occupied by the Germans.

The *Kommissarbefehl* and the order of May 13 were both in violation of international conventions on the treatment and rights of prisoners of war and civilians in occupied territories. With other orders of the same type, the regular combined German military forces became accomplices in the Nazi war crimes committed in the Soviet Union. A few days after the *Kommissarbefehl* was issued, Field Marshal Walther von Brauchitsch, chief of the Army High Command, issued guidelines giving every officer the authority to decide on the execution of commissars who had been made prisoners of war. Commissars were executed as soon as they were identified as such, whether on the front, when they were taken prisoner, or in prisoner-of-war camps. In the summer of 1941 Keitel ordered that all copies of the *Kommissar-*

befehl that had been distributed to the various army headquarters be destroyed, in an effort to remove evidence implicating the army in war crimes.

SUGGESTED RESOURCES

Bailey, Ronald H. *Prisoners of War.* Alexandria, VA: Time-Life Books, 1981.

"Guidelines for the Treatment of Political Commissars, the Kommissarbefehl (Commissar Order)." *Destruction of European Jewry Explanatory Timeline.* [Online] http://www.ess.uwe.ac.uk/genocide/destrtim.htm (accessed on August 21, 2000).

"June 6: Commissar Order." *Yad Vashem Online.* [Online] http://www.yad-vashem.org.il/holocaust/chronology/3941right.html (accessed on August 21, 2000).

Koppe, Wilhelm

(1896–1975)

Wilhelm Koppe was a senior **SS** commander in occupied **POLAND**. Born in Hildesheim, Koppe served in the German army in World War I. Following the war he was a merchant and shopkeeper.

In August 1930 Koppe became a member of the Nazi party, and in 1932 he joined the SS. The following year, he was elected to the Reichstag (Parliament). Rising rapidly in the SS, he was made a *Brigadeführer* (brigadier general) in August 1934 and a *Gruppenführer* (major general) in September 1936.

On October 26, 1939, Koppe was appointed Higher SS and Police Leader in the Warthegau (the Poznań region), a post he held until November 9, 1943. Koppe was one of the leading figures in the establishment of the **CHEŁMNO** extermination camp, where 320,000 people were killed. He was also instrumental in the liquidation of the ghettos in the Warthegau, as the western region of Poland was renamed after its annexation by **GERMANY**. In January 1942 he was promoted to Obergruppenführer (general), and in November 1943 he became the Higher SS and Police Leader in the **GENERALGOUVERNEMENT**.

After the war, Koppe lived in West Germany under the assumed name "Lohmann" and worked as a factory manager. His real identity was discovered in 1961, and he was arrested and brought to trial in West Germany. The proceedings against him were discontinued in 1966, and he was released on medical grounds.

SUGGESTED RESOURCES

Korbonski, Stefan. *The Polish Underground State: A Guide to the Underground, 1939–1945.* New York: Columbia University Press, 1978.

Wiesenthal, Simon. *Krystyna: The Tragedy of the Polish Resistance.* Riverside, CA: Ariadne Press, 1991.

Korczak, Janusz

(1878 or 1879–1942)

Janusz Korczak (pen name of Henryk Goldszmit) was a physician, writer, and educator. Korczak was born in **WARSAW**, **POLAND**, the son of an assimilated Jewish

Janusz Korczak, standing with pupils at the Rozyczka summer camp in 1938.

family. His father, a successful attorney, became mentally ill when Korczak was eleven, greatly affecting the family both emotionally and financially and influencing the direction of Korczak's life.

As a medical student at Warsaw University, Korczak associated with liberal educators and writers in Poland. When he entered into a medical practice, he did his best to help the poor and those who suffered the most; he also began to write. His first books, *Children of the Streets* (1901) and *A Child of the Salon* (1906), aroused great interest. In 1904 he was drafted into the Russian army as a doctor.

Korczak worked in a Jewish children's hospital and took groups of children to summer camps, and in 1908 he began to work with orphans. In 1912 he was appointed director of a Jewish orphanage in Warsaw. Throughout his life, an influential partner in his work was Stefania Wilczyńska, the daughter of a wealthy Jewish family who dedicated her life to the care of orphans.

Korczak wrote about the emotional life of children and advocated that children be respected. Children were to observed and listened as independent human beings, not as extensions of their parents. In Korczak's view, "to reform the world" meant "to reform the educational system."

In 1914 Korczak was called again for military service in the Russian army, and it was in military hospitals and bases that he wrote his important work *How to Love Children*. After the war he returned to Poland and to his work in the Jewish orphanage.

The 1920s were a period of intensive and fruitful work in Korczak's life. He was in charge of two orphanages, he served as an instructor at boarding schools and summer camps and as a lecturer at universities and seminaries, and he wrote prolifically. In the late 1920s, he fulfilled one of his dreams by establishing a newspaper written for and by children.

In the mid-1930s, Korczak's fortunes changed dramatically. Following the death of Polish dictator Józef Piłsudski, political power shifted to radical right-wing and openly antisemitic circles. Korczak was removed from many of his professional positions. As a result, he took a growing interest in the efforts of Zionists to establish a Jewish community in Palestine. He was particularly interested in the educational achievements of the kibbutz movement, which promoted cooperative work, learning, and living arrangements.

From the beginning of World War II, Korczak became active among the Jews and Jewish children. At first he refused to acknowledge the German occupying forces and refused to wear the yellow badge (*see* **BADGE, JEWISH**). As a consequence, he spent some time in jail. When the economic situation worsened and the Jews of Warsaw were imprisoned in the ghetto, Korczak concentrated his efforts on meeting children's basic needs for food and shelter in the orphanage. By now an elderly man, the only thing that gave him the strength to carry on was the duty he felt to preserve and protect his orphanage. Polish friends reported that they went to Korczak in the ghetto and offered him asylum on the Polish side, but he refused, not willing to save himself and abandon the children.

During the occupation and the period he spent in the ghetto, Korczak kept a diary. At the end of July 1942, when the deportations were at their height—about ten days before he, the orphans, and the staff of the orphanage were taken to the **TRANSFER POINT** (Umschlagplatz)—Korczak wrote the following entry: "I feel so soft and warm in the bed—it will be hard for me to get up…. But today is Sabbath—the day on which I weigh the children, before they have their breakfast. This, I think, is the first time that I am not eager to know the figures for the past week. They ought to gain weight (I have no idea why they were given raw carrots for supper last night)."

On August 5, the Germans rounded up Korczak and his two hundred children. A witness to the orphans' three-mile march to the deportation train described the scene to historian Emanuel **RINGELBLUM** as follows: "This was not a march to the railway cars, this was an organized, wordless protest against the murder…. The children marched in rows of four, with Korczak leading them, looking straight ahead, and holding a child's hand on each side…. A second column was led by Stefania Wilczyńska; the third by Broniatowska (her children bearing blue knapsacks on their backs), and the fourth by Sternfeld, from the boarding school on Twarda Street." Nothing is known of their last journey to **TREBLINKA**, where they were all put to death.

SUGGESTED RESOURCES

Bernheim, Mark. *Father of the Orphans: The Story of Janusz Korczak.* New York: Dutton, 1988.

Korczak, Janusz. *Ghetto Diary.* New York: Holocaust Library, 1978.

Lifton, Betty Jean. *The King of Children: A Biography of Janusz Korczak.* New York: Farrar, Straus and Giroux, 1988.

Korherr, Richard

(b. 1903)

Richard Korherr was a German writer and statistician. Born in Regensburg, Korherr succeeded academically and his early statistical publications earned him high praise. In 1928 he joined the staff of the Reich Bureau of Statistics, transferring in 1930 to the Bavarian Bureau of Statistics. Korherr's book *Geburtenrückgang* (Decline in the Birth Rate) was well received; Benito **MUSSOLINI** personally translated it into Italian, and it also appeared in a Japanese translation. The 1936 edition of the book had a foreword by Heinrich **HIMMLER**.

From 1935 to 1940 Korherr was director of the Würzburg municipal bureau of statistics and also lectured at the local university. As of 1934, he was also in charge of the section of statistics and demographic policy in the headquarters of Rudolf Hess, then the deputy Führer. In May 1937 Korherr joined the Nazi party. In 1937 and 1938 Korherr published *Untergang der alten Kulturvölker* (Decline of the Historical Civilized Peoples), and in 1938 an atlas, under the title *Volk und Raum* (People and Space).

On December 9, 1940, Korherr was appointed chief inspector of two statistical bureaus, both of which were in Himmler's domain. In December 1942 he began processing data for the **"FINAL SOLUTION"** of the "Jewish question" in Europe, a task in which he was assisted by a Dr. Simon, a Jew who was the statistician of the Reich Association of Jews in **GERMANY**. Korherr also used material supplied by Adolf **EICHMANN**'s section in the **REICH SECURITY MAIN OFFICE** (*Reichssicherheitshauptamt*; RSHA).

The result of this work was the *Korherr Report*, whose subject was the extermination of the Jews of Europe; in 1943 and 1944 he updated the report every three months. In his trial in Jerusalem, Eichmann stated that the *Korherr Report* had served him in the planning stages of the extermination effort, helping him determine how many Nazi forces would be needed to liquidate various concentrations of Jews, how many railway cars would be required, and which destinations to use for Jews from various areas.

After the war Korherr tried to diminish the importance of the report that bore his name, claiming that the statistical data were false, because they had been based on inflated figures given in the Einsatzgruppen (Operational Groups) reports. Korherr was given a post-war position with the West Germany Ministry of Finance, but he was dismissed following the publication, in 1961, of Gerald Reitlinger's book *The Final Solution*, in which the *Korherr Report* figured prominently.

SUGGESTED RESOURCES

Breitman, Richard. *The Architect of Genocide: Himmler and the Final Solution.* New York: Knopf, 1991.

Friedlander, Henry. *The Origins of Nazi Genocide: From Euthanasia to the Final Solution.* Chapel Hill: University of North Carolina Press, 1995.

Rice, Earle. *The Final Solution.* San Diego: Lucent Books, 1998.

Kovno

Kovno (Kaunas in Lithuanian) is a city in central **LITHUANIA**, situated at the convergence of the Neman and Neris rivers. The city was founded in 1030 by Koinas, a Lithuanian prince, and named after him. In 1795 Kovno was part of the Polish-Lithuanian territory that was annexed by Russia, and from 1842 it was a district capital. Between 1920 and 1939 Kovno was the capital of independent Lithuania. In 1940 all of Lithuania was incorporated into the **SOVIET UNION**; in 1991 Lithuania declared itself an independent state.

For the Jews of eastern Europe, Kovno was an important spiritual and cultural center. It was the site of the famous Slobodka **yeshiva**, and was also renowned for its extensive Zionist activities and for its Hebrew school system, ranging from kindergartens to teachers' training colleges.

> **yeshiva**
> An Orthodox Jewish seminary for rabbinical studies.

In 1939 approximately 40,000 Jews lived in Kovno, constituting nearly one-quarter of the city's total population. During the Soviet rule, from 1940 to the German invasion in 1941, the Hebrew educational institutions were closed down and most of the Jewish social and cultural organizations were liquidated. Of the city's five Yiddish dailies, only one remained in existence, and that had become an instrument of the Communist party. On June 14, 1941, a week before the German invasion, hundreds of Jewish families were rounded up and exiled to Siberia. Among them were factory owners, merchants, public figures, and Zionist activists and leaders.

Establishing the Ghetto

Kovno was occupied on June 24, 1941, the third day of the invasion. Several thousand Jews fled the city and headed for the interior of the Soviet Union, many losing their lives during their escape. Even before the German entry into the city, bands of Lithuanians had been taking violent action against the Jews. The murder of Jews continued when the Germans occupied the city and took charge of the killings. Thousands of Jews were moved from the city to other locations, such as the Seventh Fort (one of a chain of forts constructed around Kovno in the nineteenth century), where they were first brutally mistreated by the Lithuanian guards and then shot to death. A total of 10,000 Jews were estimated to have been murdered in June and July of 1941.

A civilian administration set up by the Germans, with SA–Brigadier General Hans Kramer as city commissar, issued a whole range of anti-Jewish decrees. The Jews were given one month to move into the ghetto that was being established. The assigned area consisted of two parts, the "small ghetto" and the "large ghetto," both situated in the Kovno suburb of Slobodka, on either side of the main thoroughfare. A barbed-wire fence, with posts manned by Lithuanian guards, was erected around the ghetto. The gates of the ghetto were watched by German police.

Forced Labor and Mass Murders

When the ghetto was sealed off in August 1941, it contained 29,760 Jews. In the following two and a half months, 3,000 Jews—men, women, and children—

In November 1942, 14-year-old Tamarah Lazerson described a part of daily life after electricity was no longer available in the Kovno ghetto: "My room is dark and unheated. At seven o'clock, and sometimes even earlier, I'm in bed. These are my worst hours. Memories overwhelm me and there's no way to shake them off."

Tamarah Lazerson, in *Children in the Holocaust and World War II: Their Secret Diaries,* Laurel Holliday, ed. New York: Pocket Books, 1995, pp. 128–29.

were killed. On October 28 the "big *Aktion*" (Operation) was staged, during which 9,000 persons (half of them children) were taken to the Ninth Fort and murdered. The killings were then discontinued and a prolonged period of relative calm set in, which lasted until March 1944. Of the 17,412 Jews now left in the ghetto, most of the adults were put on forced labor, mainly in military installations outside the ghetto. They were under constant pressure and harassment. Two thousand Jews, most of them skilled artisans, were organized into "brigades" for jobs related to the war effort. Another 4,600 Jews worked in the ghetto workshops, with no Germans or Lithuanians guards in attendance. Instead of wages, the Jews were given food rations, which in fact were on a starvation level. To stay alive, the ghetto inhabitants sold off their remaining possessions and used the proceeds to buy the food that was being smuggled into the ghetto at great risk.

The so-called quiet period offered some recovery time during which the Jews' basic care improved somewhat. There were still punitive measures, however. In February 1942 the Jews were ordered to hand in all their books, manuscripts and other printed materials. In August the synagogues were closed down and public prayer services were outlawed. The bureau of education and the schools were ordered closed, except for the vocational-training schools. Bans on bringing food into the ghetto and on possessing cash were strictly enforced. Hundreds of people were deported to **RIGA** or sent to work camps in various parts of Lithuania.

Internal Administration

Life inside the ghetto was administered by the Council of Elders of the Kovno Jewish Ghetto Community (*Ältestenrat der Jüdischen Ghetto Gemeinde Kauen*). It was chaired by Dr. Elchanan **ELKES**, a well-known physician and public personality, with Leib Garfunkel, a lawyer and veteran Zionist leader, acting as his deputy. Most of the members of the Kovno Ältestenrat were selected through direct elections by the Jewish community members. Forced labor and the maintenance of public order were the responsibility of the Jewish police, which had a complement of about 150 men. Appointments to the police and supervision of the force were in the hands of the Ältestenrat. A department of health, welfare, culture, and the like was maintained by the Ältestenrat. It provided various services to the ghetto population and managed public institutions such as a hospital and medical clinic, a home for the aged, a soup kitchen, a school, and an orchestra. There were concerts, lectures, literary evenings, and other cultural events. Even in the ghetto, Kovno Jews maintained their tradition of Torah study and of cultural and educational activities and mutual help, exceeding the opportunities sponsored by the Ältestenrat. Political parties were also active, initially by trying to locate their members and come to their aid. This led to the formation of Matsok (the Hebrew acronym for Zionist Center Vilijampole, Kovno), which was headed by several members of the Ältestenrat (Council of Elders) and its staff. They maintained contact with the anti-Nazi underground that existed in the ghetto. The Ältestenrat departments also provided considerable aid to the members of the underground who left the ghetto to join the **partisans** in the forests. In this, as well as in other social and communal aspects, the Kovno ghetto was an unusual phenomenon that has no parallel in the annals of the behavior of Jews under Nazi occupation.

From Ghetto to Concentration Camp

On orders of Heinrich **HIMMLER**, a concentration camp regime was instituted in the *Reichskommissariat* Ostland ghettos on June 21, 1943. In the autumn of 1943, the

partisans
Anti-Nazi paramilitary forces organized in secret to resist the occupation.

Kovno ghetto became a central concentration camp. Four thousand inhabitants of the ghetto were transferred to small camps, situated in Kovno's suburbs or its vicinity, in places such as Aleksotas, Šančiai, Palemonas, Kėdainiai (Keidan), and Kaišiadorys. On October 26, 1943, 2,800 Jews were moved to work camps in Estonia. An exceptionally cruel blow was dealt to the ghetto on March 27, 1944, when 1,800 persons—infants, children, and elderly men and women—were dragged out of their homes and murdered. Also executed were 40 officers of the Jewish police, killed for having given direct aid to the anti-Nazi underground in the ghetto. Among those put to death were Moshe Levin, the police chief, and his deputies Yehuda Zupovitz and Ika Grinberg. The remaining police became a **JEWISH GHETTO POLICE** (Jüdischer Ordnungsdienst) under the direct control of **SS** men. The Ältestenrat was abolished, and Dr. Elkes was appointed *Judenältester* (senior Jew), a position devoid of any real authority, although he retained his moral authority among the Jews.

Anti-Nazi Underground

Groups of young people belonging to the Zionist **YOUTH MOVEMENTS** resumed their activities, with the emphasis on the struggle against the Nazis. Encouragement to pursue these underground activities was given by Irena Adamowicz, a Polish woman who acted as a liaison for the underground movements in the **WARSAW** and **VILNA** ghettos and visited Kovno in July 1942. The Communists were also quite active in the anti-Nazi struggle, through the Antifascist Struggle Organization, which was headed by Chaim **YELIN**. Members of this organization sought to acquire weapons and also to establish contact with the Soviet partisans in the forests. In the summer of 1943 the Zionists and the Communists established a joint body, the General Jewish Fighting Organization (*Yidishe Algemeyne Kamfs Organizatsye*; JFO). Its purpose was to organize operational units and help them escape from the ghetto so that they could join the partisans. At its height, the JFO had about 600 members. Some were given military training, including instruction in the use of arms, by officers of the Jewish police. In September 1943 the JFO established a direct link with the partisan movement in Lithuania, thanks to the help of a Jewish woman parachutist, Gesja Glazer ("Albina"), who made a secret visit to the ghetto. This new connection enabled the JFO to send armed teams of members to the Augustów forests to set up partisan bases there. The cost of this venture was heavy, however. Out of 100 JFO members who took part, 10 were shot to death, 15 died in prison, and 14 were taken to the Ninth Fort.

At the end of 1943, 170 JFO members, split into 8 groups, left the ghetto in trucks they had secretly obtained from their Lithuanian drivers, and headed for partisan bases in the Rudninkai Forest. Most of them joined the Kovno battalions of the Lithuanian partisan movement. Altogether, some 350 Kovno Jews, most of them members of the JFO, left the ghetto in order to join the partisans. About 100 of them died en route or were killed in action.

Liquidation of the Ghetto

On July 8, 1944, as the Red Army was approaching Kovno, the German authorities began transferring the Jews to concentration camps inside **GERMANY**. Many Jews went into hiding in underground bunkers that they had prepared for just this purpose. The Germans used bloodhounds, smoke grenades, and firebombs to force the Jews out into the open. In the process, some 2,000 Jews died, by choking or burning, or as a result of the explosions. Only 90 were able to hold out in the bunkers and live to see the Red Army enter Kovno on August 1, 1944. About 4,000

Kovno Jews were taken to Germany, the majority going either to the Kaufering or the **STUTTHOF** concentration camps. In October 1944 they were joined by a number of Kovno Jews who had been held in camps in Estonia. When the camps were liberated, nearly 2,000 Kovno Jews had survived. Together with those who had held out in various hiding places in Kovno and the vicinity, they accounted for 8 percent of the 30,000 Jews who had made up the original population of the ghetto.

After the war, the survivors were joined by Kovno Jews who came back from the Soviet interior. By 1959, 4,792 Jews were living in Kovno, approximately 2 percent of the city's population. Many of Kovno's Jews emigrated to Israel.

SUGGESTED RESOURCES

Klein, Dennis B., ed. *Hidden History of the Kovno Ghetto.* Boston: Little, Brown, 1997.

Kovno Ghetto: A Buried History [videorecording]. History Channel, 1997.

Tory, Avraham. *Surviving the Holocaust: The Kovno Ghetto Diary.* Cambridge: Harvard University Press, 1989.

Kowalski, Władysław

(1895–1971)

Władysław Kowalski was a Pole who saved Jews during the Holocaust. Kowalski was a colonel in the Polish army but by the time of the German occupation, he had already retired. He was the **WARSAW** representative of the Dutch-based Philips company. Nazi **GERMANY**'s interest in the Dutch-owned company facilitated the mobility of its foreign representatives, affording Kowalski the freedom to travel around in all parts of Warsaw, including the closed-off Jewish ghetto. His first opportunity to help Jews took place in September 1940, outside the ghetto, on the "Aryan" side, when he encountered Bruno Borl, a ten-year-old boy who was wandering the streets of Warsaw, seeking food and shelter. Kowalski took the boy home, fed and cared for him, and provided him with a new identity complete with home with friends.

This led to a series of bolder undertakings. Two brothers named Rubin, a lawyer and a dentist, were helped to relocate after their hiding place was uncovered by an informer. Exploiting his freedom of movement, Kowalski smuggled seven Jews out of the Warsaw ghetto in February 1943 by bribing the Polish guards at the gates, and found safe havens for the Jews on the "Aryan" side. In November of that year he helped a family of four move from the Izbica area to a safer place with friends in Warsaw. He also offered refuge to twelve Jews in his Warsaw home. Roman Fisher, a construction worker whom Kowalski had rescued, built an underground shelter with material that Kowalski secretly brought with him inside large (and heavy) suitcases. From late 1940 until August 1944, Kowalski paid for the upkeep of those for whom he had arranged hiding places. The group hiding in his home manufactured toys that Kowalski sold in the market, thus helping to defray costs.

After the suppression of the **WARSAW POLISH UPRISING** in October 1944, and the forced evacuation of all the Warsaw residents by the Germans, Kowalski converted a basement in a ruined building into a bunker and hid there along with 49 Jews. Their daily ration consisted of three glasses of water, a small amount of sugar, and vitamin pills. They stayed hidden for 105 days and by the time they were liberated by the Russians in January 1945, they were reduced to eating fuel. More than 50 Jews were helped by Kowalski during the occupation period.

In 1947, Kowalski married one of the Jewish women he had rescued, and they emigrated to Israel in 1957. In 1963 he was recognized by Yad Vashem as one of the "**RIGHTEOUS AMONG THE NATIONS.**"

SUGGESTED RESOURCES

Bauminger, Arieh L. *The Righteous Among the Nations.* Tel Aviv: Am Oved, 1990.

A Teacher's Guide to the Holocaust: Rescuers. [Online] http://fcit.coedu.usf.edu/holocaust/people/rescuer.htm (accessed on August 21, 2000)

Kraków

Kraków is a city in southern **POLAND**, the country's third largest and one of the oldest. Kraków dates from the eighth century, and in the eleventh century it became the residence of the Polish princes. Between 1320 and 1596 it was the capital of the kingdom of Poland.

From the early fourteenth century, Kraków was one of the most important Jewish communities in Europe. In 1495 the Jews of the city were expelled to Kazimierz, a new town being built nearby that eventually became a sector of Kraków, and the history of the Jews in the two places became closely intertwined. In 1867 Jews were given the right of residing in every part of the city.

Beginning in the Middle Ages, Kraków was an outstanding center of Jewish learning and culture in Europe. During the Swedish invasion, from 1655 to 1657, the Kraków Jewish community experienced much suffering, but after the city was liberated the community gradually regained its strength. From 1815 to 1846 Kraków and its surroundings constituted a free republic, and the Jewish community prospered. Subsequently, in the period from 1846 to 1918, when the city was part of Austrian-ruled Galicia, the Jewish community grew and progressed further, with a thriving cultural and social life. In independent Poland, between 1918 and 1939, Jewish life flourished in Kraków more than ever, although in the years preceding the outbreak of World War II the Jewish community suffered from the increase of **ANTISEMITISM** in the country.

In 1540, Kraków had a Jewish population of 2,100. The numbers of Jews in the city continued to increase throughout the years. By 1939 the Jewish community had grown to 60,000, out of a total population of about a quarter of a million.

Nazi Occupation

Kraków was occupied by the German army on September 6, 1939, and the persecution of the Jews was launched immediately by one of the **OPERATIONAL SQUADS** (*Einsatzgruppen*) specially trained for these campaigns of violence. On October 26 the occupation authorities declared Kraków the capital of the **GENERALGOUVERNEMENT** (the territory in the interior of occupied Poland), and the persecution of the Jews was intensified. All future anti-Jewish decrees would be announced from this new center of the German occupation government.

A Jewish committee was organized in the early stage of the occupation, and on November 28 it was declared a **JUDENRAT** (Jewish Council). The chairman of the Judenrat was Dr. Marek Bieberstein, with Dr. Wilhelm Goldblatt as his deputy. In the summer of 1940 both men were imprisoned by the **GESTAPO**. Dr. Artur Rosen-

Entrance gate into the Krakow ghetto, c. 1940, Krakow, Poland.

zweig was appointed the Judenrat's new chairman. On December 5 and 6, the Germans conducted a sweeping terror operation in the Jewish quarters, mainly to raid Jewish property. Several synagogues were burned down on this occasion.

On May 1, 1940, a decree was issued placing the city's boulevards and major squares out of bounds to Jews. That same month the expulsion of Kraków Jews to neighboring towns was launched. By March 1941, 40,000 Jews had been expelled and no more than 11,000 were left in the city. While the expulsions were taking place, the victims were robbed of all their property.

The Ghetto

On March 3, 1941, the Kraków district governor, Otto Wachter, published a decree on the establishment of the ghetto. It was located in Podgorze, a section in the southern part of the city. The ghetto was sealed off on March 20, within a wall and a barbed-wire fence. It covered an area of no more than 656 by 437 yards (600 by 400 meters). In addition to the Kraków Jews, several thousand Jews from neighboring communities were also packed into the ghetto, mainly from Skawina, Wieliczka, and Rabka. In late 1941, 18,000 Jews were imprisoned in the ghetto. The worst problems were the overcrowding (four to five persons to a room) and the poor sanitary conditions.

Several organizations within the ghetto tried to alleviate the suffering of the Jews. Among them were the Jewish Social Self-Help Society, later called the Jewish Aid Agency, and the Federation of Associations for the Care of Orphans, or CENTOS.

Jews selling their possessions, Krakow ghetto, 1940.

On March 19, 1942, the Germans launched what they called an *Intelligenz Aktion*, a terror operation directed at the political and civic leaders in the ghetto. Some 50 prominent Jews were seized in this operation and were taken to **AUSCHWITZ**, where they were killed.

Deportations

On May 28 the ghetto was tightly sealed off and the Germans began deporting Jews to the **BEŁŻEC** extermination camp. Taking part were special detachments of the Gestapo, the *Schutzpolizei* (regular uniformed police), and a *Waffen*-SS unit stationed at Dębica. The *Aktion* continued until June 8, and when it ended 6,000 Jews had been transported to Bełżec, while 300 had been shot to death on the spot. Among the victims were poet Mordecai Gebirtig and Judenrat chairman Artur Rosenzweig, who had refused to carry out the Germans' orders. The Judenrat was

liquidated, and the Germans replaced it with a *Kommissariat*, another form of administrative unit.

Following this *Aktion* the ghetto area was reduced by half, although it still had a population of 12,000. In mid-October 1942 the Jewish *Kommissariat* was ordered to compile a list of 4,000 ghetto inmates for yet another deportation. When the order was ignored, the Germans launched a second *Aktion*, on October 27 and 28, using their usual terror tactics to round up 7,000 Jews for deportation. In addition, they shot 600 Jews on the spot. Most of the deportees were sent to Bełżec, and the rest to Auschwitz. In the course of this *Aktion* the sick, the elderly, and the orphaned children were liquidated. When the *Aktion* was over the ghetto area was further reduced, and what remained was divided in two. The first part, known as "A," contained the Jews who were working, and the second, "B," the rest of the ghetto prisoners.

On March 13, 1943, the residents of part "A," 2,000 in number, were transferred to the **PŁASZÓW** camp. The following day, March 14, an *Aktion* took place in which part "B" was liquidated. Some 2,300 Jews were taken to the Auschwitz-Birkenau extermination camp and killed there in the gas chambers (*see* **GAS CHAMBERS/ VANS**), and 700 Jews were killed on the spot. Of the Jews who were transferred to Płaszów, only a few hundred survived.

The Resistance Movement

From the start, there were underground resistance organizations operating in the Kraków ghetto. Among the most prominent were the *Akiva* and *Ha-Shomer ha-Tsa'ir* Zionist **YOUTH MOVEMENTS**. In the initial stage the underground operations concentrated on education and mutual help. The Jewish underground also published a newspaper, *He-Haluts ha-Lohem* (The Fighting Pioneer). In October 1942 the **JEWISH FIGHTING ORGANIZATION** (*Żydowska Organizacja Bojowa; ŻOB*), a united underground organization independent of the Warsaw ŻOB, was formed. Its goal was to conduct an armed struggle against the Nazi occupiers.

Heading the organization were Zvi Bauminger, Aharon **LIEBESKIND**, Gola Mira, Shimshon Draenger, and Gusta (Justyna) Draenger-Dawidson. The Jewish Fighting Organization decided not to prepare for an uprising inside the ghetto, where the restricted space offered no chance at all for an armed struggle. Instead they opted to move the fighting to the "Aryan" side of Kraków. Some ten operations were launched outside the ghetto, the most famous being the attack on the Cyganeria café in the center of the city, which was frequented by German officers. Eleven Germans were killed in this attack and 13 wounded.

Attempts to engage in partisan operations in the vicinity met with difficulties caused by the Jewish underground's isolation and the hostile attitude displayed by the local units of the *Armia Krajowa* (the Polish Home Army), which did not take kindly to Jewish partisan operations. The Jewish underground suffered heavy losses, and in the fall of 1944 those remaining decided to cross the border into **SLOVAKIA** and from there to make their way into Hungary. This plan succeeded, and members of the Kraków Jewish Fighting Organization continued their resistance operations in **BUDAPEST**, where they joined the *Ha-No'ar ha-Tsiyyoni* (Zionist Youth) organization.

On the "Aryan" side of Kraków, a branch of Zegota (Council for Aid to Jews) was active from the spring of 1943. The Zegota branch aided several hundred of the Kraków Jews who escaped.

After the war about 4,000 survivors of the ghettos and concentration camps, most of them former residents of Kraków and its vicinity, settled in the city, remaining there for a short while. In 1946 thousands of Jews who had fled to the Soviet

---

As they did in other ghettos, the Germans established several factories inside the ghetto to exploit the cheap labor now available. Several hundred Jews from Kraków were also employed in factories situated outside the ghetto, and they were daily escorted to and from their work.

Union at the beginning of the war and were now returning to Poland made their home in Kraków, where the Jewish population rose to 10,000. Several Jewish institutions were established, including a branch of the Jewish Historical Commission (the forerunner of the Warsaw Jewish Historical Institute). Most of these Jews emigrated from Poland between 1947 and 1951 in response to new, post-war waves of antisemitism. After 1968 only a handful of Jews were left in Kraków.

SUGGESTED RESOURCES

Lobel, Anita. *No Pretty Pictures: A Child of War.* New York: Greenwillow Books, 1998.

Peleg, Miryam. *Witnesses: Life in Occupied Kraków.* New York: Routledge, 1991.

Schindler's List [videorecording]. MCA Universal Home Video, 1993.

Kramer, Josef

(1906–1945)

Josef Kramer served as commandant of the **BERGEN-BELSEN** camp. Born in Munich in 1906, he joined the Nazi party in 1931, and a year later became an **SS** man. His concentration camp career began in 1934, in **DACHAU**, where he was first assigned as a guard. Advancing rapidly, he held senior posts in a number of concentration camps, including **SACHSENHAUSEN** and **MAUTHAUSEN**. For several months in 1940 he served as aide-de-camp to Rudolf **HÖSS**, the commandant of **AUSCHWITZ**. From April 1941 to May 1944, Kramer was commandant of the **NATZWEILER-STRUTHOF** camp. In May 1944 he was again posted to Auschwitz, and was put in charge of the gas chambers and crematoria in Auschwitz II-Birkenau. On December 2 of that year he was appointed commandant of Bergen-Belsen. Following his arrival there, Bergen-Belsen officially became a concentration camp, and conditions deteriorated sharply.

When the camp was liberated, Kramer was arrested by the British and put on trial, together with 44 other members of the camp staff, among them 15 women. The trial, which took place in Lüneburg, lasted from September to November 1945. Kramer was sentenced to death, as were ten others of the accused, and was executed on December 12, 1945.

Josef Kramer, in a mug shot taken before his trial in front of a British Military Tribunal.

SUGGESTED RESOURCES

Herzberg, Abel Jacob. *Between Two Streams: A Diary from Bergen-Belsen.* New York: St. Martin's Press, 1997.

Law Reports of Trials of War Criminals: The Belsen Trial. New York: H. Fertig, 1983.

Memory of the Camps [videorecording]. PBS Video, 1989.

Reilly, Joanne. *Belsen: The Liberation of a Concentration Camp.* New York: Routledge, 1998.

Kristallnacht ("Night of the Broken Glass")

Kristallnacht was a huge pogrom—a planned, violent, and organized attack—against Jews throughout **GERMANY** and **AUSTRIA** on November 9 and 10, 1938. Although the German government presented it as a spontaneous outburst provoked

Fire officials examine the exterior of the Fasanenstrasse Synagogue after it was burned by Nazis in anti-Jewish riots during Kristallnacht.

by the assassination of Ernst vom Rath, the third secretary of the German embassy in Paris, by a seventeen-year-old Polish Jew, Herschel Grynszpan, it was in reality an orchestrated event. The name Kristallnacht comes from the German word *Kristallglas* (beveled plate glass). It refers to the shattered windows of Jewish shops.

Kristallnacht occurred after a series of smaller attacks against Jews and their property in Germany and Austria following Nazi Germany's annexation of Austria (the *Anschluss*) in March 1938. The Nazis had made practical and legal preparations for the **ARYANIZATION** (*Arisierung*) of Jewish property—a move to transfer ownership from Jewish to non-Jewish hands that was intended to fatten Germany's treasury. Aryanization involved many decrees and laws that affected the Jews' public and personal status and increased their segregation from the general public. Using "infractions" of the law supposedly committed by Jews and "unemployment" of Jews as pretexts, or excuses, the **GESTAPO** and the **SS** made massive arrests of Jews. Those arrested were imprisoned in the **CONCENTRATION CAMPS** of **DACHAU**, **BUCHENWALD**, and **SACHSENHAUSEN**. Beginning in July 1938, these camps were readied to receive an even greater number of Jews. The Nazis also encouraged assaults on Jewish businesses and synagogues.

The authorities increasingly pressured Jews to leave German territory, even though the government's emigration policies made it very difficult. More and more individual Jews and entire groups were forcibly expelled. On October 28, 1938, about 17,000 Polish Jews were driven into a no-man's-land between Germany and Poland. The greatest number of them were left stranded near the border town of Zbąszyń. Herschel Grynszpan's parents were in this group, and news of their situation drove the desperate youth to his act of revenge against the Nazi regime that provided the opportunity for the Nazi's dramatic show of force that came to be known as Kristallnacht.

After Grynszpan's shooting of vom Rath on November 7, an inflammatory editorial appeared in the *Völkischer Beobachter*, the official **NAZI PARTY** publication. Sporadic rioting against Jews started the next day. On the afternoon of November 9, vom Rath died. That same evening, at a Nazi party meeting in Munich, Joseph **GOEBBELS** publicly hinted—apparently with the consent of Nazi leader Adolf **HITLER**—that this was the hour for action against the Jews.

Instructions to that effect were immediately sent out to all parts of Germany and Austria. Crowds were encouraged by the Nazi forces called the SA (*Sturmabteilung*; Storm Troopers) to attack Jews and their property. A mass frenzy broke out. Synagogues were destroyed and burned, windows of Jewish-owned stores were shattered—the broken glass littering the sidewalks—and the demolished stores were looted. Jewish homes were targeted, and in many places Jews were physically attacked. About 30,000 Jews—especially those who were influential and wealthy—were arrested and thrown into concentration camps, where they were treated with great cruelty by the SS.

This was the first time that riots against the Jews of Germany had been organized on such a broad scale, accompanied by mass arrests. Though the violent onslaught was officially terminated on November 10, in many places it continued for several more days. In Austria, it started only on the morning of November 10, but the attacks against Jews were especially fierce there. There were many arrests, and 4,600 Jews from Vienna were sent to Dachau. SS forces were officially forbidden to take part in the rioting, but these orders were ignored.

SS official Reinhard **HEYDRICH** reported on November 11 that 815 shops, 29 department stores, and 171 dwellings of Jews had been burned or otherwise destroyed, and that 267 synagogues were set ablaze or completely demolished. (In fact, this was only a small fraction of the number of synagogues actually destroyed.) The same report refers to 36 Jews killed and the same number severely injured. Later, however, it was officially stated that the number killed was 91. In addition, hundreds perished in the concentration camps following their imprisonment.

Kristallnacht was followed by administrative and legal orders issued to complete the process of Aryanization. The orders were meant to speed up the Jews' emigration, to isolate the Jews completely from the general population, and to abolish official Jewish institutions. The Jewish community was fined under the pretext of "reparation" for the murder of vom Rath. The government also took the payments made by insurance companies to cover their losses, while at the same time making the Jewish property owners liable for the repairs. Additional economic steps were set in motion during the following months. The Kristallnacht prisoners in the concentration camps who were still alive were released early in 1939 for immediate emigration or for the Aryanization of their property, often for both.

The Western press and public were harshly critical of Kristallnacht, but this did not affect the Nazis. President Franklin D. Roosevelt recalled the U.S. ambassador to Germany as a protest. The German ambassador to the United States was recalled home as well, because of "American interference in internal German affairs."

Debate continues about the causes and results of Kristallnacht, but there is no doubt that the pogrom was an important turning point. It was the Nazis' first experience of large-scale anti-Jewish violence, and it was a first step toward the eradication of the Jews in Germany.

SUGGESTED RESOURCES

Kristallnacht: The Journey from 1938 to 1988 [videorecording]. PBS Video, 1988.

More than Broken Glass: Memories of Kristallnacht [videorecording]. Ergo Media, 1989.

Read, Anthony. *Kristallnacht: The Nazi Night of Terror.* New York: Times Books, 1989.

Thalmann, Rita. *Crystal Night: 9–10 November 1938.* London: Thames and Hudson, 1974.

Krüger, Friedrich Wilhelm

(1894–1945)

A senior **SS** commander in occupied **POLAND**, Friedrich Krüger was born in Strasbourg. He served in the German army in World War I. He became a **NAZI PARTY** member in 1929, joining the SA (Storm Troopers) in 1930 and transferring to the SS in 1931. The following year he was elected to the Reichstag, and in January 1935 he was promoted to the rank of *Obergruppenführer* (general). From October 4, 1939, to November 9, 1943, Krüger was the Higher SS and Police Leader in the **GENERALGOUVERNEMENT**. As such, he was responsible for the liquidation of all the ghettos in the Generalgouvernement and for the operation of the **BEŁŻEC**, **SOBIBÓR**, and **TREBLINKA** extermination camps, where 1,720,000 Jews were murdered.

In May 1942, Krüger was given the additional title of secretary of state for security in the Generalgouvernement administration, and also became "Himmler's Representative for the Strengthening of Germandom in the Generalgouvernement." In the latter function he was responsible for the expulsion of 110,000 Poles from the **ZAMOŚĆ** area and the settlement of Germans in their place.

In May 1944, Krüger was appointed commander of the "Prinz Eugen" division of the Waffen-SS, which fought against the partisans in western Yugoslavia. On May 9, 1945, the day after Germany's surrender, he committed suicide.

Friedrich Wilhelm Krüger.

SUGGESTED RESOURCES

Rice, Earle. *The Final Solution.* San Diego: Lucent Books, 1998.

Shoah [videorecording]. New Yorker Video, 1999.

Krumey, Hermann

(b. 1905)

Born in Mährisch-Schönberg, Moravia, Hermann Krumey joined the **SS** in 1938. From November 1939 to May 1940 he served in the Waffen-SS in the Posen (Warthegau) headquarters of the Higher SS and Police Leader. Between May 1940 and March 1944 he was a member of the Security Police (Sicherheitspolizei) in **Łódź**.

In the summer of 1941, Krumey was sent from Łódź to Croatia to take part in concentrating Jews in camps. In 1942 he helped arrange at least six transports from the **Zamość** area to **Auschwitz**. He also assisted in deporting the Jews of Łódź to extermination camps, and in deporting Poles farther east.

Krumey entered **Hungary** with the occupation forces on March 19, 1944, as a leading member of Adolf **Eichmann**'s Special Commando (Sonderkommando). In this capacity, he played an important role in organizing Hungary's **Judenrat** (Jewish Council), the Zsidó Tanács, and in laying the groundwork for the destruction of Hungarian Jewry. In June 1944, in the wake of negotiations between Eichmann and the Relief and Rescue Committee of Budapest, close to 21,000 Jews were transferred to Strasshof, a concentration camp in Austria. Krumey became the head of the Special Commando assigned there. Most of these Jews survived the war.

He was arrested by the Allies in Italy in May 1945, but was not prosecuted. Rezső (Rudolf) **Kasztner**, the Zionist leader involved in the negotiations with the SS in Hungary, signed an affidavit on Krumey's behalf on May 5, 1948, and Krumey was released. He was again arrested in 1960, and after a trial in Frankfurt in 1965 was condemned to five years' hard labor, on February 3. Following an appeal by the prosecution, a new trial was held in 1968–69, and Krumey was condemned to life imprisonment on August 29, 1969. The conviction was upheld by the Federal Court of Karlsruhe on January 17, 1973.

SUGGESTED RESOURCES

"German Occupation." *Jewish History of Hungary.* [Online]
    http://www.heritagefilms.com/HUNGARY.html (accessed on August 21, 2000).

Lodz Ghetto [videorecording]. PBS Home Video/Pacific Arts Video, 1992.

KULMHOF. SEE CHEŁMNO.

Index